Bookstore

Bookstore

THE LIFE AND TIMES OF
Jeannette Watson
AND Books & Co.

LYNNE TILLMAN

Harcourt Brace & Company

New York   San Diego   London

Letter on page 71 copyright © 1981 by Diana Trilling.
Reprinted with the permission of the Wylie Agency, Inc.
"Decades" by Richard Howard.
Reprinted by permission of the poet.
Such Times copyright © 1993 by Christopher Coe.
Reprinted by permission of Harcourt Brace & Company.
Frontispiece photograph by Joyce Ravid.

Library of Congress Cataloging-in-Publication Data
Tillman, Lynne
Bookstore: the life and times of Jeannette Watson
and Books & Co./Lynne Tillman.—1st ed.
p.   cm.
Includes index.
ISBN 0-15-100425-0
1. Books & Co.—History. 2. Bookstores—New York (State)—
New York—History—20th century. 3. Watson, Jeannette.
4. Booksellers and bookselling—New York (State)—
New York Biography. 5. Literature, Modern—20th century—
Marketing—New York (State)—New York—History—
20th century.   I. Title.
Z473.B673T35   1999
381'.45002'09747—dc21   99-24661

Text set in Janson
Designed by Lydia D'moch

Printed in the United States of America
First edition
A B C D E

For readers

What is going to keep writing alive in this country are the independent bookstores. We need them so desperately. If the people who sell books don't read books or know anything about them, then it all evaporates. Too many of the small stores have gone out of business, and it begins to make you afraid for the future. Assuming that books are important—and I do assume that—then these stores are important, something fundamental to the spiritual health of the country.   —PAUL AUSTER

CONTENTS

PREFACE

As soon as Books & Co. opened on Seventy-fourth Street, I was aware of it. I live on Seventy-fourth and used to go there very frequently. Many, many times, when I would go for a walk in the neighborhood, which I do very, very frequently, Books & Co. would give me a destination, or some kind of mission to wind up someplace. Sometimes it's the museums, because there's a number of them in the neighborhood, but very often it would be Books & Co. It was just a nice place to go to, to rummage through the books and see if I could find something that looked exciting to me. Then I'd come back home and write some more. I spend my time writing.

As a young child, I wasn't much of a reader. I could write before I read, and I liked writing very, very much. I was always the class writer, always the one writing the stories, as far back as first grade, as soon as we learned. If I have time off during the day, I much prefer to sit down and write something than to sit down and read something. I only make films really to express my writing. I get up in the morning and write. I'm disciplined, but it doesn't even require discipline, because it's a pleasure. I write at home for hours, then take a walk, and when it was there, I might drop into Books & Co.

I started to read more when I got older. One has to read in order to function in the world, so I do read a reasonable amount and always have, from my late adolescence into my adult life. Browsing at bookstores and picking out books to read has been something I've enjoyed doing. But I always felt that reading was more of a necessity than a primary pleasure. You really can't keep up in the world unless you read. I've read a certain amount of fiction, because there's a certain amount you don't want to be ignorant about, but I read much more nonfiction. I like to read about science, politics sometimes, philosophy. To me, it's almost as if, if you're enjoying yourself reading, you're wasting your time, that reading should always have a didactic quality to it and a sense of purpose. If I'm reading and enjoying it, I feel, This is too light for me. I should be huddled over my Heidegger or something, trying to puzzle it out. Books & Co. had a wonderful array of subjects that interested me.

I filmed Books & Co. in *Everybody Says I Love You*, because it was one of the things in the neighborhood I was very proud of—that our neighborhood, and my block in particular, supported it. Books & Co. was a great, and deserved, source of neighborhood pride. People would come to it, renowned writers would come and read their works there. It had a real, a cultural, substance to it.

Now that Books & Co. has closed, there are a couple of bookstores in my neighborhood that I'll go to when I want a book, or if it's a specific book I want, I'll go to the nearest bookstore that has it. But it doesn't give me the same sense of being able to go into a bookstore and immerse myself in what seemed to be the kind of ambience that oozed love of books and love of literature.

The closing of Books & Co. is a severe loss to the neighborhood. The Whitney Museum and Books & Co. made up a nice little cultural scene between Seventy-fourth and Seventy-fifth streets. It was a shame to lose a bookstore of that quality. I hope there's an interest in the story of Books & Co. It's of interest to me. Books & Co. was wonderful.

—WOODY ALLEN
April 29, 1998

ACKNOWLEDGMENTS

FIRST, I WANT TO THANK Jeannette Watson for divulging her life
and thoughts to me, for being supportive to me as a writer, and for
becoming a wonderful, generous friend. Thank you, Ira Silverberg,
for introducing me to Jeannette. Thank you, Joy Harris and the Joy
Harris Literary Agency, for your constant support and guidance. My
deepest appreciation to the contributors to this book, whom I interviewed in person, over the telephone, by fax, or E-mail, for being
forthcoming, helpful, interesting, honest, funny, intelligent, and for
making this work so engaging. My gratitude to Peter Philbrook for
generously indulging me with three interviews and the resources of
his terrific mind and memory. Thank you, Ned Chase, for your support and information. My sincerest appreciation to Alystyre Julian
and Jenifer Berman, for their help in the initial stages of this project;
to Rebecca Hill, for her astute research into U.S. bookstores; and
Ronald E. Shavers, for the extraordinary job he did in transcribing the
great majority of interviews (as well as all the introductions to the au-
diotaped readings). For the even more arduous and impossible job of
compiling a list of all—almost all—the readings at Books & Co., I
want to give him a medal. Thank you, Elizabeth Schambelan, my

editorial assistant, for your intelligent eye and voice, for reading the manuscript critically in its earliest stages, for finding whatever book or information I needed, for being an enthusiast and a friend. And to André Bernard, my astute editor, for his encouragement and reassurance, my appreciation and gratitude. To his assistant, Meredith Arthur, whose efficiency and energy were constant and compassionate, many, many thanks. To the MacDowell Colony and its gracious staff, and to Hara Seltzer of the New York Public Library, Tompkins Square Branch, thank you so much for giving me quiet rooms in which to write a large part of this book. —LYNNE TILLMAN

INTRODUCTION

Bookstores and Book Lovers

BOOKSTORE is the history of Jeannette Watson and Books & Co., the independent bookstore she owned that opened its doors in 1978 and shut them in 1997. Closing the century, Books & Co.'s near-twenty years represent a significant sample of this country's literary, social, and cultural life. It is a history rich in books and people, in the lives of writers and readers. It is a story representative of its period, of issues germane to writing and publishing, to bookselling generally, and to independent bookstores specifically.

The genesis of bookstores and of writers, editors, and readers is shared. Why people love books, why they write or publish them, why they read or sell them spring from related interests, needs, and desires. Books & Co. was a nexus for literary achievements and hopes, for readerly proclivities, for human interactions—from a child's love of writing to a novelist's debut, a chance encounter to a love affair, from a casual comment to a book deal, a book's indelible effect on a reader to a memorial reading for its author.

While histories are subject to contestation and elaboration, they are essentially stories. "Story" lives inside "history," and both share an etymological root with "store." Not coincidentally, what's in a bookstore is not only books on shelves, but also the stories of those who enter—customers, staff, editors, browsers, publishers, publicists, writers. Books & Co. was literally, and virtually, filled with stories.

Readers and writers met and embraced there. It was a lover's embrace, usually metaphorical, and, in a powerful sense, *Bookstore* is a love story. Book lovers often love bookstores and are faithful to them. They discover their tunnel of love in a bookstore. It's their clubhouse, too, and, since bookstore lovers are a floating group, happy to discover a good one anywhere, the club can meet anywhere. A bookstore is also the instant meeting place for a fan club, where reader/fans can have favorite writers autograph their books.

Visiting bookstores, poring over shelves and through books, may turn into a daily or weekly ritual, a sacred moment in the secular world. Book loving and bookstore loving may even be obsessions, the book a fetishized object. If bookstores hold mystery, fascination, allure, and romance, it's because they carry the love object—the book—and are safe havens for its adoration or, at least, its discussion.

From their beginnings, bookstores have been places to meet, sites for intellectual discussion. The history of bookstores in the United States and Europe includes that of printers, printing, and the first presses, since, until the end of the eighteenth century, there was no serious distinction among these divisions. Bookstores were the outlets for printers, the first publishers, to sell their products. Colonial printers, which produced the first newspapers, were centers of information as well as its disseminators. The colonies' first book centers were in New England, especially Boston, New York, and then Philadelphia, but in the eighteenth century "traveling booksellers," auctions, and subscription bookselling altered the face of bookselling. At the century's end, only seven bookseller/publishers remained in New England.

When America met the Industrial Age in the nineteenth century, technological advances in printing—in 1840, the flatbed press and then the rotary press—led to mass-market publishing and the first large-scale publishing houses. But these houses still included bookstores, "magnificent retailing emporia," on their premises. The stand-alone bookstore that is everywhere and "natural" to us evolved over time. Not until the 1920s did the independent bookstore—personal, individual—make its appearance.

When the Civil War ended in 1865, there was a growth in reading. But as early as 1732, Benjamin Franklin declared there were "few patrons of literature," that booksellers "puff and sell the trash they deal in, and pamper and feed the depraved taste of misguided readers, while good books are neglected or not even known for lack of puffers." History records that, almost from its birth, people pronounced publishing and bookselling seriously ill or dying.

Over the years, booksellers have been troubled or concerned about unfair competition (department stores used books as "loss leaders" starting in 1870), cars, bicycles, the quantity of books published, literacy rates, poor literary quality, fewer readers, competition from other media (radio, movies, TV), the emergence of paperbacks, book clubs, discounting, and a myriad of other issues. Alarm usually receded as the latest item was assimilated, bringing with it not disaster but possibility. Radio increased interest in "pulp fiction"—detective novels—and books were promoted on radio. Book clubs, very popular in the 1920s, and subscription sales expanded sales.

Dramatic shifts occurred after World War II (during which 15 percent of the army read a book every two weeks). The advent of the paperback created a new class of book buyers, so that bookstores no longer were known to service only "the carriage trade." Then there was television. Since its inception, TV has terrified those associated with books. But books are sold on TV, too. *Roots'* popularity in the 1970s attests to that; and now there's Oprah, the singular and single-most powerful bookseller in the United States. Still, as the telephone and airplane did at the start of the twentieth century, TV, with its speed, presence, and promise of access, dismantled and rearranged the century. TV created an electronic revolution, whose seductions, virtues, and vices are much discussed and increasingly well documented.

The futurists presciently foresaw that the twentieth century was about speed, and books are a slow medium. The time it takes to read and the speed at which we live seem to conspire against books. Yet more books than ever are published and sold. In the 1960s, the installation of now ubiquitous malls created new spaces for retailers and shoppers. The chains, Waldenbooks and B. Dalton, owe their existence to malls, where they opened stores in areas not considered viable for book buying. There was also, once upon a time, a relative stability in publishing: Of the 1,000 publishing houses in existence in 1900, 191 survived until 1981 (one-quarter of them controlled by their founding families). This stability was shattered in the 1970s, with corporate takeovers and mergers that intensified in the 1980s and 1990s, speedily and radically altering the publishing body.

Though U.S. illiteracy rates remain high, in the computer age, another literacy is demanded. Books and bookstores have met the Internet, with Amazon.com and other booksellers on-line, providing a fast-service, at-home mall for books and other products. Surfing the Net takes time from reading books and develops another kind of writing and reading. The book itself is being reconfigured in computer laboratories, and its objectness in the twenty-first century may undergo a most severe kind of surgical reshaping. Bookstores, like other businesses, also contend with media conglomerates and the emergence of new concepts and practices, such as homogenization and consolidation.

Homogenization and consolidation have unpredictable consequences. The publishing industry has been on front pages of newspapers often in the last years, because the questions raised by its mergers and buyouts have wide-ranging effects. With fewer major publishers owned by a few conglomerates, how much diversity and opportunity will be afforded writers and readers? Books have always contained information in the broadest sense, and access to information, to knowledge, is critical in a democracy. What happens to bookstores, and to the industry they're part of, mirrors significant societal issues, including democracy itself. When researching this book, I talked with David K. Brown, a sales representative for fifteen university presses. He remarked, "Sometimes a buyer will say to me, 'I'll put it out, not multiple copies, but one to have for the store, because I'd like to represent that book.'" In a very real way, books represent our many identities, opinions, beliefs, our variety. Bookstores are places where that variety is housed.

But with relatively few buyers for chains, what happens to the diversity of information? (According to *Business Week*, thirty-five buyers choose all the titles in Barnes & Noble's [B&N] 1,011 stores.) Are readers, and society, depleted by homogeneity? Or is the spread of chains, no matter if the product is the same in every store, still a boon for books? Is Len Riggio, owner of B&N, a visionary or a vulture? (The shrinking of libraries and funding for them in the late 1980s, after all, made B&N's college-library environment appealing to recent graduates.) But independent bookstores don't just compete with superstores and chains. Nonbook retailers, discounters, and warehouse clubs now account for half of all books sold.

The 1980s and 1990s will be recorded as apocalyptic years for booksellers and publishers, an appropriate end-of-century condition. There are always, though, history's uncanny parallels and similarities. Benjamin Harrison, the first colonial newspaper editor, installed a coffee shop in his bookstore, the London Coffeehouse. Even a coffeehouse in a bookstore is not new, though its first (and even second) appearance may have been revolutionary.

When the first booksellers convention or book fair, organized by Matthew Carey, took place in 1802, fifty booksellers attended. Carey called his organization the American Company of Booksellers. By 1998, its relative, the American Booksellers Association (ABA), represented 4,047 independent bookstores. (Membership fell from 5,132 in 1991.) In April 1998, the ABA and twenty-six independent bookstores filed a suit against B&N and Borders in federal court, claiming that the chains' "secret" deals with publishers put them at a "competitive disadvantage" and posed "a threat to their survival and the diversity of American bookselling." Both chains deny this.

Whatever the outcome of the suit, there is no doubt there has been a shakeout and that independent bookstores have been shaken. In 1990, the first year of the superstore, the Bowker Almanac records there were 6,996 general-interest bookstores, in 1996, 7,090, a gain of 94 stores. But during that period, according to *Publishers Weekly*, approximately 800 superstores opened, so it appears that about 700 smaller, general-interest bookstores, including some chain outlets, closed. The ABA, which keeps an informal tally, reports that from 1993 to 1998, 221 independents shut down. (There is no definitive count of independents that have gone out of business.) On the other, happier hand, 1997 saw the pace of decline slowing for independents' closing. But B&N's attempted purchase in 1998 of Ingram Book Group, the biggest U.S. wholesale book distributor, aroused great concern about its potential "Microsoft-like" control of bookselling.

The crisis in independent bookstores springs not only from a shakeout in the market, but also from larger questions about what a general-interest bookstore is; what a general education is; what an educated person needs to know, and even what constitutes being educated. Bookstores contain ideas—about education, for instance— and are ideas about what readers and writers want and need. Their ability to present differences, conflicting viewpoints, varieties of imagination, and to be different in themselves is invaluable. Threats to their diversity are portentous.

When we think about the past, though, we often imagine golden ages far different from our own, without such threats. But as early as 1930, when the independent bookstore as we now know it had just come into being, H. L. Mencken wrote, in "Lo, the Poor Bookseller," an essay that appeared in *The American Mercury*, about, in part, the "cheap book experiment":

> People will no longer go to bookstores as they do now, to browse among books and to be educated in reading; they will make their selections from meager and shabby stocks with piles of camera films to one side and bales of hot water bags to the other. Buying books will cease to be the pleasant adventure that it has been ever since the invention of printing.

Jeannette Watson wanted her bookstore to be "a pleasant adventure." In fact, the business of books is filled with idealists and optimists like her. The people who start bookstores usually do so because they love books and want to do something worthwhile with their lives. To them, books are essential and important, and the fate of books and bookstores is urgent, inseparable from their lives and life itself.

When I began researching Books & Co.'s history, I discovered how inextricably it was part of Jeannette Watson's life. I'd never met Jeannette before. I was not a native informant. I'd never read at the store. I'd bought books there from time to time, attended some readings, it represented my books, but it wasn't my bookstore. I knew almost nothing about its history. Though I was a writer, I also knew very little about how a bookstore worked. My job, I told myself, was in part to make that understandable—how a bookstore operates, how books get chosen and why, how a philosophy animates each independent bookstore. I also wanted to look at the roles of editors, publicists, sales reps, and publishers, who figuratively deliver books to bookstores.

Jeannette Watson once told me her store was a "nineteenth-century idea." She told me she wanted her love of books to be communicated in an ideal place for them. Writers sometimes invoke the "ideal reader," publishers the "general reader." Muses for each group, these ideal types are inventions, probably necessary illusions. And just as authors, in a way, create their readers with each new book, traditionally, independent bookstores create their customers. No two independent bookstores are exactly alike in selection of books or ambience.

I interviewed Jeannette more than twenty times over six months, in her office, her apartment in New York, her home in Stowe, Vermont. We examined scrapbooks, looked at memorabilia, photographs, and letters. I read through all the files, all the letters. Jeannette xeroxed pages from her diary that she'd written since the bookstore had begun, and I read those. I looked at old programs and fliers and familiarized myself with the store's past.

I interviewed others who were significant to Books & Co.'s history and to Jeannette. Initially Jeannette gave me a short list of names, and from those names, the list grew and grew. (Through a third party, I tried to arrange a meeting with Burt Britton, Jeannette's original partner, but he did not wish to be interviewed.) I interviewed more than sixty-five people, in discussions that lasted anywhere from fifteen minutes to two hours. I talked with writers, customers, editors, buyers, other independent booksellers, publicists, friends of the store and of Jeannette.

Writing this book was a combination of doing history, cultural history, and biography. I hadn't expected it to be biography. Once I started working with the material, I realized I needed to tell Jeannette Watson's story. The impulse to start Books & Co. was hers, and her desire and commitment gave birth to the store and kept it going. Writing her biography from the interviews was like being a portraitist. Jeannette was, in a way, my material, my primary source material. If she were sitting for me, sitting in front of me, then I was using many of her words, her expressions, to draw from and paint with, interpreting them and augmenting them to make a continuous, fairly chronological narrative. (In a sense, I turned information into narration.) The interviews, of course, did not go from A to B. I asked many questions, and we talked about many things, sometimes in no specific order. From the interviews, letters, and her diaries, I had to establish links between events, make inferences and segues, and forge conclusions that seemed appropriate, using Jeannette's actual words when possible. I decided to keep her voice in the first person, like the other contributors, to maintain the book's immediacy and directness. I had to think as if I were Jeannette and recall events in her life as if they were mine. (It was as if I were writing her autobiography.) It was a strange experience, something out of Mind Invaders, and as much as I appreciated the dedication of biographers before, I respect them even more now.

More conventionally, I did oral history, too, organizing the other interviewees' material, selecting and editing commentaries to interrupt Jeannette's story. These interventions would amplify or diverge from the tale she was telling, and there was an enormous number of possibilities. The range of topics and expression was gloriously broad, beautifully articulated. (The reader of *Bookstore* will find a fuller discussion of some of the issues touched upon in this essay and much more.) But Jeannette's voice kept the narrative going; she was the engine. Others could stroll down memory lane and bring into it other memories and themes. I wanted to include as much as I could. This book's design was to showcase, along with Jeannette's life and her store's, many other lives and ideas, the way good bookstores do.

People go to bookstores for many reasons; people read for many reasons. We enter these stores with expectation. Perhaps we readers want to find ourselves in everything we read. But if it's in a book, and much is, booksellers try to fulfill the reader's demand. It's not an easy job, just as writing books or publishing them is not. A bookstore is not only a cultural space, but also a social space and a place for fantasy and desire. It is a business place, too, subject to the market, to changing business practices and consumer tastes, and all of this is in the story of Books & Co. To me the store became a living entity, a house full of voices, many of which are presented in *Bookstore*. I hope that *Bookstore* will live as a kind of book of books, a book for people who love them and who care about the fascinating business of bringing them into our world.

—LYNNE TILLMAN
June 1999

Sources used for general background and information were *Publishers Weekly, Business Week, The Bowker Library & Book Trade Almanac,* the ABA's Web site, John Tebbel's four-volume *A History of Book Publishing in the U.S.* (New York: R. R. Bowker, 1981), and the *New York Times.*

Bookstore

When I was growing up, books sheltered me. They carried me away from everything I knew, to worlds I wanted to know and visit. I was very shy as a child, and I'd read all day long. I'd read for five hours without moving, and sometimes I'd go outside, climb a tree, sit on a limb, and read there. Reading was my life, my happiness, for those hours, for that day.

When I was little, I loved magical, fantastical books. *The Wizard of Oz*, fairy tales, *The Little Princess*, *Little Women*. I must have been intrigued by spiritual matters even then, because I read the Bible often. I wasn't a saint. I remember praying to God: Remove some of my younger sisters. He didn't, fortunately, and I stopped praying for that. I'm the oldest girl of five. My younger sisters are, in descending order, Olive, Lucinda, Susan, and Helen, and I have an older brother, Tom Watson III.

My father called her "Madam-Nose-in-Books." I think he used to take her books away when she was naughty. He had an angle on all of us, and that was hers. I'm right behind her, the middle child. Growing up, we all argued

1

about the usual things, but now Jeannette is the person I look up to probably most of anyone in my life. She tells me I'm a very rewarding person to give advice to, because I always tell her how it's been absolutely correct and how much it's helped me. —OLIVE WATSON

I was raised in Greenwich, Connecticut, but I didn't feel part of the suburban world. I didn't like knowing just one kind of person, and I hated every second of the elementary school I attended, Greenwich Country Day. I was so very shy and so embarrassed by my background. The kids often teased me, Oh Watson, you're so rich, you're so rich, and I'd start to cry.

She told me once about going to school the day after an article had appeared previewing some new IBM machine and disclosing how many shares of the company her father owned and the value of those shares. The kids had taunted her about it, she said. Not that *their* fathers didn't also run companies and own huge chunks of the stock. But IBM was the most glamorous big company in the world, and Tom Watson was on the cover of *Time*. When she got home that day and told her father that she'd been picked on, he sat her down and said, "Jeannette, I want you to get something straight: We are *not rich*—we have *some money* but we are not rich." I've always loved that. —STEVEN M. L. ARONSON

Our house was beautiful. We kids had lots of animals, even a pony. Meadowcroft Lane was not yet a suburb. The end of the lane was full of blackberry bushes, and we could stroll down the lane and pick blackberries. We had a pony cart, and we'd ride it up and down the lane. Greenwich was still quite rural in the early days. I remember quaint details from my childhood, like the smell of the laundry, and seeing the clothes hung out on the line, the smell of clothes dried under the sun, which is indelible. Every Sunday we had a big lunch, quite a formal affair, and when I think about the present and my family, it's a different life. Our Sunday lunch is sandwiches, salad, soup, none of the formality with which I was raised.

At thirteen I went to Miss Hall's. I loved boarding school, where I formed lifelong friendships. I even love going to the reunions now, because though I may not see these women for years, we have so much to talk about. We were sequestered from the world, the way boarding schools were then, and that was a relief to me. I was so shy, I didn't want to go to dances or be around boys. I wanted to read.

Reading was my great escape into realms I could only imagine. Rasputin and Lawrence of Arabia were two of my youthful heroes. I came to them on my own, since my education really took place in the library. When studies ended, rather than working more diligently on my homework, like algebra, I'd go into the library and follow the alphabet. I reached the *R*s and discovered Rasputin. There were many books on him in the old school library, and I became obsessed with reading about Russia during that period, with Rasputin's effect on the czarevitch, the tzar's son, the hold he had on the czarina as well as on the group of women he'd collected around him, all obsessed with him. I was fascinated, too, by Lawrence of Arabia and read the *Seven Pillars of Wisdom* and every biography written about him. Lawrence was another charismatic, formidable character. I was taken with brave adventurous men who had motorcycles, like my father.

In that family Jeannette was the bookish one, curled up with books, while the others were much more physical, out in the world, more like her wonderful father, Thomas. He was one of the most extraordinary people I ever met, truly charismatic—a cheesy word now, charismatic, but he was, to the point where if he told you that something was so, it was not only so, but you would back it with your own life. For example, once he invited me to fly up to Stowe for

3

a skiing weekend, and we were to meet in Westchester. A blizzard came, and the airport was closed. Actually one of Jack Kennedy's close friends was also supposed to be going up with his girlfriend, and when they saw the storm and the airport closed, they begged off, but Tom said, "I'm going out, do you want to come, Brendan?" I said, "Of course I'll come." Because it was Tom Watson. It was a plane he had not flown often before, and he was going to fly himself—he had a copilot, but he had a book of instructions spread on his legs, and then he said into the microphone, "I'm taking responsibility for this flight, and I'm getting out of here." They put the lights on and we went off in the snow. When we got up in the air, it turned out that the airport in Stowe was also closed, and Tom had gotten in touch with somebody and they opened up another airport somewhere else, and we came down at another airport, newly plowed, just for us, and Tom. This was the commonplace. Another time I had to get back to New York, and Tom said, "I have a helicopter that has something the matter with it, and I'm flying it to Boston to get it fixed. I'll give you a ride to Boston, and you can catch a regular commercial flight." Again, no hesitancy on my part; here's a helicopter, which I hate, and there's something the matter with it, and we're going to take off. It was summer, and Tom had his shorts rolled up, and on the way off of the island and down to Boston—he was making notations on his bare skin, his upper thigh, and I thought, Here I am, thousands of feet in the air, with a man who's had a massive heart attack and had just recovered from it, and there are certain extraordinary notations on his upper leg, and if he had another heart attack, what do I do?—how do I read the upper leg of a dead man? I knew Tom would get me to Boston. There wasn't a chance in the world that we wouldn't get to Boston. That's the way he was.

—BRENDAN GILL

My mother was very beautiful. To this day people almost gasp when they see her. When I was thirteen, I found out she had once been chosen one of the ten most beautiful girls in New York and flown to Hollywood. She was in a movie called *Vogues of 1938* in which she sang a song. Mother said everyone stood around holding their ears when she sang. She couldn't sing a note. They had to dub her voice. And she dated Jimmy Stewart. I remember thinking, How can my life ever measure up to this? How could I ever do anything as glamorous as be chosen one of the ten most beautiful girls in New York, be flown to Hollywood, be in a movie, and go out with Jimmy Stewart?

My father was handsome, glamorous, and very frugal. Daddy found ways to drive home from New York without paying tolls. He told my mother she should buy Wonder Bread from the factory instead of the store because it was cheaper. His father, his namesake, Thomas Watson, was a self-made man from a very poor family.

> My father went from rags to riches, but what impressed me was how close he came to staying in rags.
>
> —THOMAS WATSON JR.,
> *Father, Son, and Co.*

At age forty, Grandfather was fired in a traumatic manner by his boss at National Cash Register. But then he went on to be like a Gatsby. His was an amazing story, an American story, from poverty to a grand house off Fifth Avenue. It was an enormous double townhouse, and later it became the home of Rebecca Harkness Dance Company. (Ironically, about five years ago, I was asked if I'd like to purchase it for my bookstore.)

Grandfather was a friend of FDR's. He was a Democrat and, during the Depression, made a fortune by dint of his optimism—Watson optimism—because instead of laying off workers, he hired more and produced more adding machines. With the advent of the New Deal, the machines were immediately needed. He credited much of his success to my grandmother, Jeannette Kittredge, after whom I was named. I remember when I was little, Grandfather taking me to his office. Seeing it, being there with him, made a very strong impression. One time he even let me accompany him on a "special" business trip, to the Endicott office.

Before my parents married, my mother was a model, helping to support herself and her family. Mother was frugal, too, never one to throw money around. And though my father was extremely wealthy, he kept to a budget and forever worried about money.

My father's business was part of my life from a very early age. Daddy brought home business acquaintances for us to entertain. He'd tell us, "This is your bread and butter." My sisters, mother, and I would reply in singsong, "Bread and butter, bread and butter, bread and butter." As a family, we were all involved in the company, just as IBM was famously involved in the lives of its employees. There were even IBM country clubs. So from the beginning, there were two families—our family and the IBM family. The two were entangled. Daddy once told me that, as a young man, he would have to talk to the employees if they were planning to divorce.

He was the most successful businessman of the middle of the twentieth century, who, by the way, never taught his daughter to use a computer.
—ALEXANDRA ANDERSON-SPIVY

My father did incredible research every time he took us on a trip, so we would be informed of the country's history. He never gave a strict history lesson, there was always some humor. My father read everything, poetry, history, nonfiction, and, as children, we were definitely encouraged to read. My mother always read, too. We have scrapbooks from all the trips; I must have thirty from a family reunion three or four years ago, and going all the way back. My parents chronicled everything. Actually, we were interviewed on a Dictaphone by my father every trip, probably every night or every other night. Then it was edited. We were expected to remember something and talk about it; that was definitely part of the traveling.

—OLIVE WATSON

Daddy admired my love of reading, and I'd tell him the plots of novels sometimes. I remember we'd been reading *Crime and Punishment* at Miss Hall's, and I told him about Raskolnikov, how he felt because he was so intelligent he was beyond the law and had the right to murder the old woman. Daddy found that very interesting and used it in some speeches. Later in the bookstore, he was always asking us to tell him what to read, as if there were an absolute list, and I'd have it. Daddy always wanted to read the one hundred great books.

My mother went to New York University, and she always gave me books. I was in the Korean War, and in Korea, my knapsack was not army equipment, it was books; she was loading me up all the time. Sometimes I'd have to write her, Hold up, don't do anything until I've finished what I'm reading, because I couldn't carry them all around. Interestingly enough I worked for Jeannette's father at IBM. Somebody went through my personnel records and found out that I was a reader of books. I'd been a journalist before I joined IBM, so I was called in to a high monkey-monk's office, and he said, "You read—do you still read?" I said, "Yeah." He said, "The chairman here is concerned that the senior executives of this company are too imbalanced—their backgrounds are in the sciences, or engineering—they're not in the arts, they've never read a novel, they've never read philosophy." I was trying to figure out what this guy was getting at, and he said, "Would you teach a course? We'll pay you for it, extra, and it would be done at night and wouldn't interfere with the daily work schedule." I said sure. He said Tom Watson Jr., who was the chairman when I was there, was enamored of the Great Books course from the University of Chicago. He asked, "Would you go through the course and see if you could handle it?" I said, "Most of the stuff I've read, but some of it I haven't, and I'll go through it and let you know very quickly whether I can do it." I did it for the next three years, taught a Great Books course at night. Roughly, it was like a roundtable, about twenty-five at a time, and they were very studious, very good. This was around 1958–1961, when IBM still had its headquarters at 590 Madison Avenue. Watson wanted his executives to have this other dimension—he felt that it was something they were lacking.   —BUD POMERANZ

Daddy loved poetry and used to recite "The Hermit of Shark Tooth Shoal" for us. It turned out to be the first book I published, the Christmas after he died. We all had tried to remember the words of this Robert Service parody, but couldn't. A friend sent it to me, and I printed it up beautifully for the family as a Christmas gift. Olive could recite it, too, but we'd all ask Daddy, "Please say 'The Hermit of Shark Tooth Shoal.'" It was one of our treats, and he recited it extremely well. It's likely I love hearing people recite and read aloud because of him.

I went to Yale with Jeannette's first cousin, Walker Buckner Jr., and I met her, I think, through him when she was at Sarah Lawrence. I must have been invited to her coming-out party years before, because, years after, I found the invitation. Our friendship really began one summer in the mid-seventies when I was renting a small house in East Hampton next to the big house she was renting. That house, by the way, now belongs to Nora Ephron. Jeannette didn't have much self-confidence then. She was highly intelligent, good-looking, had a good character, a good sense of humor, but she didn't know what to do with herself. She did know that she wanted to spread her wings more widely. So she had the ambition, and she also had, as her father—let's remember—had represented to her, "*some money.*"   —STEVEN M. L. ARONSON

I went to Sarah Lawrence and majored in early childhood education, training to be a nursery school teacher. I met Jane Stanton Hitchcock, Barbara Lazear Ascher, Jacqueline Weld, and Alexandra Anderson-Spivy. Then I married Ralph McElvenny in my junior year, became pregnant, graduated, and gave birth to my first son, Ralph.

We were both seniors in college, both pregnant with our first children, and we were both having terrible morning sickness. That's how I first knew her. We would sort of look at each other and turn green. We spent a lot of time talking about what we wanted to be when we grew up. And a bookstore was one of many things she was considering, and then that seemed to be, if my memory serves me correctly, that seemed to be it. That was the big one. There were other things; I remember she talked about social work school. But when she came upon the bookstore as an idea, it seemed like the natural, perfect thing, because she was such a wonderful reader and had such a passion for books. Long before Joseph Campbell came out with his advice to follow your bliss, she was doing it.

—BARBARA LAZEAR ASCHER

Then we moved to Grosse Point, Michigan. I adored Ralphie and loved spending time with him. I read to him all the time. But Grosse Point was suburbia, where the men went to work in the big city, and the women stayed home. Women didn't even visit museums in Detroit, because the city was considered dangerous. This was not the interesting life I wanted for myself. The bright lights were Jody

Said and Bicky Kellner. We found each other and became fast friends. Bicky and I had children the same age, and we'd wheel them in their strollers and talk about what we wanted to do. Bicky was probably the first person I spoke to about my great idea: I was either going to be an anthropologist or start a bookstore. That was about five years before the idea became a reality.

Eventually, I was living in New York, where I'd longed to be. I had divorced; I had Ralphie. I found work as a mental health worker. I'd volunteered to do community work at a project at the Stratford Arms Hotel, where some of the older people who had recently been deinstitutionalized, released by the State from mental institutions, lived. I started as a volunteer, three days a week, and then I became a paid worker—my second paid job. I was in charge of the sixth floor. There were several major problems on the floor. Often we'd have to call an ambulance, because some of the people were seriously ill.

There was a woman who wouldn't bathe or clean her room. I tried to encourage her. I'd get clean clothes for her and talk to her, and finally—I probably could be arrested for doing this now—I said, "Today you are going to take a shower. We're going to take a shower together." I went into the shower with her, with my clothes on. I washed her hair, I washed her all over, I put her in clean clothes, and, after that, I made her visit the alcoholism counselor—she was a recovering alcoholic. I went through her room. It was horrible to do. I don't think I would do it now, but there were the rights of the other people on the sixth floor. Her room stank. I threw away a lot of stinking, disgusting rags. I'm sure they were important to her, but I threw them away, cleaned up her room, and went home. The next day, one of the other social workers told me the woman had said, "Jeannette has imprisoned me in my clothes, I can't get out of them." She couldn't go to the bathroom; she couldn't figure out how to get out of her new clothes.

There was a woman named Marina who was very depressed. I'd bring in nail polish and lipstick—the remedy for any problem—and paint her fingernails. I'd put lipstick on her. She liked that. Sometimes I'd take her to light candles in church, and we'd say prayers together, which comforted her. I also started a reading group. One day Daddy came to the welfare hotel and sat in on one of my groups. All the women fell in love with him. He was so dashing. They kept asking, "When is your father going to come back?"

I went to Afghanistan with Jeannette and her father in 1975. I had just met my husband. Jeannette and I went on the "White Diet," and I said, "If you eat everything white, you'll lose weight." Unfortunately, everything white was vanilla ice cream and spaghetti. About halfway through, Jeannette said, "I don't think this diet's working, Janie." I said, "But there's no meat. No meat!" I remember on the plane to Afghanistan, which is just a hellish flight, a twenty-four-hour flight, Jeannette brought a book that was a thousand pages long. By the time we got to Frankfurt, she was halfway through. It was a book I'd read, something like Thomas Mann, something I knew pretty well. I said to her, "You're showing off. You didn't read that book. You did five hundred pages. I'm going to give you a quiz." And I did. She had read every word, and we had a long discussion about the book. By the time we got to Afghanistan, she finished the book. She had to take along a suitcase of books, because this girl reads like a devil, fast, comprehensively. I went to Evelyn Wood and read slower after the first lesson. We had a ball with her father in Afghanistan. He was wonderful. He could be the most charming man. He was so handsome, incredibly charming, and in some ways he was like Captain Ahab. He was kind of megalomaniacal, and deservedly so, and very strong. Jeannette's a survivor. He was a difficult parent.

—JANE STANTON HITCHCOCK

Though I was very attached to the people at the Stratford Arms, after doing this work for three years, I felt depressed myself, frustrated.

The most one could do was maintain them in that community, and one never saw any forward movement. They were not able to move out or on, and, as much as I tried to help, and all of us tried, it seemed futile. They didn't get better. And, I felt driven to have something that nobody could take away from me, something that would be really mine.

In 1975, I got out of architecture school, nobody's building a thing up in New England, and John and I came to New York. We had a son, so we were looking for work, looking for schools, looking for the basics. My older sister, Pam, invited me to a luncheon with some friends of hers. I was about twenty-seven. I thought that I had arrived and had come to the capital of sophistication, because up in Rhode Island and in New Jersey, where I grew up, women didn't go out to lunch typically in the 1960s and 1970s. Jeannette was there with Jackie Weld, my sister Pam, and everybody ordered white wine spritzers. I didn't know what they were. I thought, This is it! This is so exciting. These women are incredible. Jeannette was single and extremely witty. The repartee at that luncheon was very sophisticated. I was saying very basic things like, "I need to find a nursery school. I need to find a job. Where do I get groceries?" In the 1970s, women who had children were always portrayed as being burdened and dragged down. Single was what you wanted to be. Jeannette embodied it. She had friends, hey, she drank white wine spritzers at lunch! She was the feminist movement at its best, but with a great sense of humor and kindness. I was trained as an architect, but at the time she met me, basically I was a mother with a child in New York City, stuck at home in an apartment when everybody was off having careers.

—CLARA DALE

I found out I needed hip surgery, an osteotomy—a piece of bone had to be removed from my hip, in order for it to go into the socket more easily. I have a condition called congenital hip dysplasia. The hips are displaced, and, though I'd been born with it, we didn't know it when I was a kid. If only I'd known, I thought, I wouldn't have had to play field hockey all those years and suffered such humiliation. The doctor said it would be a year's recovery. I'd be in the hospital for two weeks, home recovering for months, then on crutches and a walker. A long time recuperating. I was extremely upset. This unhappy prospect accelerated my thinking. Then, like a miracle, I had a dream. The dream came almost immediately after I was told I needed surgery. I dreamed I was in a bookstore, surrounded by books, hundreds of books, and the place had two floors, and it was cozy. It looked like what would become Books & Co.

> Jeannette's dream was to start a bookstore, my dream was to write my book, and these dreams were going on simultaneously, and the idea behind these dreams was that one day I would read my book at the bookstore, which I did get to do with great happiness.   —JACQUELINE WELD

Throughout the ordeal, the operation and the long recovery, the dream sustained me. I was determined there would be a bookstore at the end of the tunnel. One day I invited my friend Steven Aronson out for lunch. He was the only person I knew who was actually in publishing. I told Steven I wanted a bookstore that would look very old fashioned, be like a private home, and carry wonderful books. There would be events, parties, and gallery openings. Steven thought it was a good idea, and he introduced me to others, like Brendan Gill, who was also very encouraging.

> I knew her father but I met her through Steven Aronson, and they were nearly contemporaries—and I'm sort of a father figure to Steven, who is now about fifty—and I'm eighty-two. I was the godfather, or whatever you want to call me, of the bookstore.   —BRENDAN GILL

I was like a midwife to the birth of the bookstore. I was the copublisher of Harcourt Brace Jovanovich at the time, and in a position to put her in touch with all kinds of useful people: architects, critics, editors, writers, and of course readers—that is, customers! I proposed her as a Fellow of the Morgan Library, which in those days was a very august thing to be, and I would have put her up for the Grolier Club, too, but they didn't admit women then. I just ransacked my address book trying to pull out the right contacts for her. —STEVEN M. L. ARONSON

My father said he would loan me half the money to start—we each put up $150,000—but he wanted to make sure I could face failure. He asked, "Are you sure you want to start this because what if you fail, how can you deal with failure?" I thought about it overnight. The next day I told him I'd rather try and fail than not do anything with my life.

Jeannette talked to a lot of the bookshop owners, and I remember that a couple of them weren't that nice to her. They thought, She's a dilettante. She's the daughter of so-and-so . . . They didn't take her very seriously. But Jeannette was serious. She is a person who is very low key, but very intense underneath it all. When she wants to do something, there isn't anything that's going to stop her, and she wanted a bookstore. —JANE STANTON HITCHCOCK

I always think, What if Jeannette had been a man? There's been a lot of condescension toward Jeannette— (a) she's the child of Thomas Watson, and (b) she's a woman. She was never a dilettante. She wasn't a dilettante in school; she wasn't a dilettante when she was married and had her first child. She was a shy, somewhat insecure woman, who had great privilege, but was never frivolous.

14

Great wealth immediately makes people think that what you do is more self-indulgent, even when it's not, so you have to fight this image.

—ALEXANDRA ANDERSON-SPIVY

Like her father there's an enthusiasm in her and a true sweetness of nature. In bookselling, and in running a store and running any commercial enterprise in New York, there's a lot of disappointment involved, and Jeannette must often have been frightened at the cost of things. Her father didn't want her to be hoodwinked by people in the business world of New York, which is a dog-eat-dog world on any level, no matter what it is—even on its quasi-respectable level of having a bookshop. So he was worried that Jeannette might have been making a big mistake or at least getting in over her head. She was then very young and obviously vulnerable, so when I was very keen about her doing this, I, an old gentleman, gave a kind of sanction to what Jeannette was doing, which Tom was grateful for. Always expressed afterwards was his gratitude that I had encouraged her to go on with this thing. I was being parental, I was saying as a good parent to another good parent, Trust her, she's on the right track, this is going to cause her to bloom, to flower, to become who it is that she has it in her to become, it shouldn't be stopped. There was always the silent hint underneath all this: You can afford for her to make an experiment. All experiments succeed, but if it happens to fail, that will also prove something.

—BRENDAN GILL

I wanted a community, a salon, a place for discovery. There was no bookstore I liked. I hated walking into most of them and having people running at me, like the perfume salespeople in Bloomingdale's. I wanted a store that represented the way I felt about books.

Reading a book was an imaginative journey, and that's what I wanted Books & Co. to be.

> My response to her wanting to open Books & Co. was caution: "There are a million stores out there. Why would you do this?" I didn't picture it in 1976. There was nothing in my reference bank for it. She had a vision that didn't exist in New York at that time, and she pursued that, in spite of the doubts or the lack of enthusiasm of her closest friends. Now, she did get support, and we all said, "Great . . ." But I didn't really get it until later.   —CLARA DALE

When I was a child, I remember thinking, I don't have any talent, none. In a sense I was able to convert my passion, my love of reading and books, into my talent. Tono, a Japanese intellectual, once lectured at Martha Wilson's Franklin Furnace, an artist's book archive and performance space. He described how erotic reading was. He said, Turning a page was like spreading the legs of a beautiful woman. Sexist, perhaps, but reading was like that for me, erotic, almost sexual. Nothing came between me and my book.

I was able to segue my desire into a career. Right after I was finished with surgery and had recuperated, I decided to find somebody with whom to start the bookstore.

> She needed to have a partner. I asked my friend John Lahr who *he* thought was the savviest person in the bookselling business and he agreed, "Burt Britton." I gave Jeannette Burt's name. That was the first she'd heard of him but she called him up.   —STEVEN M. L. ARONSON

It was like a mantra: Burt Britton, Burt Britton, Burt Britton. Everyone insisted, "You must talk to Burt. He runs the review books department at the Strand." Burt had his own empire there. Fran Lebowitz told me every time she needed money she would take the review books she had received in the mail to Burt, and he'd buy them. He was very generous. All the writers liked him.

I had known Burt for many years by the time Books & Co. started. The second I started writing for little magazines—and I cannot stress the word "little" enough—I would get books in the mail. You can tell that no one really wants books—you can tell how highly valued they are—by the fact that a nineteen-year-old kid writing for a magazine with a circulation of six gets inundated with hundreds of review copies. The books you didn't want you would bring to the Strand, which paid a quarter, I think, of the retail price, so basically this accounted for, at various times, between a quarter and a third of my income. I remember once getting seventy dollars cash. My rent was $121.78. So that was a very substantial sum of money. I always felt Burt gave you more than you were supposed to get—he would take the books, and it was like watching a card shark shuffle a deck of cards. It was the only experience I've ever had in life where I got more than I thought I was going to get. —FRAN LEBOWITZ

I used to live at Twelfth and University. I would walk down to the Strand if I got stuck on a paragraph, because it was only a block away, so I spent a lot of time there. Burt had a lot of respect for writers and writing. He held an odd kind of salon in the basement. You'd get acquainted with Burt, then he'd say, after he counted up your books, "Are you looking for anything?" or "Can I get you anything?" because he had the books they were going to send to schools or libraries before they put them out on the shelf. A lot of writers also bought their books at the Strand; they were half price. You'd schmooze with Burt and maybe with somebody else. I knew one guy who went to the Strand every Saturday, got his money for his books, and took it to Le Petit Cochon, a place down the street that made various kinds of pâté. He turned his books into pâté. I remember going to the Strand with my older daughter, she was about twelve, and introducing her to Ralph Ellison. It was one of those rare times when I told my child, "You remember that man." —CALVIN TRILLIN

Arranging a meeting with Burt was like a scene in a John Le Carré novel. Burt would call from a phone booth—he wouldn't phone from the Strand—and he'd say, Meet me at Bar X, downtown, 10 P.M. Very mysterious. I went to Bar X, we met, and talked. He seemed interested. After more meetings and talk, I asked him if he'd like to go into business with me, and he said yes. An agreement was drawn up and signed, then we started thinking about what kind of books we wanted to have.

Burt liked writers like people like movie actors—they were big stars; they were his movie stars. He got the idea at some point that he would have these guys do self-portraits, sketches of themselves, and all these people came in to the Strand. He knew their work, and he would get them to sketch. Almost everybody responded, and they came up with interesting likenesses and caricatures of themselves, so he became a sort of literary personality himself. Random House did a book of it, and he became something of a celebrity among literary celebrities.

—ALBERT MURRAY

Elizabeth Bishop created a drawing of herself for Burt's book before her watercolors were known at all—and a ring and the word *imaginary* lurching toward it. Mark Strand turned himself into a medallion; Harry Mathews gave a very severe presentation, like his prose. There's a shaggy Menippean satire about the whole. —DAVID SHAPIRO

Burt was a great bookman, with wonderful knowledge, and of course a charismatic guy. He was a sort of tall, ruggedly handsome guy, and he always smoked these little cheroots.

—THEODORE WILENTZ

Right after the agreement was signed, a space was discovered. Somewhat earlier I'd told my friend Dick Spizzirri, who was a lawyer, about my bookstore dream, and he asked, "Why haven't you started?" I said, "I can't find anyone to start it with me. I can't find a space." He was adamant that I should get started. He was also altruistic. One day he phoned and said, "I've found you a location, 939 Madison Avenue." I phoned Burt immediately. We were tremendously excited.

Tom Watson and I had in common an interest in architecture—he had revolutionized corporate architecture by choosing another friend, Elliot Noyes, to be in charge of the architecture for all the new IBM buildings which were being built all over the country, all over the world, and so he also thought, Brendan must know something about that, too. So then of all things, Jeannette was going to choose this miserable shaky falling-down brownstone. Going into a building like that would not be the kind of thing that Thomas wants for an IBM place. He wouldn't really think it was a prudent thing to do, and in fact, when Jeannette and I went down in the basement I remember the first time—there was this brick column holding up some of the floor tenders. I touched it and the pillar rocked back and forth. I wouldn't have dared to tell Tom that the building was a wreck, but it was mendable. It could be put in sufficient order, and of course books are a very heavy load, so it was a chance-taking building, but it was a wonderful location, and it had a quality of age. It had what Henry James called "the tone time," and that's very good for a bookshop, the right sign. It felt homely, domestic; it was domestic—it had been a house. It was a tenement house, a row house, and it would have been built probably anywhere between 1875 and 1885. That would be roughly its age. The whole row, all the way along, as they were expanding up Madison, were probably begun as ordinary residences, with three or four Irish greenhorn servants up on the top floor. They weren't designed as tenements, then they became tenements, and the Whitney owns them all now. It's a rabbit warren, all nasty little rooms going every which way, but it was a perfect location, in a radically imperfect building, but also with very good intentions. One could sense the kind of bookshop that Jeannette was going to have, in the sense that the personality of the proprietor was everything. It's odd to think that one can have ten thousand different books in a space, written by all of those different people, and nevertheless, by the choice of the books, the books represent something about the personality of the owner. And one of the great things from the beginning was the feeling that the building had had a history, that it had a life, that there was something in the walls, beyond the walls, and then the books somehow mated with the locale, and so she was right to choose that risky building.   —BRENDAN GILL

Burt spent a day standing outside 939 Madison counting the number of people who went past. It was the good side of the street, we decided, since more people walked on our side. The space was two floors, with a basement. The street floor was about 1,000 square feet, the basement 750 square feet, and the second floor was the same amount of space as the first. The downstairs had been a deli, the upstairs an art gallery. What became my office had once been Maria the dressmaker's. In the back was an empty apartment. We could break down the walls, put all the spaces together, and build the store I'd envisioned—with a place for the staff to eat. That was important, I was told.

I've lived at 937 Madison since 1966. I'm told there was a pharmacy at one time, before the Whitney was built, and there used to be a Gristede's on the corner. Downstairs was a women's hairdressing parlor, and they had attendants. There has always been controversy on this block, always somebody fighting somebody else, and when I moved in, the tenants were fighting with the hairdresser. The two women dressmakers came in and shared their space, which is quite large, with a man called Mr. Fix-It Master, an Italian, who fixed everything. People would come with their vases and whatever. What was so funny was these old-fashioned seamstresses, sharing space with this strange Mr. Fix-It Master. What was so extraordinary is, in this neighborhood, no elegant trade is going to climb up the first rung of stairs. So they would meet their best prospective customers halfway down the stairs, gush all over them, and keep them from walking up. On the second floor, there was a woman I became very close to. She was ninety when I came in, and her name was Victoria Villars. She was so chic. She spread rumors about being an illegitimate child of Sarah Bernhardt. She was very old school. She worked for Thomas Beecham, the conductor, in London. One day Vaslav Nijinsky came by, and said, "*Je suis* Nijinsky." Victoria Villars must have said—I don't speak French—"Why bother me about it?" Also on the second floor, we had a very talented music teacher named Betty. At sixty she rode a bicycle around the neighborhood, which I thought was quite remarkable. And the woman across the hall from her did children's designs for cartoons. I was a floor above somebody who committed suicide, a young man in the back. After that a distinguished woman from one of the book publishing families came in and lived in the back. She was a very intelligent woman. We've had wonderful people here in the past.

The environment has changed radically. Unfortunately you can't explain that to anybody, nobody believes you. The sad thing about growing older and older is nobody believes you. Life couldn't be what you say, you exaggerate. Just like the films from the fifties. I used to write, and I worked in the studios, Hollywood, for a couple of years. Publicity, reading scripts, nothing that mattered. I didn't have the discipline. You can't tell anybody now what went into films then, and what they did for people and what they were, compared with all this nonsense we have now, where everything has to explode all over the place. Nobody believes you. I was born before the First World War, and I took part in parades in 1916. I wore a Scottish kilt in the parades, when the cry was "Kill the Kaiser!" The children were all into that. Then we had a terrible influenza epidemic, in 1919, and wore little handford bags. As if that meant a damn thing, but we wore them to school. The stability was so touching in those days, up until World War II. In the Depression we never locked our doors. Regardless of Chicago and Capone and all that nonsense, there was a stability in the people and in the nation, and it died out then. —DUNCAN BENTLEY

In October 1977, we signed a fifteen-year lease for 939 Madison with Judson Realty, for $60,000 a year. An enormous amount of work had to be done before we could open our doors to the public. And we hadn't found a name yet. Burt had always wanted to call a bookstore "Books." But one day, while my father and I were having lunch, he suggested, "It should be 'Books & something.'" He wrote on the tablecloth: "Books & Sympathy," "Books & —." We couldn't come up with it. In the middle of that night, I awoke and thought: "Books & Co. Books & Co." I liked the pun—there was company and books, but there was also the play on company as a business. Theoretically, a moneymaking business. I wasn't thinking of Shakespeare & Co., I was thinking of people and books.

One day I bumped into Burt, and he tells me he's leaving the Strand to become a manager of a bookstore. He tells me it's going to be up on Madison Avenue, a building with two floors. I immediately say, Two floors!—because he said it was small—two floors, Burt, that's most inefficient. He says that may be, but there are other business reasons for it. He said she has very definite ideas of what she wants. She wants to hold readings and whatnot. She wants these two floors and already had picked them out.

—THEODORE WILENTZ

We found our name. Over the years, the bookstore has been influenced so much by friends and their interests, and by my customers, and so many things have happened because of all of them, the name became ever more apt. Kathleen Howard, who works at the Metropolitan Museum of Art, came into the bookstore every week since we started. She was a big reader and a devotee of Mark Morris, the choreographer. She told me about Morris, and I began following his work, though not as devotedly as Kathleen. There was a genuine, intense cross-fertilization between the customers, writers, and me. The store grew into its name. It earned it with time.

People want to have a sense of contact with the authors through the bookseller. Somehow it's an osmotic thing, just as Sylvia Beach was of Shakespeare & Co. in Paris in the old days, a place that was irresistible to people—and it always helped that James Joyce was in the back room. To people who are interested in books, being in the presence of a book is almost like a sacred activity, since we don't have any sacredness left, or almost nobody goes to church, or people who go to bookshops don't often go to church anymore.

—BRENDAN GILL

I'm a bookstore junkie. For some reason, I was never drawn to libraries. Since I was a child I always wanted to have the book. I started buying books when I was about nine. Of course, I was reading before then. My mother owned some books, good books, and as Christmas and birthday presents I was given classics then thought appropriate for children, like Swift and Lamb and Hawthorne and Alcott and the Brontës and Stevenson. But it always felt as if the world of books was my world, as opposed to the world of everyone around me. Books were an instrument of self-creation, and as I recall the feelings I had as a small child it's almost as if I were born with the idea that I would have to create myself. I was sure that I was not going to have a life like that of my mother or anyone else I knew, and books were the great passport elsewhere. Each one a magic carpet. But, as I said, my mother did have books, most of which I read very early, and the one that really marked me, as I remember, was *Les Misérables*, which I read when I was eight. It was a transforming experience. I discovered what it was to live inside a book for a long time—the edition my mother had was in six volumes! I discovered social injustice. I discovered, so it felt, the thickness of the world. And shortly after, I started buying books of my own. Most of my tiny allowance went for books—especially once I discovered the Modern Library when I was ten. I loved that this was a series. Great books. All I had to do was read them all, which meant buying them one by one. I couldn't imagine giving a book that I loved back to a library. I had to see them in the bookcase in my bedroom. They were my guardians, my friends.

—SUSAN SONTAG

After we'd begun working, I went to bookselling school. The American Booksellers Association offered a weeklong course in Boston. I studied every aspect of running a bookstore—bookkeeping, inventory, how to order, how to manage a bookstore—and every part of it was interesting to me. It made me recognize even more strongly that this was absolutely what I should be doing. I studied my lessons, but I didn't, unfortunately, follow all of them. Still, my dream was coming true. A bookstore on Madison Avenue, with Burt Britton, who knew everybody.

Burt also knew almost every contemporary writer and his or her work. I'd read the classics in school, but he knew contemporary fiction. He worshiped writers and literature. Burt was an original character. I hadn't met anyone like him before. He was sort of bohemian, bearded, wore work shirts, blue jeans. I thought he was really cool, part of the other life I wanted to have when I was a child. We shared a love of books, and that was our bond. In the early days, when we were thinking of titles—who was going to be the president, the vice president, of our venture—Burt said, "Can't we just be the King and the Queen?" A very good idea, I thought.

> In 1975 and 1976, I was quite good friends with Burt. I knew in my heart this was not going to work. Burt had the most astronomical knowledge, which meant he wanted to purchase every book in the world, immediately, which he went out and did. It took Jeannette four years to bail out from that. But it was a great moment, actually, when Burt finally could buy all the books he'd ever wanted. In spite of just learning the business, Jeannette instantly understood what tone to set, because she loved books. She followed her heart. The image was perfect, from the beginning.
>
> —ALEXANDRA ANDERSON-SPIVY

Burt had brilliant ideas, one of which was to open the store with all the books signed by their authors. I'd drive to outlets and pick up cartons of books, then we'd go to the writer's house to have them signed. The very first author we visited was Allen Ginsberg. We drove to Allen's apartment on East Tenth Street around a quarter to twelve at night. I yelled "Allen!" at the top of my lungs. He threw down his key, and we walked up several flights of stairs. Burt had to carry all those boxes of his books up all those stairs. Ginsberg signed every book, and then, in a sweat, Burt had to carry all of the boxes down. For a while I stored the books in my apartment, but once we had 939 Madison, and the space was ready to receive them, we brought the books there. There were many, many signed books in my apartment.

Then they had to be shelved, and Burt's friends helped out. Burt excited people about the bookstore. He was so charismatic, he could charm well-known writers even into shelving books. Alice Trillin, Harold Brodkey—they were there, helping out, eager to see the store thrive. Ellen Schwamm helped, too, and in fact, Harold Brodkey, an early member of the Books & Co. family, and she met while shelving books. One night, Ellen invited everyone working in the bookstore for dinner, and it was that very night when Ellen fell madly in love with Harold. She left her husband and went off with him. Ellen had once taken a class with Anatole Broyard, who thought Harold was one of the greatest writers ever, so she was in love with him, in a sense, even before she met him.

Burt and I agreed on how the store should look, on getting as many books as possible signed, on what books should be in the store. Our mandate was literary fiction, poetry, and signed books. Books & Co. was going to be a writers' hangout. Initially I wanted to separate women writers from men writers, shelve Jane Austen and George Eliot and the Brontës in one section, but Burt said, "No, a writer is a writer; they should all be together." He was right.

I wanted to allow for a certain kind of experience, for discovery, I wanted Books & Co. to be a salon. So the store had to have a specific look. I knew what that was—it had to look the way it did in my dream: cozy, comfortable, lived in. I remember going with Brendan Gill to the Customs House, where I bought bookcases and vitrines. They contributed to its look of being a nineteenth-century bookstore.

When I grew up, if I wanted a book, I went to the library. My whole family did. There were very few bookstores throughout America. To me, books are the highest form of art and culture because they are the key means of communication among people. A good bookstore is even in a small way a repository of this art, the knowledge of centuries and indications of things to come if they're good stores. When I was co-owner of Eighth Street Bookshop, Burt used to drop in; that's how I knew him. Burt thought quite highly of the Eighth Street Bookshop. It was a key bookshop for a number of reasons, including the fact that we had a sense of the times, a sense of the value of writing and the value of writers and customers. Eighth Street was part of one last chain, one half of a chain of stores that were mostly lending libraries, books, cards, and whatnot. After World War II, they started selling them off. My brother, Eli, and I saw this happening. I wanted to get back in the book business—I'd been away in the army, but before I was in the army, I had some partners in some small shops in the West Bronx, which was like England then, and they were more or less like a lending library books, cards, so forth. By the time my brother and I went to Eighth Street we had ideas developed and some knowledge, and we were out to make it a real bookstore, and as soon as we could we got rid of everything but books. Eli had gotten a job at the Greenwich Village shop, and a month later they put up that plus some more stores for sale. We bought the Greenwich Village shop. That was 1947. At that time the book business just couldn't be compared in size with what it is now. I have seen such incredible growth in the book business, including the retail end. Paperbacks made a tremendous difference—it made bookstore-going not just something for the upper classes or special people; it made bookstore-going part of everyday life. This, too, remember, came after a period of well-being in the U.S. You get a country living through a history of building itself up, and then it gets to a point where it's ready to spend more time with its culture. But the fact is that the paperbacks did help—not only were they inexpensive, they made people feel at home in bookstores, and people came and bought. I remember giving what was a very large order for the initial ten books from Anchor Books—I know they included Henry James, *The Awkward Age*. The enormous growth has been a joke to me often. People will say to me, Oh, the book business is sad, nobody reads anymore, and I say, the business is bigger today than it's ever been. Early on in the American Booksellers Association, the whole convention was in one hotel, the exhibits in a relatively small space downstairs in the lobby, with all the attendees staying in one hotel. Coming early, you could stay in the lobby and watch everyone arrive, booksellers, salespeople, editors, publishers, like you were at a small family affair. Have you been to an ABA today?   —THEODORE WILENTZ

I remember talking to Donald Klopfer about when he and Bennett Cerf started Random House. The two of them would go out and sell America books. They would go to the one bookstore in Mississippi, the only bookstore—it wasn't exactly a burgeoning literary culture out there. A book was a much more stand-alone cultural artifact than it is now.   —JONATHAN GALASSI

Burt kept a secret list of great books. He loved Vance Bourjaily's *The Violated* and Hannah Green's *The Dead of the House*, which I loved, too. He introduced me to the work of anthropologist Tobias Schneebaum, whose *Keep the River on Your Right* became one of my most treasured reading experiences. The bookstore opened up other, even exotic, realms to me, just as books themselves did. When Cartier-Bresson came in to sign, in 1979, he told me that everyone should take photographs. That way, he said, everyone would look at things differently.

It was a mecca to me. At Brentano's and Doubleday, there was no personal relationship with anybody. The different people that Jeannette had working for her would very nicely impose on the customers the kind of writing they liked, which made it all the more interesting. Jeannette was frequently on the floor, and she was always interested in her customers and what they were reading. She told me she used to go through the house charge accounts—I had a charge there—to see what people were reading. The books were always listed on each person's sheet.

—BUD POMERANZ

Books & Co. became such a part of our lives. First, it was in the neighborhood, which gave a sense of neighborhood, and second, I found it impossible to walk past it without going in. I found it impossible to get out of it without an armload of books. Books are my great extravagance. One funny thing about going into the bookstore was that you usually saw a friend there, but even if you didn't, everybody looked vaguely familiar. You thought you'd met them before. —LYN CHASE

I lived two blocks from Books & Co., so I started going there as soon as it opened. I went there on a daily basis. Jeannette could tell you, or anybody who worked there, I was there every day, five days a week. As a child I was seriously dyslexic. They didn't know what dyslexia was in those days, they just thought it was a kind of mental illness. I couldn't read for a long period of time. The one thing I would do that held my attention for stretches of time was drawing. So I learned to draw. Then miraculously I had the kind of dyslexia that started to dissipate at the onset of puberty. I was extraordinarily lucky in that. But by that time I had begun to develop strategies for dealing with it. I really taught myself to read by reading *Planet*, pulp magazines. They were called detective, or planet, magazines, cheap magazines that came out with sensational science fiction stories or private eye stories. It was where a lot of private eye writers got their start in the forties. They were visually written and had very, very strong narrative lines, so they'd hold my attention just a few beats longer. The dyslexia's never completely gone away. I'm still learning strategies to deal with it. But I love to read. I love to read with the kind of energy you put into reading when you can't read. Consequently, I read all the time. I'm a very slow reader, and I don't make much progress, but I read all the time.   —ROBERT BENTON

Burt selected most of the books, some of which went on the Wall. The Wall was his invention. It was intended to represent a complete spectrum of hardcover books, with as many translations as possible, of the great works of literature from Shakespeare to living writers. When you entered the bookstore, it was on the left. The entire left wall consisted of important works of literature.

The Wall was a wall of fiction that very few people could have. That's where Burt's knowledge was at its best. If you went down that wall, you could come back day after day and still have a meal. At that time, it was just a remarkable thing that he did. No question. He took her idea, worked out the stocking, and the nature of the stock he put in was fine. If you have a bookseller's heart, you have a sensitivity to writing, which is related to what's going on.
—THEODORE WILENTZ

All of Burt's favorite writers would be on that wall, contemporary writers along with the good classics. Some of these were very popular writers—John Cheever was a big favorite of his. He knew all of these people from the Strand over the years, and they would come in, and in a matter of less than two months, the bookstore was a hit.
—ALBERT MURRAY

I've been in the publishing business for twenty-three years. When I first came to New York, in 1975, the first bookstore I got attached to or interested in was Gotham Book Mart, which represents the old literary bookstore. It was more or less in the last days of the Frances Steloff era, but it still had that aura of literary history. People would give book parties there still, and she was still around. And the whole sense of literature as central to the culture was different then than it is now, so I was very intrigued by that. Poetry is my thing, and it had a very strong poetic resonance. When Books & Co. started up, it was a lot spiffier, and it had an uptown aura. Jeannette had Burt Britton, and it was somewhat glitzier. But what it had that I think was the key to establishing the success of Books & Co. was the Wall. All the books that classified as litera-ture got on to the Wall, and the idea was they stayed there, this was the canon. The other thing, which I associated with Gotham and stores of that ilk, was that instead of featuring commercial books, Jeannette would feature new books, imports, things you couldn't find—odd books, strange books. The store catered to people like me, who aren't necessarily interested in the new book you can find in every bookstore, but in things that are new, but that you have to look for. Maybe some weren't even legal imports, but they were British books, foreign books, so you were always discovering things. Jeannette made it into a kind of clubhouse in the sense that you felt that when you were there you were with like-minded people. The Gotham went a different way, and Jeannette stepped into that breach and made a kind of center out of it. It was very homey.   —JONATHAN GALASSI

The Wall became famous, people talked about it. Writers came to see if they were on it, happy if they were, unhappy if they weren't. The horseshoe was downstairs from the beginning, too, and that, too, like the Wall, never changed. As soon as you entered the store, there it was. The salespeople and cash register were in the center of the island, which was created by the horseshoe counter. Customers could walk around it, browse, and see what we thought were the most interesting current titles. Later, I hung photographs of favorite writers and customers on the walls downstairs, and that too became famous. People liked to find themselves there or identify the people who were.

> When I was working at the Whitney Museum, I virtually went into Books & Co. every day. I could relax, sit on the couch upstairs and talk to the booksellers, the staff, whom I always enjoyed. They were always people I knew, so it was a real place for me to get out of the Whitney and be with what I love most—books. The first thing I did when I entered was go around the horseshoe. Then I saved going to the other parts of the front as dessert, after going into the back. I checked what was on the main table in fiction, on the main table in the second section, then back to see what was in art and history, then circled back and went upstairs, checked that out, then I went back down and said, Oh! there's still something to check—that was in the front. I knew I had entered the halls of the immortals when they put my photograph on the wall. —JOHN G. HANHARDT

I was a bit of an embarrassment, because I was reading at two or something, or so my parents tell me. My father I wouldn't normally believe, because he used to brag irrationally about me, but my mother, as in a classic Jewish household, would contradict everything. And she agrees that I was reading very, very early. I remember reading Comic Classics Illustrated. They had a version, I seem to remember, of a Bible. There would be Isaiah, standing there in his little pajamas, with an enormous bubble coming out of his mouth, with the whole of the prophesy of

Isaiah. Or Elijah being fed by the ravens. I thought this was very cool. I remember, where I grew up in Leigh-on-Sea in Essex, there was an old used bookstore that was full of old almanacs. It had things like the *Life of Napoleon*. But I remember one of the first things that I saw was an old photographic history that was published in 1936, I think it was, for George V, for the twenty-fifth anniversary of his coronation, so it was actually a kind of history of Britain from the death of Queen Victoria to baby George V, the most boring king of the twentieth century. It had lots of pictures and little text. The trench warfare in the First World War . . . I remember it had embossed blue covers, and it was very heavy, and the photographs were all kind of sepia brown. I was very, very fascinated by this book. I would come back to the bookstore to look at it, and it was two shillings or something, more than my pocket money. But I kept on coming back, and in the end the bookseller gave it to me, he was so tired. I must have been about six or seven. It was very nice. I must have been this rather comical little figure, at the time. There was something about the smell of old books; they had a rather pudding-y smell. I was very interested in, literally, the smell of different papers in books, old books and new books. I remember an old British publisher used this very pulpy, soft, kind of doughy paper that was wonderful. You could press your little thumb into it, and it would make a little indentation. And others, Dent, for example, had a very shiny, slightly strange stock, quite like coated paper. Somehow the actual tactile qualities of books appealed to me. Foxing—when really old books develop brown spots—was very interesting to me. These strange, measleslike blemishes would appear. And when I first saw my first wormhole, that was incredibly exciting, too. I kept on looking through wormholed books to see if the worm was still there, or the body of the worm was. Wormholes that have really eaten their way through pages go sideways through the book, so there's a pattern from one page to the next. I thought those were amazingly interesting. I was living in the seaside, and my other great passion was to beachcomb, and you would see seaworms and tiny critters burrowing. Books seemed to me to have this kind of oceanic, almost primordial quality. I loved all that as much as I loved the first pictures. Very sexual, very sensuous.

—SIMON SCHAMA

The image of the store was essential, and the window was an important part of it. We had a point of view, we were a curatorial eye focused on books, a gallery of books. The first window featured Barry Hannah's *Airships*, and in July 1978, a beautiful edition of a Colette book filled the window. Lee Radziwill came in to buy it.

I met Lee Radziwill, but I didn't know who she was. She bought two Colette novels and talked about Colette. I remember her saying, "I've read everything Colette's ever written." I said something like, "Oh that's nice," and she laughed. I met many people there, many writers. John Bernard Myers, for one, who wanted to read E. F. Benson's Lucia novels. He put his arm around me, he had a cane, and I walked him around the store and chatted him up. I knew who some of the people were, but I didn't know who other people were. I started working there, because I needed a job desperately, and John Ashbery said, "Books & Co. is always hiring people. Why don't you get a job there?" I got the job—this must have been '78, that's when I met Jeannette. She seemed very nice and bubbly, and Burt seemed dour. Jeannette thinks I worked there for a day, but I think I lasted five or six weeks. I never showed up on time, the store opened at 10 A.M., and I never got there before 10:30. One of the people I worked with was Steve Taylor, the guitarist who accompanied Allen Ginsberg on a lot of pieces for many, many years. We'd go out to eat afterwards, usually to complain about the bookstore, or whatever it was we complained about, and I decided I shouldn't do this very often, even though I liked Steve a lot, because what I wanted to do was write. So I'd work, go home, make dinner, and write, which is one of the reasons I was always late the next day. I'd write until three or four in the morning, go to sleep, get up, and try to get to work.

—JOHN YAU

Books & Co.'s official opening and party was set for October 18, 1978. We were ready earlier and, in a sense open to the public, but we didn't want to open officially in the summer. Burt hired Abbie Zabar to create our logo, which was printed on the invitations. Burt not only understood the importance of the look of things, he also knew the people who could create it. Ed Koren designed our original shopping bag, with drawings of creatures all over it, and the bag won a design award. Actually the creatures were caricatures of Burt, very droll drawings. It was a great shopping bag, but very expensive to produce.

Burt always had two things on hand—a case of bubbly water and a case of red wine. He would stand there with a cigar hanging out of his mouth and say, "Andrew, Andrew, get him a glass of wine." He'd be in the middle of conversation with, say, Richard Avedon. Off you go, get a glass of wine for this person, and Burt would have a glass, too.

—ANDREW BERGEN

I learned how to work the cash register, my station for the next year. Burt felt because he was the one who knew the writers and the books, we could save money by my being the only one who worked the register. I was so flustered when Lee Radziwill bought her Colette, I forgot to charge her sales tax and was much too embarrassed to run after her for it. But I made a much bigger mistake the first year. Every night we used to count the money; we didn't take in that much money as we were just starting. One night, there was a hundred-dollar bill, but it was a fake. Betty Lou, who Burt had brought on as an assistant, said, "Do you remember who gave it to you?" I said, "Yes, an extremely rich woman, a friend of Steven's, from an old family." Betty Lou said, "Call her and tell her."

> I had dropped notes off to something like a hundred people I knew who lived in the neighborhood and were able to buy all the books they wanted—and, for that matter, all the everything else they wanted, too. I said that a good friend of mine was opening a bookstore and that I hoped they'd go there often and give her a lot of business. On my list was a woman who was famously rich and social—exactly the sort of customer Jeannette needed to cultivate. And the woman did indeed take my suggestion and begin frequenting the store, which for her was conveniently next door to the Whitney Museum of which she was a trustee. She always paid Jeannette in cash, but one time she paid with what turned out to be, as they say, funny money. Jeannette turned to me for advice—"What should I do?"—and I said, "I know this woman very, very well, and here is what I would do: absolutely nothing. Eat the loss—if you call this to her attention, you'll only embarrass her and end up alienating her." But Jeannette didn't listen—she informed her that her C-note had been counterfeit. The woman never set foot in the store again.
>
> —STEVEN M. L. ARONSON

With more retail experience, I learned to swallow those kinds of losses.

Burt and I were too excited about ordering books. The basement filled up, the shelves were bulging and on the verge of collapsing. Books were in piles everywhere. One day the phone rang, but I couldn't find it. It rang and rang, one of my first calls at the store. Finally I found it, and it was Alex Sanger. I had just seen Alex at my cousin Liz Buckner's wedding. The concurrence of events in my life at this moment was phenomenal. The dream, hip surgery, finding Burt, finding the space, beginning the bookstore, then Alex. It was the perfect time, and I was as happy as I'd ever been.

Liz's wedding was on a Saturday afternoon, and I remember thinking, I don't know whether I'll have a good time. I didn't feel like getting dressed up. But I heard a voice, my mother's voice, saying, You have to go to the wedding. You never know who you're going to meet. I put on a pretty chiffon floral dress. It was cut low in the front and was a trifle racy, because one didn't wear much underneath, and it had a very low back. It came with a shawl, which made it a bit more demure to wear at a wedding. The dress was very soft, drapey, flowy, romantic-looking. I was having quite a good time, wandering around, when suddenly, a very handsome young man walks up to me—just my type—dark hair, big brown eyes. He said, "Aren't you Jeannette Watson?" I said yes. He said, "I'm Alex Sanger." I had known him years before in Fisher's Island, but Alex was two years younger than I. I would never have even looked at him at that point— he was my sister Olive's age. We had a nice chat, and he asked me to dance. He was a wonderful dancer, but then I had plans for the night, and he did, too. He said he would call me. A couple of days later, Burt and I were sitting in the store with a sales rep, when the phone rang.

My grandmother was Margaret Sanger. I was nineteen when she died. She had three children. My uncle Stewart was the eldest, then my dad was the second, and her daughter Peggy was the third. Peggy died at age four, basically of neglect, although pneumonia was the official reason. My grandmother was in exile for about a year in England when she was under indictment here. She left the kids behind, it's a long story. Peggy just didn't understand where her mother was. My grandmother came back, and a week later Peggy contracted pneumonia and died. A couple of things got my grandmother involved in reproductive rights for women. Her mother was pregnant eighteen times and died at age forty-nine. My grandmother became a nurse, after a couple of false starts, and nursed on the Lower East Side. She was called into cases of women dying from self-induced abortions. She put the two together and said there's got to be something better we can do for women. I became the head of Planned Parenthood New York, on January 1, 1991. I had been a partner of White and Case, left there in 1988, went into the manufacturing business, but in the summer of 1978, I was a practicing lawyer. I was really young, we were really young. Jeannette and I were both divorced. We saw each other at Liz's wedding. Liz was one of my oldest friends in the world. I was walking across the dance floor, kind of one side to the other, kind of cruising around, and Jeannette walked the other way across the dance floor. I hadn't seen her until then. I looked at her and stopped. "Aren't you Jeannette?" She looked at me a little strangely and said yes. I said, I remember meeting you at here, here, and here. We'd first met when we were little kids. She looked at me a little less blankly. I asked her to dance, and we were married six months later. At some point on the dance floor, though, or when we were sitting down, I asked, "What are you doing?" She said she was starting a bookstore on Madison Avenue. I remember being very intrigued. She said, "We're under construction, and I've got a partner." I'm sure she mentioned Burt's name. I remember her talking about wanting to have all the best literature in the store, all the ages of writing. She had told me the name of the bookstore, and I remembered it. Books & Co. I waited until Monday, playing hard-to-get, and called. The phone rang and rang, ten in the morning, eleven. At about the tenth ring, Jeannette picked up and said, "Books & Co." I said, "Hi, it's Alex. Are you busy?" She said, "No, this is the first phone call we've ever gotten, and I couldn't find the phone." It was underneath a pile of books.

—ALEXANDER SANGER

Male–female relationships were so complicated at that time, I'd never know whether I was supposed to pay or not. I'd married when I was twenty-one and divorced at twenty-six, and change was coming fast in the field of dating, where we need anthropologists to explain us to ourselves. But Alex was courtly, which I really loved. I am a romantic, and I've lived with him happily ever after.

> That was the beginning of a big transformation in her life, the start of Books & Co., and at about the same time Alex came into her life. It was a wonderful beginning. It's why I believe there are second acts in American lives. It was the beginning of a fabulous second act.
>
> —BARBARA LAZEAR ASCHER

On October 18, 1978, we had our grand, official opening, a day-into-night gala. We were open and going, celebrating from morning to night, and in the evening there was a splendid party. Many writers and friends came: Calvin Trillin, Fran Lebowitz, Paul Auster, Nora Ephron, James Merrill, Richard Howard, Howard Moss, Freddy Eberstadt, Isabel Eberstadt, Ogden Nash's daughter, and many others. And much of the same crew remained a part of the family at Books & Co.

> It was still a very heady moment in the cultural world. There were bookstores on Fourth Avenue, there was Max's Kansas City, there were still salons where the art world went. There was certainly nothing like Books & Co. when she started it. The last bookstore like it was Haywood Wakefield, on Madison Avenue and Sixty-fifth Street, started in the early forties by Betty Parsons, Ila McDermott, and Marian Willard. It closed in the mid-sixties. What Jeannette created was an instant salon. She provided a meeting place for writers, where writers felt nurtured. In a way maybe Eighth Street had done it, but it wasn't as cosmopolitan. Eighth Street was still more downtown-ish, more bohemian.   —ALEXANDRA ANDERSON-SPIVY

Remember Fourth Avenue when they had all the second-hand bookstores? You had to beg those guys to sell you a book. You had to scream and yell to get their attention because they were reading. You remember those old grumpy horrible guys? You would say, How much is this? They'd grumble, I don't know. Put a figure on it. Could you give me some idea of how much? So booksellers always agreed not to make a lot of money. What they didn't agree to was what's happened since the chains came in. No one can agree to that, because that's not just agreeing not to make much money, that's agreeing to starve to death. It's very hard to get people's consensus on that.

—FRAN LEBOWITZ

The bookstore was written up everywhere. Burt knew how to get publicity and, every time a piece came out, he'd place a hundred copies on the counter. Word of mouth spread quickly. In that way the store was doing fantastically, but Burt and I didn't keep track when ordering books. It's the lesson I didn't learn in school—bookkeeping, crucial to any business. We didn't even have a desk for a bookkeeper. We were paying Madison Avenue rent for nine months, and the store wasn't officially open. For those nine months, money went out, only. I had to keep putting in more and more money. We were ordering hundreds of copies of books, which the authors would happily sign. In those days, Ann Beattie, who was a friend of Burt's, would sell well, but many of the authors, who were also good writers, were much more obscure and didn't sell well at all.

She's got incredible business genes from her father and her grandfather. I think almost at the beginning she didn't want to use them, because the bookstore was just chaos when it opened. Burt was a quirky genius in his own way, but the place was a financial land mine. They didn't know what books they had, they didn't know how many books they sold, Burt was giving books away, and Jeannette didn't care.   —ALEXANDER SANGER

Burt recommended that Theodore Wilentz advise us. As Ted and his brother, Eli, had started New York's legendary Eighth Street Bookshop, he was a highly respected expert in the field.

Going to a store should be an experience, special, and to me it's a special experience when it's a good bookstore. Burt helped create that. Jeannette was very quiet and unsure of herself at the time, but she knew what she wanted, yet she was very much in the background. It was as if she had given over control to Burt. In fact when they had trouble, Burt recommended they call me in as a consultant.
                                                    —THEODORE WILENTZ

I was at the cash register every day, while Burt was talking to all the exciting authors. I felt a bit like Cinderella. I had the bookstore, I loved being there, I was near books, and though I didn't mind working the cash register, ironic as it was, I wanted to be acknowledged as one of the owners. But I wanted to maintain to the outside world that there were no problems, and I never talked about our trouble. When Paul Goldberger's article appeared in the *New York Times* on the architecture of the bookstore, he called it Burt Britton's bookstore. I wasn't mentioned.

At the beginning, I did think she worked at the bookstore for Burt. I thought she was a beautiful blond woman who was there to stand behind the counter. It took me a while to realize that actually that wasn't the case. I think she needed to be recognized for herself and for her own journey. I've always liked people who have made a life for themselves from places that are unexpected. I think I might have discovered this about her quite early.

—ANN LAUTERBACH

We had informal readings at the store, but we decided to have an official reading on January 9, 1979. Harold Brodkey introduced it. Poets John Hollander, Richard Howard, Howard Moss, and James Merrill read. It was spectacular. Burt was able to draw prestigious poets to our store, create a stellar lineup, an important literary event.

It was a big lineup. It was fun to do because we all were enthusiastic about the store, and it was fun to read the poems. It was a somewhat uncomfortable audience, because that space is so ungrateful, and I remember it was hot. We were all sort of squeezed in there, but it was the audience that in those days was interested in coming to hear these poets. I don't suppose that's changed very much. After all, Jimmy and Howard Nemerov were stars and famous, and Howard Moss and I had a certain acclaim in New York, at least where we were known. Howard was a very important figure because of the *New Yorker* connection. I was sort of pushing along, and the four of us had a good time. There's something about giving a reading in a bookstore that's particularly nice—you feel you're surrounded by the things that you're reading, that you can buy them, and it's much better than reading in a hall. I loved being at Books & Co. and using it. It seems to be an absolute, like having to have a fix—to buy books, to have them. It isn't that I don't like libraries. I use them and am happy to. I have a rather bookish family, and I was writing from the beginning. I wasn't always necessarily writing poems. In a sense I'm much more of a reader than I am a poet. I'm what's called an intellectual, and I was always an obsessive and compulsive reader. It's the part connected to all this, my love of bookstores, books, poetry. I don't think the bookishness and the poetry are necessarily the same thing, but the bookishness and my character are. I read all the time, late at night, late into the night, and nothing has ever stopped me, including my social and personal life, which seems to have been vastly impinged upon by reading, which is the most important thing in life, much more important than anything else I do. I'm sociable and affable, but I would rather read than do anything else. My family settled in Cleveland, Ohio, in the 1840s. They were German Jews, who came in that wave of immigration. I think my great-grandfather was sort of a glorified peddler. They became rich—my family owned a factory that made men's clothes. My grandfather, when he went on his wedding trip to Italy for three months—people did these things much more grandly in those days—decided that he and his wife must know Italian. There was a German organ maker who had sold his shop in Cremona, Italy, and come to the States in the beginning of the century or a little before. My grandfather, who died in 1926, before I was born, had commissioned him, Richard Laukhuff, to teach him and his fiancée Italian before their honeymoon. Then when they came back, Laukhuff, who had worked in my grandfather's factory, wanted to become a bookseller, and my grandfather set him up in business. My mother bought all her books from Richard Laukhuff, who turns up in Hart Crane's poems. He was the person in Cleveland who sold books, and Hart Crane used to go to his shop all the time. I bought books from Richard Laukhuff when I was a kid. In fact, Laukhuff's was the first bookstore I was ever in. I remember being given the run of the shop. I put Laukhuff in a couple of poems, including a poem I wrote about Crane, which is about bookstores. I could well have read my Hart Crane poem at that first reading in the store. It would have been very likely.

—RICHARD HOWARD

43

II *Laukhuff's Bookstore.*   I am fourteen, I live
on the Diet of Words, shoving a ladder around
high shelves while the German ex-organ-maker
smokes with a distant nightmare in his eyes
("You have heard of Essen," he murmurs, "you never
will again": it is nineteen forty-three),
his body on hinges, his elbows hovering wide
over the *Jugendstil* bindings (Werfel, Kraus . . .)
like a not-quite-open penknife. "Hart Crane?

He came here to marry the world . . . You understand?
Maritare mundum: it is the work of magic,
Mirandola says it somewhere, to marry the world . . .
And not much time to do it in, he had
to read all the books, to marry, *then* to burn . . .
It is one kind of greatness to grow old—
to be *able* to grow old, like Goethe;
it was Hart's kind to refuse. You understand?"
Laukhuff is asking *me*, laughing through smoke

his postponing, renouncing laugh. No, I don't—
that much I do. I climb down, clutching *The Bridge*
and hand it over. "Will I understand this,
Mr Laukhuff? Should I buy it?" "Cross it first.
You won't, but there is a certain value, there is
poetic justice in the sense of having missed
the full meaning of things. Sure, buy it. Spend
all you have, your mother will give you more."
The German penknife closes with a click.

Marriage, Hart. The endless war. The words.
Cleveland was our mother-in-lieu. We left.
                    —from "Decades" by Richard Howard

Around this time, Jackie Onassis sauntered in, looking gorgeous, muffled up in fur. She told me she loved the bookstore and

liked the Wall. It gave her so many ideas about books to read. She said she would come back, and she often did.

Hannah Green's was our third reading, and then we had a reading by William Goyen. He was a fine, modest man from Texas, a wonderful writer, and not as well known as he should have been. Goyen read from his unpublished autobiography, and it was a very moving night. On the night Bernard Malamud read, he proclaimed, "First there was Shakespeare & Co., then there was Books & Co. I'd like to thank Jeannette Watson and Burt Britton for having these books on their shelves." It was a gratifying moment.

Truman Capote came in often in the first years. He'd ask, "Do you want to go to the Carlyle?" and we'd run away together. He wasn't drinking, so we'd go to the Hotel Carlyle and order Tab. Truman would gossip and tell me shocking stories. He quoted Brendan Gill as having said, "A woman can never be too rich or too thin." I love reading people's diaries, and being with Truman was like having a scandalous diary read aloud. He showed me the announcement of Lee Radziwill calling off her wedding, and said, "I sent her a very expensive wedding present, I hope I can get it back." But one day Truman came in, probably right after having a hair-transplant operation, and there was a bloody gash on his head and blood on the collar of his coat.

Although, by this time, the store seemed to be doing well, there were big internal and financial problems. Ted Wilentz was troubled by what was happening at the store, and I was unhappy. I imagine Burt was also. It wasn't working.

> I had found Burt very likable, but if you have a staff turning over too much, not only don't you have the knowledge you need, but it's bad for the morale. And there was the attitude toward Jeannette. She did not have any book business knowledge. Burt did not have what I call new book knowledge. And I remember discovering that he had rented the top floor of the next-door building just to store books. That's Madison Avenue. It's not a warehouse area.
>
> —THEODORE WILENTZ

By then Alex and I were married. One evening I went to his law office to meet him for dinner, and our bookkeeper—who was not a professional—phoned me there. She said, "We're $30,000 overdrawn at the bank." She didn't know how it had happened. It was the day of absolute reckoning.

> Finally she figured it out and realized, "I've got to run this like a business." She took hold of the reins and turned it around, but I think there was resistance to even do that. Two weeks after it opened the store was just about bankrupt. She realized she had to buy out Burt and get the store out of bankruptcy. —ALEXANDER SANGER

During the first year of the store's life, books kept sprouting everywhere, growing like weeds. My father would come in, see the piles, the disorder, and become incredibly annoyed. "You're taking in $800,000, but you're spending way over $1 million." Later, Daddy said, "You have got to take responsibility for this. You can't blame it on Burt. It's your store. It's your money." I had to take action and change the situation.

> She went to talk to her father about it. She was trying to sort out different ways to refinance the store, how to buy out Burt, what was his interest worth. She would go to her father and come back and talk to me, go back to her father. It was very, very difficult. At one point he said, "I've got an idea. Jeannette's problem is that the store's overstocked with signed books that can't be returned. What I'm going to do is buy Jeannette's inventory from her and put it in my garage. Then, as the store gets on its feet, she can buy the inventory back from me and sell it." And that's what they did. He bought over $150,000 worth of books and had them trucked up to his garage in Greenwich. Jeannette got cash to refloat the store, and then bought out Burt. It was brilliant, but it wasn't easy. Her father was

paid out over a couple of years. He hadn't put money in, but he was a 50 percent shareholder of the store. It was a combination of his "genius," if you will, and creative ability, Jeannette's money and her creative ability, a fifty-fifty partnership.　　　　　　　　—ALEXANDER SANGER

My father's involvement in the bookstore gave me courage at the beginning. It gave me confidence that he thought enough of the idea to put money into it. When we got into trouble, his offer to buy the books was a boon to my spirits and to the store. He always took chances and was always an adventurous man.

I started out shoveling books in the legendary basement. The first few weeks I was there I just worked like a dog. There was this massive quantity of inventory that we were trying to organize and in some cases I think probably pack up for returns. We were moving it from one place to another and trying to determine if there was anything down there that should be upstairs, possibly we could sell it. It was a long time ago. God, I was earning $3.65 an hour.

　　　　　　　　—SUSAN SCOTT

Daddy was vigilant about his business investments. Right before he went to Russia, as ambassador to the Soviet Union, and even before the store's first-anniversary party, he hired a lawyer, George Gillespie, to come in every week and monitor our practices. We were not to order too many books, and we were to make sure books were being returned.

Burt was there for about three months when I came around. That was a very complicated process. It was a very intense struggle for a while, which I managed not to become directly involved in. There was a lot of crying and door slamming, all this strange stuff going on.

　　　　　　　　—PETER PHILBROOK

Our face to the world was happy and bright, so business went on as usual, which was always a little unusual. When Kurt Vonnegut's book was in the window, he came in and thanked us. Then he left, and I raced after him to get him to come back and sign. That day Neil Simon and Marsha Mason came in to sign, too, and the next Robin Williams bought $500 worth of books. Celebrity sightings were a regular and thrilling part of the Books & Co. day. Over the years, John F. Kennedy Jr., Edward Albee, John Cleese, Elmore Leonard, Roy Scheider, Isamu Noguchi, Candice Bergen, Jacques Derrida, and many others stopped by.

Our first-anniversary party was a glamorous affair. Nora Ephron, Patricia Bosworth, Calvin and Alice Trillin, Fran Lebowitz, Ann Lauterbach, Jackie Weld, Clara Dale, all our friends came, everybody. But things were going so badly between Burt and me that Burt didn't appear. I played the role of the wife who's forced to cover for her husband's absence. Where's Burt? everyone asked. I'm sure he's coming soon, I lied. We had just signed a new agreement, and Burt was upset. When he didn't come to the party, the split became public. To me it signified that it was all over.

> I always liked Burt. I always thought he was a riot. I would go in there and say, "I have to buy a present for someone." He'd say, "All right, talk to me." He would want to know all about the person's quirks, what they did, who their family was, then he would walk over to the shelf and pick something out. He rarely missed. He was really great at doing that. He loved books, but the partnership didn't work. She would come home, after some horrible day, and collapse. Whenever Jeannette goes into an emotional collapse, she says, "I'm going to bed. Bring me some tea and anything by Jane Austen." I'd bring her *Pride and Prejudice* or *Sense and Sensibility,* and she would drink tea, read, and fall asleep. That was her way of calming down and getting out of the twentieth century. She views herself as a nineteenth-century person. She says, "That's the century

I would have been happy in . . ." I say, "You would have been miserable. The bathrooms didn't work."

—ALEXANDER SANGER

The dream had become a nightmare. Our initial laxity with bookkeeping, the numbers of books we ordered and couldn't return because they were signed, the overstock that overwhelmed our small space, the staff turnover, the discontent between me and Burt, all of this created the enormous problems that meant the store could fail. It could close.

Finally, a divorce agreement was drawn up between Burt and me. We all met at the lawyer's office, with my accountant, Arthur Ruden, a gutsy character. He'd once been the accountant at Eighth Street. Months before, Burt had taken out insurance on both our lives, and Arthur said, dryly, "At this point you'd be better off dead." The store owed hundreds of thousands of dollars. We owed everyone so much money—everyone. People would call the store: May I please speak to Ms. Watson? I'd say, I'm sorry she isn't here right now. May I take a message?

Had things worked out, Burt would have owned half of the bookstore. He put everything into the store, so much effort and devotion. He worked seven days a week, fourteen-hour days. In retrospect, I'm grateful lawyers were brought in early enough, to document the problems and maintain oversight. As difficult as it was, everything was done in an orderly fashion. I wish the marriage of true book lovers had worked out, but instead the divorce papers were signed in January 1980. Burt left.

My father said, "I think you should close the store now." Then he said, "If you close it now, you can blame it on Burt. But if you keep going, it'll be your failure." I said, "I'd like to try!" After Burt left, many writers came to the store, stood around, and said, We're so sorry Burt left. They hadn't any idea of what had gone on.

There was a lot of talk about how Jeannette had come in with her money, taken over this great literary thing. Some of the writers boycotted Jeannette. But slowly, she won us over. Calvin Tompkins and I, who were married at the time, were urged not to go there. But Jeannette won everybody over. —SUSAN CHEEVER

Jeannette Watson's dream of opening up a literary bookstore became a nightmare almost as soon as she opened the doors. The bottom line was that the store lost $70,000 in sales of $600,000. . . . *Publishers Weekly*, 1980

When they split up, you didn't really have to choose sides, because Burt disappeared. —FRAN LEBOWITZ

Within one year Burt had put that store on the map. He had gotten so many write-ups, all within a year, from the *New Yorker* to *People* magazine. He created the Wall, which was a great idea, and it became a great publicity and promotional device. —THEODORE WILENTZ

Life in the store changed immediately. Andrew Bergen said, "We're going to do a window, pick the books you like, let's do it." I walked around and chose some favorites: Hannah Green, Jane Austen, Edith Wharton, Cynthia Ozick, I can't remember all of the authors. I hadn't been allowed in the window before, and it was an incredible treat, almost a guilty pleasure. Books, customers, talk, authors, readings, and now the window. Here we were on Madison Avenue, just doors from the Whitney Museum of American Art. Thousands of people passed the shop every day, and what they saw was the window, our view on the world and the world's initial view on us.

I loved doing the summer window. I'd bring in a beach chair, bathing suit, dark glasses, and a Diet Coke—the summer reading window. One of my favorites was for *White Trash Cooking* by Ernie Mickler. Peter Philbrook bought Wonder Bread, mayonnaise, potato chips, ketchup and put pictures and recipes of food like Scooter Pie, okra omelet, potato chip sandwiches into it. The book was published by Jonathan Williams of The Jargon Society. People thought it was hilarious, and we sold a lot of copies. Some might imagine it wasn't a Books & Co. book, but it was.

> The Upper East Side is a unique place. It's got a tremendous amount of wealth, and yet our location, being next to the museum, allowed for a mixture of people; it wasn't just the neighborhood folks, it was also people from all over the city and all over the world. I worked at Books & Co. from probably the autumn of 1979 until March of 1985. There was a desire on both Jeannette's and Burt's part to create an atmosphere where people felt they could stay and chitchat. In time, that was more possible for somebody who, like me, had just been a clerk. In time, I had more responsibility. I didn't have to be making sure I was always ringing up sales. I don't know if there's anything special about what I did. I think that the circumstances were unique, so I don't know that they translate to anyplace else. I always said after I left Books & Co., I would never work at another bookstore. It would never be as much fun. I'd never have the freedom to buy the kind of books that we were able to buy, or the freedom to sell the kind of books that we were able to sell.
>
> —ANDREW BERGEN

I had a strong awareness at readings, particularly by a first-time novelist, of their significance to writers. It was very rewarding to encourage them, and the readings were an idea and ideal of Books & Co. from its inception. It became my mission to present young writers, new writers. Patricia Bosworth was involved with the bookstore from the time we opened. She wrote a marvelous book, *Montgomery Clift: A Biography*, which she read at Books & Co. And there were Susan Cheever, Ted Mooney, Susanna Moore, who all read their first or early books here and visited often. Every book Ann Lauterbach published we presented and supported.

I remember feeling very excited that I could read there. At that time, more than later, the audiences were your friends, so there was a sense of a public place that had the possibility of a certain kind of intimacy and camaraderie. It's what the bookstore stood for. When my first book *Many Times, but Then* came out, doing the reading was a seminal moment—there have been a few of them—when you think you've entered the world of New York writers—the literary world, as it were. I had published a couple of very small chapbooks before *Many Times*, but everything up until then had been one's effort on one's own behalf.

—ANN LAUTERBACH

There's a significance, too—almost a drama—in introducing readers to books. Dramatic because books can and do change people's lives. I've felt that importance as much as I've felt it about introducing new writers to readers. Burt used to say, "It's just as easy to read a good book as a bad book." If people were given the right book, they could experience something wonderful. One woman told me that she wasn't a reader until the bookstore opened, but because of my suggestions, she was reading Balzac. It's what I'm most proud of doing over the years.

Before going to architecture school I had been a good English major. I read books like texts. Dickens, Milton, we analyzed them and then regathered our data, then we wrote an analysis or our interpretation, and it was always to interpret the language, to understand the author, but the sensual pleasure of reading had escaped me. It had just never been what I think Jeannette had experienced—getting lost in language. I enjoyed what I read, I was taught by some wonderful teachers who could convey the power of the language, and I enjoyed writing short stories, but reading for pleasure was not something I did a great deal of. Jeannette's romance with literature edified reading, which was influential to me, to say the least.   —CLARA DALE

Ted recommended Stan Lewis to be the second buyer/manager. Stan had had his own bookstore, a rare books store, Parnassus. We tried selling rare books, but they're hard to display. We couldn't keep them downstairs, they were too valuable, and it didn't work. Stan stayed for about a year and had some good ideas, like the newsletter, which he produced beautifully. I continued the newsletters, which were sent to our house list and featured the books we loved most. It was a place for me to write regularly about the novels, poetry, and nonfiction I found most compelling. The staff, too, always contributed, and that way we provided greater diversity and range of opinion and taste.

Burt had begun the art gallery upstairs, and Stan set up some shows. Especially memorable was the Steichen exhibition. But Stan's lasting contribution was the couch. He found it at B. Altman's. I'd always wanted a really nice couch for upstairs, and this couch was deep green leather and very comfortable, good to sit on, to read on. It was with us for nineteen years. The couch was worn in by all kinds of people sitting and reading, quietly absorbed. It was one of my favorite views, people reading on the green couch.

I had been in love with Books & Co. from the very first time I came to New York with my college girlfriend, Dara. I was in graduate school, in Iowa, in the MFA program, and it was 1979. We wandered around the city all day in a sort of combined fit of ecstasy and terror. We went to the Whitney and stumbled back out; we'd been out on the sidewalks by then for about fifteen hours, and I said, "Look, there's a bookstore." We walked in, and I knew immediately. You can just tell when you cross the threshold that there's something profound there. That it's more than just a bookstore. I don't know what it is. I think all those great books must actually exhale something into the ether. Dara and I looked through the books and went upstairs and realized there was a big sofa up there, just sat on it, and no one was going to tell you to get out, no one was going to tell you to buy anything, you could just sit on the sofa. I felt like a refugee who had suddenly been picked up by a boat. We sat on that sofa for an hour, reading books of poetry we couldn't believe she had. Dara picked up books from the philosophy section. Jeannette has stuff that you could find other places, but you'd have to really search for it. I was just starting to write and sitting on that sofa with Madison Avenue roaring around below through the glass, all these books around us, I kept thinking, This is that thing that's been in the cartoon balloon over my head. This is what I'm sitting in my shitty little apartment in Iowa City trying to create and get to.

—MICHAEL CUNNINGHAM

We carried literature from many countries, and when people were trying to decide which translation to buy—we often had several of the same book—I might make a recommendation. But usually I'd suggest: Why don't you take the books upstairs and sit on the couch, read a few pages from each, and see which you like best? It was so pleasant upstairs, so quiet. We never stopped people from reading in the store. On weekends, kids were sitting on our floor. We had no coffee machine, but anyone could go next door to the New Wave Coffee Shop, get a cup of coffee, come back, sit upstairs, and drink it.

Romare Bearden and I were very close friends. At first, we'd stop in to see Burt, and we met Jeannette, liked her, and they had a staff there, enthusiastic young people who knew the stock, and it was growing, and they were adding. We'd go in and browse and then we would go next door and eat, because we spent a lot of time next door, and you'd find people who were really at Books & Co., in this little restaurant next door. We were there when Roy Scheider of *Jaws* was there, Raquel Welch and her then-husband. There were all kinds in and out of there during those early days.

—ALBERT MURRAY

I came to the Whitney in 1978 as Librarian and Associate Curator for Special Collections, so I run the library, the archives, put on the occasional show. I think of Books & Co. as a kind of late-1970s idea of the literary culture, a world that's a little bit lost. We're one step further away from a reading culture. It was always pleasant to go in there and see art encompassed as part of a much larger reading world. Robert Darnton theorized about the crisis in reading of 1790—that there was a certain point, pre-1790, when it was an intellectual belief that one could know and have read all of the classics, but as printing expanded, scholars were staying up all night just to keep up, and the possibilities for what you should have, could have, read changed. There was some kind of break. You realized you couldn't do it. Years later everyone decides to be specialized; probably there's a lot less ambition, and there isn't that same sense of an intellectual, or intellectual culture, who must be in command of this vast knowledge.   —MAY CASTLEBERRY

Before Stan left, my staff took me out to dinner, to discuss how the store was doing, what could be improved. There was a lot of intimacy and staff involvement. I've always been interested in the people I work with, but when I started Books & Co., I was thirty-two. The employees were anywhere from twenty-two to twenty-five. We were closer in age and had lots of parties and dinners. When Ted Wilentz asked, with Stan gone, who out of the staff can be the manager? I said, Peter Philbrook. Peter was very brilliant, very shy, but he knew so much about books, had worked at another bookstore, and had worked for a woman, too, so I didn't think that would be a problem. I invited Peter to my apartment and explained that Stan was leaving. Would he be the manager? Peter was so shy he could barely look me in the face. But he said yes.

Andrew Bergen, Peter, and I were promoted, the right thing happened. It was a wonderful moment, like a small moment in a small bookstore in a very big city, and it was a moment of pure joy. Andrew did the art buying because that was his expertise, and I inherited the departments that were of no consequence to Peter. On and off, I did some of the children's buying and cookbooks and a few other things. Eventually both Andrew and I sat in on trade fiction most of the time because it was of interest to us.

—SUSAN SCOTT

The bookstore started doing better, even well. That made me very happy, as did Saul Steinberg, who told me he loved my office and thought it looked like a harem. I said he could draw in it anytime.

My first official title was floor manager, the person in charge of the staff, day-to-day operations, and when Jeannette asked me to be the manager, I was pretty young or perceived as being young. It was also a sort of triumph with me and Andrew and Susan. I may have always liked to do things in a consultative, committee kind of way. As time wore on, it just seemed clear that it was an unnecessary duplication to have a buyer and a manager, and it came to a point when I decided I was going to be the buyer, too, and so Chuck Campbell, who was a great guy, left. In a store that size, I would think it would be difficult to have a buyer and a manager. I had developed a clear sense of what needed to be done. Buying interested me, and control was what ultimately interested me. That way at least I was responsible for the store, what the store was, and that's what I think a manager is. Jeannette wanted to be fully informed and know what was going on, but she didn't want to deal with the day-to-day business. That was my job.

—PETER PHILBROOK

I gradually learned how to sell books, to talk to customers, to support writers, and to run the store with the staff's help. For a while Sylvia Friedman worked as our bookkeeper. She had once worked at the Gotham Book Mart and was very friendly with the legendary Frances Steloff. Sylvia invited Alex and me to dinner with Steloff. By then Steloff must have been ninety-three or ninety-four. She was very vivacious, still vital, and, she told us, she could stand on her head. It was a thrill to hear her reminisce about the Gotham. She spoke of paying the clerks thirty-five cents an hour! She told us she fired Tennessee Williams for being late on his first day of work. She was beautiful and full of enthusiasm.

At dinner that night, she taught me an important bookselling lesson. Steloff said, "You never say to customers you're out of a book; you walk them to the section. Even if you don't have the book, they may see something else they like." I repeated this at every staff meeting.

We used to fly up to Gotham Book Mart and get all the stuff on the front top shelf, Auden, Spender, Day Lewis, a fantastic collection. We'd fly from Tuskegee over the weekend or on cross-country training flights. I discovered Gotham in 1942, when I came to New York on a delayed honeymoon, because we had married in 1941, and my wife was still a student. She had one more year to go and had a summer job up in the Berkshires, she and her friend, who were majors in home economics, so they could get jobs with families vacationing there. This is 1942, I was called back in 1943. We came to New York in 1942 and spent some little time there, and then the others went on up to Massachusetts. I went on to New York with my WPA writers guide, a classic. It was helping New Yorkers find their way home, because they didn't know where they were, but I knew the whole thing from the map. The Gotham suited my tastes. I found when I went in all these pictures of people I admired, and when I came back to New York in 1947 to go to grad school, all these people giving parties, so I met people out of Greenwich Village—Delmore Schwartz, Ruth Stephan, Nicholas Callus. Read the journals *The Tiger's Eye* and *Chimera*. All that you could find at Gotham, the avant-garde stuff, and there was the section, We Moderns. It was a very literary background. People would try to put you into a civil rights context when they talked about the development of the American intellectual. They get confused when they deal with me because my world is not that world. My world is what is available in the United States.   —ALBERT MURRAY

My first purchases were at the Gotham Book Mart. The Gotham was where I found a very important anthology: Donald Allen's *New American Poetry*, which I proceeded to memorize and imitate when I was thirteen, going from Duncan to Creeley to O'Hara. Years later the Eighth Street Bookshop and St. Marks had a real charm. It was at Eighth Street that I met Allen Ginsberg.

—DAVID SHAPIRO

When Fran Lebowitz came in to sign *Social Studies*, I committed an act of aggressive bookselling. I had her personally inscribe six copies and then I charged them to six people. I'd just had my second child, and Fran suggested we call him "Fran." But we called him Andrew Campbell Sanger.

I would usually develop a routine about a certain book. I would concentrate on certain books at any one time and develop a whole spiel about it. I would find the right book that seemed to grab the most people—and there was a pleasure in doing that—there was a sense of satisfaction that you could sell two hundred copies of a book that might otherwise not sell at all. That's a blast. Not to say that many of those books I didn't really love, and it was wonderful that I was selling them and exposing people to them, but it also had a sinister quality to me. Still does.

—PETER PHILBROOK

Selling a book is a minimalist art, since less is definitely more. Give away too much of the plot, and people lose interest. Many reviews tell too much story and provide too little interpretation. To sell a book, I'd say, "This is wonderful, you'll enjoy it, the writing is extraordinary, but I don't want to tell you too much about it." That was sometimes sufficient, since one's own enthusiasm for the book carried weight. Sometimes I presented more of the book's ideas, talked about its structure, depending upon my judgment of what the customer needed to know.

I felt selling books was like being a doctor. You just asked for symptoms and could make a diagnosis. I used to say, What was the last book you read and loved? And then go from there. People love to talk about themselves and so then you've given them an opportunity to tell you what they love and then that just makes it easier for you and then they're happy, too, because they're talking about themselves. Some of the customers wanted their hands held by one of us specifically. We each had our own following. I don't mean that egotistically—Peter especially had his own following. There were any number of people for whom no one would do but Peter. All of the rest of us at one time or another had a few customers like that. Nobody had as many as Peter.   —SUSAN SCOTT

There were opportunities to talk, and I know Peter made some good friendships. In the early eighties, there was a tremendous amount of money around. This was also the early Reagan years, before 1987. Property values were skyrocketing, the stock market was doing very well, there was money. The exchange rate between the estates in Europe was very good, which was very good for Books & Co. and the work I did, because we imported books and they had a great markup. If you looked at all that, every single customer interaction, on a busy Saturday or Sunday, could be very interesting and potentially fruitful. A lot of money was made. We sold a lot. —ANDREW BERGEN

Selling books, talking about them, I'd remember their stories and themes again, with all the delight they gave me. I'd return to that pleasure, which was what I hoped to communicate. I came to believe that, philosophically, talking about books was an extension of friendship, with the writers and the customers. Knowing the writers' work, especially when they're starting out, unknown and unsure, and letting them know you know it, can make a great difference to them.

I went up to the counter to buy a book, and Peter Philbrook recognized me, he knew who I was. That didn't happen very often to me in 1979, 1980. I don't think a writer could have been more obscure than I was then. As Nathaniel Hawthorne once put it: "the obscurest man of letters in America." Needless to say, I was touched by Peter's kindness, and we eventually became friends. After that, whenever I was in the neighborhood, I would stop in, and that's how I came to know the store. Curiously, though, I had been visiting that building since the mid-sixties. My aunt and uncle lived there. When I started writing poems and stories as a high-school student, my uncle, Allen Mandelbaum—poet, professor, translator of Dante, Virgil, Homer, and others—was the first person I showed them to. He taught me many important lessons about literature in that building. In some sense, you could actually say I turned into a writer there. How eerie that Books & Co. should eventually move in downstairs. Of all the tens of thousands of buildings in New York! —PAUL AUSTER

A camaraderie and friendship existed between the staff and me. We celebrated every birthday with a Greenberg's chocolate cake, chocolate being my most cherished vice. It became a Books & Co. tradition—cake, a party, all of us singing "Happy Birthday." There was an intimacy and a shared purpose, too. At that time, the house charge accounts amounted only to about twenty people, and many of them were my friends. So at the end of the month I did the additions and sent out the bills. It was all very close and personal. For the early readings and other events, I'd bring banana bread or muffins to the store.

> One is always introduced to somebody when one walks in there, because she knows everybody, so there's always this sort of marvelous, Do you know so-and-so, and then you get to shake hands and say hello. It's the best part about New York, actually, this idea that suddenly something can happen and everything is shifted. The ground is slightly shifted.   —ANN LAUTERBACH

Peter, Andrew, and Susan were the backbone of the bookstore, each worked at Books & Co. for many years. Their presence, the stability, was extremely important. The triumvirate absolutely helped to create Books & Co.'s identity.

> I took over the art books, which was, from my point of view, a good move, because they're the ones that brought in a lot of cash. I ran that section of the store along with architecture, photography books, and eventually I was the buyer. I memorized every book we had, not on purpose, but just by handling them, by being around them. I had my own taste, what I read, what I was interested in, but in terms of knowing the stock, it's a question of being interested in it, being around it. There's no real mystery. The opportunity Jeannette gave people working there was to sell their taste. It's not that often you get to do that,

particularly when it comes to books. You can't do that at any of the big stores. You can't do it either at most small stores. Most small stores are dominated by one person, one ego sort of rules, and while that always was true to some degree at Books & Co., depending on the management, there wasn't anyone who has ever run that store who wasn't going to let somebody who was having a run on a book not get more of it, unless they were a fool.

—ANDREW BERGEN

I had one customer who got to know me after a while and he came in regularly, usually on an evening when there was a reading. He'd say he needed a new book and usually would not comment on the previous book at all. He'd say he didn't want it to break the back of a twenty-dollar bill, just put it in a bag, didn't want to be sold on a book, didn't want to know anything about it. He just wanted it flipped into a bag, and he'd take it away. He would set financial limits. Maybe he'd be in the mood for a paperback, maybe in the mood for a hardback, which at the time didn't break the back of a twenty-dollar bill. Rarely if ever commented favorably or unfavorably about my previous selections. Just wanted a new book. Potluck. I waited on him all of the years I was there.

—SUSAN SCOTT

We achieved our imprimatur from the books we carried— unusual books, literary fiction, university press books, books people couldn't find everywhere. These came to be known and spoken of by the publishers' sales representatives as a Books & Co. book. Some of the reps worked with us for years, knew our taste, knew what to emphasize from their list. Something literary, not commercial, though hopefully both, like a Joan Didion book—well written, maybe contemporary European or Eastern European literature. But it was also the staff—knowledgeable, personable, there every day for years— that earned us our name.

I used to go down to Jaap Reitman's, the art bookstore in Soho, until Jaap Reitman threw me out of the store one day. I'd go see what he had, then buy it for the Upper East Side. There was no other way I was going to find out about stuff. Jaap threw me out in about 1983 or 1984, because he had gotten wind of what I was doing—writing down titles. I didn't feel I was actually stealing any business from him, because of where our location was. But he wasn't too thrilled. It's closed now. I went again after I left the book business. In fact I stumbled in in the last few days of its existence. I always enjoyed that store. It's a tragedy that it's gone.   —ANDREW BERGEN

Peter, who was manager and buyer for thirteen years, Andrew, and Susan were all so capable. I could trust the entire store to them. But I learned an important lesson early on: One could find a good manager more easily than a buyer. The buyer was crucial. Peter was a brilliant buyer, uncanny.

The basic thing in stocking is the owner or manager or whoever is the key person responsible for the buying. You can't stand over the buyers while they're ordering each book. You have to pick people who will buy the way you want them to buy, allowing for their own individual taste, allowing for the fact that in some cases they may know more than you. You've got so much room—you've got so much money and credit—which is a part of it, a large part. This is the nature of the store: You want to have a cookbook section, an art book section, you want to specialize in fiction. The nature of the store determines what you buy. The retail book business is a tremendous amount of paperwork, and it's a small-money business. You're not selling mink coats. Even a forty-dollar book is not that terribly expensive, and that's an expensive book. The gross profit should be roughly sixteen dollars on a forty-dollar book, 40 percent. If that was net profit, that's a different matter. You have unsold books, stolen books, damaged books. Maybe 36 percent net. Remember that the giant stores are much more than bookstores. They've made themselves into entertainment complexes. Today a café is part of a store. —THEODORE WILENTZ

A bookstore creates its character, its sense of itself, through the buying decisions, and that is, I suspect, nowhere more evident than at Books & Co. We were arrogant enough not to feature best-sellers. We'd put them under the stairs. What we did order in ones and twos was Danielle Steel. We were much too snobby about literary tastes to buy that stuff and display it prominently. During the eighties, we didn't need to sell it. We had found a niche, and again we had garnered, with the buying decisions we made, a big chunk of literary New York who could come to our store and find a good book, not just the book that everybody else was reading. If we played our cards right, we could make it into the book that everybody else, at least in their set, was reading.   —SUSAN SCOTT

Peter developed the philosophy section, which became famous. Since he was here almost fifteen years, imagine how well people knew him, and how well Peter knew their exact tastes and reading habits. Sometimes he'd order a book in advance for someone, knowing that the person would want it.

I remember advocating that we have a philosophy section, and Stan thought it was a good idea, so I just started working on it. It gradually took up more and more space, from being on one side of the wall upstairs to being on the other side, too, so it was almost the entire room. At that point it was one of the largest philosophy sections in the city. I was primarily addressing my own interests most of the time. To a certain extent the interest is in everything, though the section was always in a certain way leaning toward some kind of fashionable continental philosophy. One week I decided I didn't like Foucault, we had less Foucault. It was much less geared toward analytical philosophy or philosophy of science. It certainly found an audience. I don't imagine there's a lot of people who decide they'd like to pursue philosophy after they leave school, but I think there's a certain market among the people who come to the Whitney. The section was also critical theory, which was riding very high at that point. At the same time we had the first reading, probably, outside the Columbia University area, for Julia Kristeva, and I think we had the first reading Baudrillard did. It wasn't like people in the early eighties were breaking down the doors to come, either. This was before all the books were translated and published. He wasn't that well known.

—PETER PHILBROOK

Peter was a reader after my own heart, very intense, rather dour, not folksy like Burt, and very, very attentive. As I discovered how many literary passions we shared I came to have complete confidence in his judgment about what I would want to read. I'd come into the store and he'd greet me with, "I put this aside for you because I know you're going to want it." And whether I'd heard of the book or not, they were often quite arcane, I invariably bought it. And he was always right. Sometimes what he put aside for me were new books by writers he knew were favorites of mine (and of his), like Thomas Bernhard, or retranslations of Kierkegaard, whatever. Sometimes, if I hadn't been in the store for a while, he'd send me a book I hadn't asked for. And he never made a mistake. The only time I ever surprised him was after I started writing *The Volcano Lover* and had placed an order by phone with one of the clerks for some scholarly tomes on eighteenth-century British naval history, the Napoleonic wars, etc. As I recall, he called me and said, "What's going on, Susan?" I had to reassure him that I hadn't morphed into somebody else, but that I had to do some background reading for a new novel. "It's what some people, though not me, dignify by the name of research," I told him. "I call it boning up." It was an ideal relationship of sorts, to have the manager of the best bookstore in town as an accomplice of mine in the great project of reading only what's worth reading (that is, what's worth rereading). It wasn't always convenient to get up to Books & Co., but Peter had hooked me. I wouldn't have dreamt of disappointing him and doing any of my book buying a little more locally. —SUSAN SONTAG

Andrew was not just knowledgeable about art and art books, he also loved to read and was a very compelling salesman. When he really liked a book, he could sell a hundred copies of it.

Because the store was next to the Whitney, there was always an art component to it, and at that time the art market was beginning to shift. People with money were beginning to get interested in buying a new bunch of painters, sculptors. There was also beginning to be an interest in art books, in terms of value, and there was some real value attached to books. The Whitney had an Edward Hopper show, and suddenly this monograph that had been worth nothing two years before was selling for $300. Suddenly value got out of whack. —ANDREW BERGEN

It reached the point where it was bookstore therapy. I'd say, "Andrew, it's a three-alarm day. I need to get away, and I can't get on a plane." He'd say, "I've got just the book for you." They introduced me to books I never would have seen. I never would have read Robertson Davies on my own, basically, because he wasn't widely advertised.

—CLARA DALE

Andrew ran the gallery for a while, curating the shows, and then, after he stopped, someone else did and put up a show with a photograph of a naked man clutching his genitals. By then, my children were walking in and out of the store, and I felt it wasn't entirely appropriate for a family bookstore. So I took over the gallery, and we continued to have a lot of nudes on the walls, but no men clutching their genitals. When you run a store like Books & Co., there are offers and proposals, not to say propositions, every day, all the time. People wanted shows here, and wrote me or dropped by. I'd look at their work and decide whether to do it. Sometimes friends or customers suggested shows, and we'd do those. I tried to be open to all suggestions and to support loyal customers.

Jeannette's way was once much more common in the less formal art world of the past, having small exhibits, putting them up for a month or two months, without a lot of fanfare, but in fact giving people good exposure on the walls of the bookstore. She also encompassed a kind of interest in the visual arts—again open, experimental, generous. She literally put up what she liked.

—ALEXANDRA ANDERSON-SPIVY

We developed an extensive photography section. Photo books were popular in the eighties, and for a while, we did a very good business in it. Our gallery also featured many different photographers. Early on we were fortunate to have an Andre Kertesz show and an exhibit of Geoffrey James and later Lynn Davis. Lynn exhibited her photographs of Tibetan monks. She wanted to show this work in our gallery, because its ambience suited her religious sensibility.

When Lynn Davis had her pictures of the Buddhist monks—an amazing exhibition—it was quite interesting. Lynn would show those pictures in the bookstore, but wouldn't show them in a gallery. She felt some kind of affinity with Jeannette, felt that this was an appropriate place to have these pictures, because the work wasn't a commercial project. Jeannette must have had a hundred exhibitions in there, an ancillary part of the program, giving another layer, another texture, another piece of the cultural pie, combining those unexpected people together. I don't think really for the past ten years there's been that kind of crossroads anywhere. Everything's become much more segmented and specialized.

—ALEXANDRA ANDERSON-SPIVY

I was particularly proud of one exhibition: photographer John Albok. Albok was great friends with Andre Kertesz, a fellow Hungarian, and took photographs of New York in the thirties and forties. He went almost daily to Central Park and photographed there, documenting the park and New York. But he supported himself as a tailor. It was Albok's daughter, Ilena Albok Vitarius, who first contacted me about his work. Albok died in 1982, and in 1987, we used an Albok photograph for our Christmas card. Ilena wrote: "Dad would be so honored to know you chose his card as your Season's Greeting to your friends. I get chills every time I see it." We also showed photographer Grace Knowlton and many painters, including my cousin Walker Buckner, who had two shows. Another exhibition was the work of one of my great friends and earliest customers, Romare Bearden.

"In the late seventies, I used to take the train from New Haven to New York on Saturdays, to spend afternoons with Albert Murray at Books & Co. on Madison Avenue. We would roam—often joined by artist Romare Bearden—through fiction, criticism, philosophy, music. Murray always seemed to wind up fingering densely printed

68

paperbacks by Joyce, Mann, Proust, or Faulkner; Bearden, typically, would pick up a copy of something daunting like Rilke's 'Letters on Cézanne' and then insist that I read it on the train home that night. In those days Murray was writing Count Basie's autobiography—a project that he didn't finish until 1985."

—from "King of Cats," HENRY LOUIS GATES JR.,
The New Yorker, April 8, 1996

Romie and I did a lot of book buying and browsing together as well as a lot of gallery going. Books & Co. was right where the galleries were, right next door to the Whitney, so that was right in our orbit of activity, and it was our kind of bookstore, like we thought of it as a British bookstore, and it had all these quality books. And anarchists, we were made so welcome and invited to come back that it was convenient. We would go looking at pictures, let's say on Saturday mornings and other times, too, but certainly we would do the New York Saturday morning art gallery–combing thing, so it became our regular stop. —ALBERT MURRAY

What can be better than introducing the work of someone you love? In 1980, Fran Lebowitz read from her spectacular first book, *Metropolitan Life.* She was a great reader, not only of her own work, but also of others'. For years I relied on her judgment and recommendations: Stephen Millhauser, Deborah Eisenberg, Mary McGarry Morris. Fran introduced Deborah at her reading. She also singlehandedly, doggedly, brought John O'Hara back from the dead and wrote the preface to *The Portable John O'Hara.* Fran became a major friend of the store. She attended many of the parties and was so brilliant, so funny, talking and eating. Fran loves to eat.

I'm an exceptionally talented eater. I'm very interested in food. I think about food quite a bit. I read cookbooks. I love to eat, but I don't love to cook. Not liking to cook probably is just part of my general slothfulness. There are a lot of things that conspire against me working, probably the primary one being I'm just incredibly lazy. I'm slothful. You cannot imagine how lazy I am. I never understand all these people saying they love to work. They'd work whether they had to work or not. In fact, I know a number of people who don't have to work, but work. I think of them as fools. I was born to be an heiress. I could easily fill my days with pleasure. I have everything necessary to be an heiress, except money. Jeannette is an heiress, and she works. Absurd. Every writer would like to have a bookstore. I would love to have a bookstore. In fact, if I win the lottery I plan on having a bookstore. A bookstore with a door policy. It would not be open to the general public. There would definitely be someone at the door, and that person would be me. Jeannette lets you smoke in her office. Very important. She's a real bookseller. All booksellers should be like Jeannette. I don't mean, obviously, exactly like Jeannette, but owning a bookstore, being a bookseller, was never a very lucrative endeavor. It's a passion as opposed to a business in the sense that if you're going to go to all the trouble of going to work every day and having a store, almost any other kind of store would be more lucrative. Almost any other thing that you could think of that people could sell people want to buy more than books. I'm a bulk buyer. I buy many books at a time. I went to Books & Co. about once a month, but Jeannette would also send them over to the house—a full-service bookstore. It's better for me to call, in the same way if you were a drunk, it would be better to call the bar, because then just the number of drinks you initially started out wanting would come to your house. It would be better to call and say, Would you send six Martinis over, than to go to the bar where you would have endless drinks. I read when I'm supposed to be writing. I read all day. I know about being a junkie—this is what I do instead of heroin. It's much more expensive than heroin. But it's more glamorous. Ever since I learned to read, I'd spend most of my time reading, less when I was a kid because I had to go to school all day. I had to go to school, which really interfered with my education. I decided to be a writer when I learned to read. I should've realized that I was going to be a reader, but somehow I thought I would make that transition more easily than I have. I'm reading so I don't have to write. I'm not writing because I'm reading. I reserve all of my terror for writing. —FRAN LEBOWITZ

It wasn't easy sometimes getting the writers we wanted. I triumphed with Diana Trilling. First she agreed to give a reading, but then her publicist at Harcourt Brace said she wouldn't. Trilling wished to seclude herself to write her memoirs, and no longer wanted to read from *Mrs. Harris*. I wrote to Trilling, telling her I'd already printed 4,000 brochures with her name on it. I asked if she'd be willing to read from something else—an unpublished work, perhaps. Her letter in reply was a triumph in its own way.

Dear Ms. Watson:

    The mails are not to blame for my delay in replying to your letter of December 17th—it has been sitting on my desk while I try to figure out how to answer it. I feel awful about reneging on a commitment even when it doesn't create embarrassment at the other end, but in your instance, when you've already announced my appearance in February, I find myself in a terrible dilemma. On the one hand, there's your awkward situation for which I'm responsible by withdrawing. On the other hand, I've cancelled *all* the reading engagements that were arranged for me and how can I justify my reinstating the appearance at Books & Co. but not elsewhere?

I notice that in your announcement you say that I will read from *Mrs. Harris* and "other works"—perhaps this gives me a way out. I can think of the occasion as a *general* reading and not especially as promotion of the Harris book, from which I would then read only briefly. Would you give me a couple of weeks to ponder whether this is a decent solution?

By the way, I'm not taking refuge to write my "memoirs" or certainly not in the conventional meaning of that word. Although it is autobiographical, it stops at my marriage, at the age of 23. That's when most people would want my memoirs to begin!

Cordially,
Diana Trilling

Sometimes authors would write to me asking for readings or signings. William Goyen, for instance, wrote asking for help with his new book, *Arcadio*: "Books & Co. is the only place I'd care about having an autographing gathering. . . . I believe we could sell a lot of books."

When Susan Cheever read here the second time, from *A Handsome Man*, she was teamed with Susanna Moore.

After college I became a high school English teacher. I swore I would never be a writer. I changed my name. I went to live in Colorado, and I got married. But that was as good a way as any. I remember the reading I gave at Books & Co. with Susanna Moore. Nan Talese was our editor. Relationships with one's editors are more intense than one's marriages. What I remember is that I was having a clothes crisis. Nan Talese said, "Susanna's just going to wear her old Givenchy." I just died. I spent most of my early career in a state of fear and intimidation, which sounds stupid. My first book party was at Elaine's, and my parents were scared to come. My father was as scared as I was. I had to say to Elaine, "When these two short people come to the door, please be nice to them. They're my parents." I was just scared all the time. For my book *Elizabeth Cole*, Jeannette gave the party at the store. It's a very social place, without being a scene in a bad way. There are so many horrors in publication. One of the horrors is which of your friends is going to give the party. Is there going to be a party? It's worse than a birthday. Jeannette said, "Let me give the party in the store after the reading." It was perfect. —SUSAN CHEEVER

It's extremely important for writers to be involved in gathering an audience for their readings. Sometimes nobody showed up, which was horrible. I'd say to the writer, Please invite people, tell your friends, we want a crowd. But writers and publishers sometimes imagined that for a reading at Books & Co., nobody would have to do anything; there would be an audience. That was never true. There's so much going on in New York, the store had to work for every audience. It had become harder and harder to sell and promote poetry and literary fiction.

Jeannette had created the store to represent the backlist— and the Wall was meant to have the great works of literature. If the publisher didn't have the ingredients for the Wall, the Wall was going to become rather anemic. We did our best to make sure that we kept stuff in stock over time. The change in the tax law in 1987, when publishers were no longer able to write off their backlists, their warehouses which held their backlists, was a big problem. At the time of that shift, you could still rely on some of the distributors to have some older stock to buy, but that slowly changed. Publishers have taken advantage of it in a negative way by reissuing books at inflated prices. You had a nice hardcover that cost you very little to produce fifteen years ago, but you now produce a cheap paperback for probably about the same as it cost you to produce the well-made hardcover. You sell it for almost the same price as you would have sold a hardcover ten or fifteen years ago. The main issue that bugs me—they're badly made, and they're expensive. —ANDREW BERGEN

After the new tax law in 1987 [that taxed inventory], it became very important for publishers to control their printings, not have too many books sitting around, and also, when books get returned, books that haven't sold, to deal with them, pulp them or remainder them, to control inventory very closely. Things have changed a lot, because all the bookstores and all the publishing companies have incredible computer systems now. They can keep track of their inventory very closely, but it's an ongoing concern. Even at Penguin there are memos that come around several times a year. We're either considering remaindering or pulping books, and sometimes it's just so hard to look at these lists. Often we can just say, No, you can't possibly put this out of print, and then it's fine. A computer program picks up everything. —PAUL SLOVAK

If it were an unknown writer reading, and first novelists usually are, I feared no one would buy the book. I started throwing dinner parties at my apartment to celebrate the work, the writer. If people were invited to my house afterward, I figured they'd feel obligated to buy the book. They didn't. People would RSVP: I can't come to the reading, but I can come to the dinner. I wanted to say: You can't come unless you go to the bookstore and buy the book. Susan Cheever always told me I should be more aggressive.

Sometimes I would just flog a book, anybody who came in that I knew, anybody who asked what was good—I would sell this book. The only problem in that case is I probably had reached such a fever pitch, I just kind of slammed it down on the counter and said, You have to read it. I didn't do that very often, only a few times, and I think people probably bought it to get away from me.

—PETER PHILBROOK

It occurred to me that I was ideally suited for publishing, because I had been surrounded by books my whole life. I had worked in libraries, both growing up and at university. So I came to New York, started applying, and actually my very first job was at Penguin—I've been here my whole career since 1983, first as the publicity assistant to the director of publicity. I love bookstores, and in my job, I've cultivated the independents over the years and gotten to know them all. They are the booksellers that can really sell our literary titles, because they read, care about books, and hand sell them—they recommend them to people. We send authors to them for readings, and there's a sense that there's twenty or thirty—some of them have closed now— very key independent bookstores that together could account for a significant part of the sales of literary writers' work. One personally cultivates the buyers, gets them reading things early. Many of the stores started producing newsletters and keep mailing lists, so that every month they send out a newsletter that not only has all of their upcoming events on it, but different people in the store write little essays about books they've read which they like or forthcoming books they recommend. Some of these mailing lists can be up to ten thousand people, so it's a very effective tool for making people aware of books, because it's gotten harder to get reviews than it used to be. A lot of newspapers and magazines aren't running nearly as many reviews as they used to, and there are more books being published.

—PAUL SLOVAK

To promote new writing and writers, in 1980, I had started a foundation, the 939 Foundation. It lasted about five years. The advisory board included editors Aaron Ascher and Seymour "Sam" Lawrence, and writers such as Carlos Fuentes, all of whom recommended writers for the series.

> I would not feel well if I were not supporting it as much as I can. I think you are dealing with matters whose time has come. Given the difficulty that younger writers find publishing first books or even appearing in periodical publications, I think it takes more than a good agent, it takes an atmosphere, a literary world, to sustain these authors, convince the publishers and find outlets.
>
> —CARLOS FUENTES,
> April 4, 1982 (from a letter)

We had readings every week, and the foundation paid a salary to Barbara Penn to run the series, send out announcements, and do publicity. But though the bookstore and the foundation were meant to be different entities, the separation was not clear to many. We had to charge admission to support the series, and I wasn't entirely comfortable with this. The staff wasn't comfortable with an outside person managing the series. I learned that one can't easily bring in a manager, or anyone, from the outside, to manage the bookstore or to run events. It was better if the person emerged organically from within, so the person would understand the nature of the store. The foundation was my attempt, though, to create more attention for writers and readings, not to have the readings function only as extensions of the bookstore.

> Readings are a very effective tool in terms of getting an author's book out into the world and getting people to talk about it. I think more than anything else books sell by word of mouth and by recommendation.
>
> —PAUL SLOVAK

I remember introducing Jamaica Kincaid there a few times, and other writers. It's funny, it's not an ideal place either to go to or give a reading, because it's such a small space, but there was a very nice family feeling about it. It was sort of like being in your living room. It was a very good place to get something going, a kind of catalyst.

—JONATHAN GALASSI

I love reading my work aloud. In fact, the touring that I do when my books come out consists almost entirely of bookstore readings—that, and a few interview shows on National Public Radio. Of course, being an eloquent reader of your own work has nothing to do with being or not being a good writer. If you're good at reading to an audience, the skills you employ are those of the actor in you that you repressed in order to become a writer. It's all about speaking up and knowing when to pause. The most seductive reader I ever heard was Don Barthelme. His phrasing was magical. Right now the reader of his own work I find most thrilling to listen to is James Fenton.

—SUSAN SONTAG

I fault the writer for being a bad writer much more than for being a bad reader. —FRAN LEBOWITZ

Our events were resolutely varied, eclectic, attuned primarily to the literary community's needs. In 1981, we held a benefit for PEN—The NYC Poetry Marathon, a reading of poems about New York, from Howard Moss's anthology *New York: Poems.* Among the readers were John Lithgow, Tammy Grimes, Barbara Feldon, Christopher Walken, Patricia Spears Jones, John Guare.

There was an incredibly broad range of material presented through the readings. Very unpredictable, which is one of its charms. You're not just going to get the novelist of the week, the intellectual darling of the week. You got the most famous along with the most obscure.

—ALEXANDRA ANDERSON-SPIVY

We sponsored a Bloomsbury evening with a Virginia Woolf reading, to support the Royal Oak Restoration Foundation's project; Nigel Nicolson commented and reminisced. There was a James Joyce Centennial reading, a tribute to Delmore Schwartz, a commemorative birthday reading for Elizabeth Bishop. Ted Joans read from Langston Hughes and André Breton, and Barbara Guest read from her much anticipated biography of H. D.

My favorite bookstore event, only because my niece reminds me, was when we went into the bookstore, I think it was a Saturday morning, and who walks in but Dustin Hoffman. My niece even at age six knows who Dustin Hoffman is and thinks this is just unbelievable. He kind of snoops around, people leave him alone, and then he appears at the cash register. He picks up a volume of D. H. Lawrence poetry and starts reading "The Snake." He recites it in a very loud voice. Everyone gathers from all over the bookstore to listen to Dustin Hoffman reading. Then he puts down the book and sees my niece, goes over to her, takes her hand, and kisses it. She's now twenty-one; she still hasn't washed that hand.

—ALEXANDER SANGER

I got Dustin Hoffman to read a D. H. Lawrence poem about meeting the snake at the well at a Paul Metcalf reading. Dustin Hoffman would come into the bookstore and one time he told me he was reading Kenneth Koch and liked Koch's poems, and wanted to read other people. I said, "There's a reading, Paul Metcalf—he's really good, you should come," so he came to the reading, and then he really liked the reading, and somehow, I and maybe a couple other people said, "You should read something, Dustin," and he grabbed this D. H. Lawrence poem and read it aloud. —JOHN YAU

An intimacy developed between us and our customers. It became a hallmark of Books & Co.

I'm not a businessperson—so this is a more idealist attitude than any business-oriented person would consider to be a valid approach to bookselling, but for better or for worse, it continues more strongly than anything now that I'm in the children's book world. I've used this as a way to put good literature in people's hands. If that meant that money changed hands and a business grew, so much the better. And I earned a living. If I get health benefits because of it, fine. That was a secondary effect. I really felt that the bookstore was in the business of connecting people with wonderful books to read. That's what our mission was. I think, as far as Jeannette was concerned, it was that. I think she had that vision for the shop. But my own personal vision as a worker was that when I picked up a book and sold it to somebody, then someone had gone home with a good book. When someone's gone home with a good book and reads it, the world is a better place.
—SUSAN SCOTT

Over 70 percent of the people who came into the store didn't want to be helped. We recognized that by the way they walked in. They moved purposefully past the register, didn't make eye contact, and didn't want to be greeted. For them the bookstore was a solitary experience, and they wanted to make their voyage alone.

The secret best-seller at Books & Co. was Maurice Blanchot's *Death Sentence*. No one knows this, but when it came out from Station Hill, it must have been the early

1980s, Andrew and I sold hundreds of copies of that book, particularly to every pretty woman who came into the store. But no one ever came back and said, "WOW! What a great book! Or that was interesting"—never, ever heard a word about it. It has a different jacket now, but at that time it had a kind of black-and-white image, a very strange image of a woman's face, which was totally inappropriate, and Blanchot apparently didn't like the cover and complained about it, but there was something about it. It was very early eighties, dark and punkish. A brilliant book, translated by Lydia Davis. I never saw those people again. Maybe they were horrified and wouldn't come back.

—PETER PHILBROOK

Peter had that sort of smoky, romantic, antihero intensity, and was always reading. He hadn't gone to college. He was just a bibliophile from top to bottom and would go on these fads: this week it was all French literature from the eighteenth century, and he'd be reading all the books.

—MAY CASTLEBERRY

If I weren't a bookseller, I'd read all the time, so when it turned into my work, I could guiltlessly squirrel away with my lover the book. Luckily, I'm a fast reader and often read several books at once.

She can plow through a book a day. She'll be reading about eight books simultaneously. This is a totally prejudiced remark—she has got the most amazing critical sense of literature, about what is good, bad, and why. I'm going to cause a lot of angst for her readers out there, but about three times a year, maybe four, she will say to me, "This is something you have to read." The other 350 books she will have read during the course of the year, she'll say, "Don't bother."

—ALEXANDER SANGER

I adored selling Carlos Fuentes's books. The first time Carlos Fuentes read here was for *Burnt Water*. We threw a party afterward. Then, as we got to know each other, he'd visit me in my office. One time, after I'd just read *Aura*, Carlos stopped by. My son Ralph was visiting, too. Ralph was about nine, and I was talking about ghosts, telling Ralph about *Aura*. He turned to Carlos Fuentes and said, "Do you really believe in ghosts?" Carlos said, "I certainly do, and not only do I believe in them, I write books about them." We joked that Carlos would come to our apartment, dress up as a ghost, and chase Ralph around, so that Ralph would believe in ghosts, too. *Aura* was a short, beautiful ghost story. I preferred the bilingual edition and often recommended it to people.

Carlos Fuentes's wife's name is Sylvia. Beautiful woman. Someone's kid had just drowned, a writer's kid or a friend's kid, had drowned swimming, and they were talking about it in the bookstore while Carlos was there with his wife, and maybe a Mexican TV crew was filming them while this was going on. Sylvia said something like, "Carlos, if you were in your study writing and one of our kids was drowning in the lake, you'd never come out to rescue them." He said, "You're right."   —ALEXANDER SANGER

When Jeannette first opened the bookstore, she asked a writer — it might have been Carlos Fuentes—"What am I going to talk to all of these writers about?" He said, "You're going to talk to them about sex and clothes." It's true. One of my first visits to the bookstore, a writer asked, "Where did you buy those boots?" That's really all anyone wants to talk about. I've always been very nervous when writers want to talk about Mallarmé or Proust, because you know they're probably terrible writers. The really good ones want to know where did you get that outfit.

—JACQUELINE WELD

Carlos Fuentes sent Gabriel García Márquez to the store, Isabel Allende visited, and Octavio Paz became a good customer. Alex and I followed Paz to any reading he gave, within reason.

Books & Co. supported not only Mexican literature, but also Latin and South American writing. But I read many Mexican writers, and we had many Mexican customers. We shipped hundreds of books to Mexico City. One very charming customer had us mail him books to Sin, Mexico. We loved his address.

> Jeannette took a major position on Latin American literature, people like Carlos Fuentes, and she's a great admirer of Llosa, the Peruvian writer. I went to several Fuentes readings at Books & Co. In fact, Jeannette's grandmother endowed the Mario Vargas Llosa chair at Syracuse University. —BUD POMERANZ

Every year there were two or three books that became special to me, that I knew would be important to me for the rest of my life. Later, these books went onto my special table, Jeannette's table, we called it. I'd rotate the books, always returning my secret, special books to it. What happened when I first read one of these books was physical. I'd experience a tingling in my toes, a sensation that was powerful, erotic. I'd say to Alex, This is it, this is it. I had that sensation when I was reading Ted Mooney's *Easy Travel to Other Planets*, the story of a love affair between a dolphin and a woman. It became one of my favorite interspecies love affair books. People swimming with dolphins and then. . . . I thought, But how does one go from swimming with them to having sex with them? The more elevated course would be, first, you swim with them, then after about five classes, you have sex. Even married people could have sex with dolphins, and it couldn't be considered adultery. Could it? God, I thought, that was exciting. We ordered a hundred copies of *Easy Travel* and sold them fast.

My first book, *Easy Travel to Other Planets*, came out from Farrar, Straus, in the fall of 1981. I was working full time at *Art in America*, so I had been writing every morning between 4:30 and 9:30, and I had led quite a reclusive life. I went to Books & Co. I was thinking I would just buy my books and go, but I was told—they called me at Farrar, Straus and asked me to go and sign some copies. When I got up there, they had an enormous number of copies, and it was in the window. It was a surprise; I didn't know. That's when I met Jeannette and discovered that Andrew Bergen had bet the Farrar salesman that he could sell a hundred copies of it in the first week. And had done it. He won a bottle of champagne. It was really quite thrilling. Jeannette is wonderful in that she not only has very good taste, if I may say that about someone who admires my work, but she has the enthusiasm to pass that taste along to others. I came to work at *Art in America* a couple of weeks later, and there was this enormous, gorgeous flower arrangement sent to me by a secret admirer, who turned out to be Jeannette's friend Pat Thorpe. I did a reading at Books & Co. two weeks later, improbably enough with Richard Sennett, who had just published his one and only novel, *The Frog Who Dared to Croak*. David Rieff was our editor. I read the first chapter, which is the only part that works, I think, as a short excerpt. It also includes the dolphin seduction, for which I was to become notorious. Apparently, it turns out, women don't really want men, they want dolphins. I didn't know that when I wrote the book. I became entranced by dolphins when I was nine or ten. My parents took my sister and me to the Caribbean. I was swimming out by myself, maybe a hundred yards from shore, and was surrounded by eight or nine dolphins. I guess I was young enough for them to do what they're famous for, to see if you are OK and breathing, which is how they take care of their children. When their children are born, they have to be careful to get them up to the surface to breathe. . . . I touched them, their skin is amazingly sentient. You can feel it when you touch it. It made a deep impression. Nothing seemed frightening. It was extraordinary. —TED MOONEY

William Wharton's *Birdy* was another favorite interspecies love story, about an adolescent boy who becomes lost in a fantasy bird world, imagines he's a bird, and has an affair with another bird. It was so inventive, I relished it. I haven't thoroughly investigated what it is about animals and humans falling in love and having sex that moves me. Though I don't know of any anthropologist doing research in that specific area, I'd want to read about it if there were, or, better, research it myself and become a pioneer in the field. One day William Wharton walked in, and I asked him to sign his book. We went next door, to the New Wave Coffee Shop, and I was able to tell him how I felt about *Birdy*.

I always thought I helped get Elmore Leonard a little more attention than he was getting right at the moment, because I was able to sell his books to some Hollywood folks, who then turned his stuff into movies, and maybe they hadn't known about him before. This was the early eighties. Roy Scheider came into the store all the time, and he would eventually make a very good version of a Leonard novel, *52 Pick-Up*. The guys at Madison Avenue Books turned me onto Leonard. So there was the sense that you could sell anything and that you could perhaps get somebody interested in an author, and it was perhaps somebody who had some influence, and all that was possible, and you felt that, you thought about it, and you made an effort to please. —ANDREW BERGEN

They knew I liked certain things, or they would have something that they liked. That was what was terrific about it. I first started reading Richard Russo there. *Nobody's Fool* was given to me before its publication, but I first bought and read *Mohawk* and *The Risk Pool* there, his first two novels, and from that, developed an enormous respect for Richard Russo's work. —ROBERT BENTON

Another fulfilling day was when W. P. Kinsella entered the store. *Shoeless Joe* was one of those first novels that made my toes tingle, gave me that old literary, sexual feeling. I made everyone in the bookstore read it and told Carl Lennertz at Random House about it. He wasn't Kinsella's publisher, but he put it in his newsletter. We did a baseball window, featuring *Shoeless Joe*, and when Kinsella arrived to sign, he was wearing his baseball hat and uniform. He was overwhelmed to find a big window for him on Madison Avenue. The book's advice was, "If you build it, they will come." It's a line I often think about. Anything you want to do, you have to have the faith to make happen.

May 12, 1982
How nice of you to invite me in to sign books! I will always remember signing my first baseball. I really appreciate the enthusiasm you are showing *Shoeless Joe*.
> Very best regards,
> *Bill Kinsella*

I heard a marvelous rumor right after I left your store. "There is no W. P. Kinsella: Salinger wrote *Shoeless Joe*." Spread the rumor!

Five years had passed in a flash, and in October we began planning our fifth anniversary party, celebrating on May 23, 1983, with a party at the Puck Building on Lafayette Street. Earlier in the evening, we had a star-studded reading at the Madison Avenue Church, which we'd sometimes use when we needed more space. Louis Auchincloss, Andre Gregory, Erica Jong, Grace Paley, and Calvin Trillin all read. The party and reading were a fund-raiser for the 939 Foundation's reading series.

I remember introducing Mary McGarry Morris. I told Jeannette I thought she should read there, and this was her first novel. I remember I was looking through a bunch of papers—I always write everything on tiny little pieces of paper—and I found a tiny scrap of paper. There's one word on it—"vanished." Now if I were of a more occult turn of mind, perhaps I would have been interested in it in that way, but I tried to figure out, what is this word. I'm a slow writer. We save every word in my house, and this word could be valuable to me. I'm not just tossing this word out—if I find six more, I have a sentence. Then I was in a bookstore and saw a book called *Vanished*. I remembered that John Waters had told me, You should read *Vanished*, and I had written down the title instead of the name of the writer. I bought the book, the store had only one copy, and I loved this book. Then I told Jeannette about it. So Jeannette called the publisher and Mary McGarry Morris read. To me the most extraordinary thing about her as a writer is that she wrote this first novel without telling anyone. In other words, she lived in a house with her husband and her children, and they never knew she was writing a novel. However, I learned nothing from this encounter. —FRAN LEBOWITZ

I liked being on the floor, talking about books, organizing events. Being a buyer is quite different, more like being a writer. You spend a lot of time alone in a room, thinking, studying catalogs, determining how many copies to order, which is sometimes based on what you've sold in the past. When the publisher's sales representative comes in, the buyer and rep will go through the catalog book by book. The rep will explain what the publisher's plan is: how many copies are being printed, whether the author will tour, whether, in our own case, the author has a New York connection. I loved dealing with the reps, and, after a while, knew them well. Some sold to us for twenty years, and though I never met their children, we'd know each other's kids through conversations. And I was the one who bought the children's books.

I've been a sales representative in the New York area for just about thirty years. Eighteen of those years I was with Macmillan, and when Macmillan bought Scribner's about thirteen years ago, my friend was running the company, Frank McCormick, and he asked me to come to Harcourt, because Mr. Jovanovich, when there was a "J" at the end of Harcourt Brace, asked him to get the trade division rolling. I've loved working for Harcourt ever since. Basically I've been calling on the same accounts. Years ago, there were more bookstores than there are today. I used to have the suburbs. I didn't have Manhattan, because there was so much. I had Connecticut, other parts of upstate New York, plenty to keep you busy. Then, one day, they said at Macmillan, "You gotta have Manhattan." I said, "Fine. No problem." I was used to the suburbs' way of ordering books. If there was a major book, they'd order maybe ten of a title. When I came to New York, I called on the stores on Madison Avenue, and I remember going into Books & Co. We had a book about France. They were talking about the book, and usually I never like to say a number—unless I really know the people—there's a pregnant pause where you don't say anything. So, the buyer was going like he really liked the book, and I said to myself, I'm going to be brave. So I said, "Why don't you take twenty-five?" To me that was a big number. He said, "You know what? You're right. I'll take 125." I said to myself, "Ed, for once in your life, keep quiet. Get a New York brain in your head." Books & Co. really introduced me to the buying power of these stores. Again, I'm going back twenty years. . . . I became a rep when I got out of college. I took business and didn't have any idea of what I wanted to do. It was '64, and there was the Vietnam War. I didn't want to go, naturally nobody wanted to go, and luckily my mother worked at a fabric house, Lowenstein on Fortieth and Broadway, and one of the people she worked with was a sergeant in a National Guard group in Flushing. And he said there's an opening, so I was able to get into the National Guard, and that stopped me from going to Vietnam. I was tied up for seven years, going to meetings, summer camp, it becomes a real pain. But when I think of it now. . . . On lower Manhattan about five years ago, I met one of the people I trained with in California, and he told me that most of the people in our company died. They used to mix the National Guard with the regular draftees. It was all just basic training. So as much as I used to bitch about it, they all died. When he told me that, I tried to remember their faces, and I remembered we were just young kids, full of life. You're twenty-two, twenty-three. God, I'm getting sad thinking about it. They're faceless now, but it's so sad. Once I got the National Guard out of my life, I was able to look for a real job. In those days, there were jobs all over the place. I went to an agency still not knowing what I wanted to do, not being a reader at all throughout my life, and I was getting married, and I went into this employment agency. He had a cigar box—today you have the computers—and this was mom and pop, dinosaur time. He was going, "All right, do you like books?" He said, I still remember, "It pays $8,000 a year." I said, "Books, books, whatever." I always liked to talk to people, I even used to love blind dates. I just like to talk to people. So I said, "Sure, I'll try it. I'm getting married, no problem." Then I found out that I enjoyed it. I loved it.   —ED SOLOWITZ

One of our best titles was the relatively unknown *Rum, Sodomy, and the Lash: Piracy, Sexuality, and Masculine Identity.* Peter boldly ordered quite a number—we took a big position—and we sold them all. Our readers demanded the unusual book; we supplied it. Peter had several extraordinary and unique orders, including Eco's *The Name of the Rose* and Patrick Süskind's *Perfume: The Story of a Murderer.* He ordered seven hundred copies of *Perfume,* and we sold all of them. Years later we might have sold a hundred copies. The climate was different then.

We published Umberto Eco's *The Name of the Rose.* I was talking to Peter, I had a good relationship with Peter, and he says, "You know why this is our book?" Like this is made for them. He says, "Eco comes into the store." I said, "I would think so." He said, "What do you think?" I said, "Well," I was really puffing out my chest and said, "maybe we should go for a couple of hundred." My wildest dream.   —ED SOLOWITZ

I was famous for ordering two books. Eco's *The Name of the Rose* is often quoted to me as one of the largest orders ever for Eco. I think that was the first time Eco came into the store—he signed faster than anybody I've ever seen. Then he came in a lot. He's a real bookstore hound; his favorite bookstore is the Strand. He's a serious book buyer and buys fourteenth-century manuscripts. The other book was *Perfume.* I was passionate about it, I read it in one night. I don't think it's a great book, but it's a perfect book in a lot of ways, and they were flabbergasted, Knopf or

Random House, at how many I ordered. Probably only 200 copies, maybe 250, but it was probably something they thought they were going to go flog and sell 20 of, getting the initial order. I knew something of the buzz the book had gotten in Europe, which was true of the Eco, too. I always tried to pay attention to what was happening when the book was published in Europe. But that was often a delusion, too; a big success in France might bomb here. When the book came in, I'd do a dramatic window. I love doing windows—I didn't photograph them, and oftentimes I can't remember what I did, but I must have done an entire window for *Perfume*. One of my very favorite windows was when *Heidegger and Nazism* by Victor Farias came out. It was a very controversial book and had touched off a lot of the so-called Heidegger debate in France. When it was published in English in the late eighties, I did a combination—that book and another one went into the window. I blew it up, made it huge, a hilarious passage from Thomas Bernhard's *Old Masters* about Heidegger, and there was an image of Heidegger's wife sitting and knitting him socks, so the window was this giant book, Bernhard's book, and reams and reams of yarn with needles sticking out. The window disturbed some of the devotees of Heidegger who complained it was disrespectful.

—PETER PHILBROOK

Creating the windows was one of the best parts of the job. We put a lot of thought and energy into them, and had a lot of fun concocting them. We usually designed a traditional Christmas window. For all retailers, Christmas is the major time of year. People bought expensive books, and in the good days, in a good year, we'd sell a huge number of books. Christmas for us, then. Andrew Bergen created the most beautiful Christmas window ever. He bought a substance that looked exactly like real snow and placed real, but small, evergreen trees all around. We put books around the trees, and it looked exquisite. One year, a picture book on Frank Capra's movie *It's a Wonderful Life* came out from Random House. We rented a TV, continuously played a video of the movie, and there was a tree, too, with ornaments I'd collected over the years.

At Christmas it's fresh vegetables; the whole vibe changes. The product is fresh and people want it and you've got to get it in the store and get it out of the store, and if you don't have it, you're missing out. It's much more like vegetables used to be than they are now. Probably used to be when strawberries came into town, they were snapped up fast, and now there are strawberries all the time so we don't see it as that special. Maybe there's a few products in the vegetable stand—Jersey tomatoes—go for it. Christmas is like that in the book business. If you don't have that new book—however silly it might be—you lose out, and if somebody's mentioned it somewhere in some publication, everybody wants to have it. I remember there was *Karl Bodmer's America*, a University of Nebraska Press book, an oversized art book, sixty-five dollars, and we sold a few. Then it got some press, I knew about it, and we were able to keep it in stock. We were one of the few stores able to make some money off that book, so that was an example, a Christmastime thing, and who would have guessed that that would have hit. University of Nebraska is not known for publishing art books, but it did a beautiful book. Karl Bodmer was a very interesting guy from Germany who traveled out West with some German prince in the 1830s–'40s. He saw a lot of tribal groups that would later disappear. Most bookstores didn't even get the University of Nebraska Press sales rep visiting them, but university presses knew they could sell their books in our store. People were coming in with money to burn in the week before Christmas, and we would go to a book distributor, Peter and I, and fill up shopping carts with books. Everything we bought one day would be gone two days later, then we'd go again. I think that happened for a couple of Christmases.   —ANDREW BERGEN

I usually decorated the Easter windows, another tradition—old children's toys, beautiful Easter eggs, bunnies. In one window, I placed my children's rocking horse, a Raggedy Ann doll, and some other of their old toys. I loved selling the children's books, and every spring, when many come out, we celebrated them. I also wanted to remind people we carried children's books, so I'd find our prettiest ones to display. I remember Edmund White reading from *A Boy's Own Story*. The next day a man came into the store and picked up Ed's book. He said, "I'm buying this for my young son, what do you think?" I said, "It's a wonderful, wonderful book, about a young gay man's awakening." He didn't buy it.

A bookseller's anxieties are: running out of a book, not having a book, being expected to have every book published ever when people ask for it, and customers wondering why you don't—I think it was not knowing why we didn't have a book or not understanding the reason we didn't have a book and always having to answer that, that was hardest. I certainly represented plenitude, but there were often gaps in that plenitude that were hard to account for. I always thought Books & Co. worked as a book boutique. That's how I always wanted it to be—we have this, we have this, if you don't like it, you know, that's OK, but this is what we're interested in, what we have. I got interested in fly-fishing. We had fly-fishing books. Did anyone care that we had fly-fishing? Fly-fishing was next to art criticism, next to Foucault, and it made perfect sense to me.

                                          —PETER PHILBROOK

We ordered our books carefully, curating the store, and like curators, we cared for our flock, our customers. In turn, we were cared for by the sales reps. They were helpful and kept us up to date. Ruth

Liebmann, Mike Rochman, Eddie Ponge, Marilyn Abel, Tim Mooney, and Ed Solowitz visited us for years. They all spoiled me in a way, inviting me to parties, movie screenings. It wasn't that I wanted to go to hundreds of glam parties—I had children at home—but I appreciated being invited. Especially to a party thrown by Liza Minnelli, which Alex and I did attend. But I loved staying home at night, because my day was like a perpetual party. When Alex worked in a law firm, before he became president of Planned Parenthood New York, he went out more than I did. His day was spent doing something deadly like writing a will, but mine was exciting. I was talking about books, or people's lives, and then, at home at night, I could read more and have more to talk to people about the next day. And I had all the bookseller perks.

The reps knew our mandate, to buy unusual books, and though I saw us as a general bookstore, we couldn't carry everything.

There's ground zero: we won't take the book at all, it's not for this store, we're not interested. Next step up is representing it—take two—and we'll see. That's the classic thing, the standard thing to do with first novels, fiction, a lot of things, you just have it in the store, and then you remember it. Generally with a publisher like Random House, you'd take everything, maybe with a few exceptions in areas we didn't carry—sports, knitting. The next step would usually be five, and that would mean you might put it out on the counter. If you could go over five, it could mean it might be there for a decade. Maybe the author had some track record, maybe they had another book that we'd sold a couple of copies of, or it's what the expectations of the reviews might be. Maybe there was a little bit of pressure from Knopf—they wanted us to take a few more—that kind of thing. The stages—ten or twenty-five or fifty, all the numbers were usually pretty arbitrary because there were cases—Eco and *Perfume*, again—examples where you'd be making some kind of mini-statement. Something like Updike—you'd get 100 copies, I don't know if that's still the case. Also you get a higher discount from the publisher the more you build up the order. Whether you get 100 or 150 of the Updike, you weren't necessarily deciding I'm going to sell 300 copies—it's how many am I going to sell in this amount of time; how am I going to spread the money around, because the bills fall due in a certain order. If you order in September or dial in your order in the summer, when they come in October, when are you going to have to pay for them? You're dealing with thirty-day invoices, which you really only pay in ninety days, so you're constantly juggling these things. If you're doing it from a strict business standpoint, you're probably looking at it one way. I was much more focused on what we were selling.

—PETER PHILBROOK

The reps present their list twice or three times a year, usually in the fall and the spring. The ones who knew us would say, You wouldn't even want to look at this. You wouldn't sell it at Books & Co.

We'd sit on that leather sofa, and we weren't disturbed. Talking about a book, you should say, "No calls unless the roof is burning down." Books & Co. were very professional. But I've been to other accounts over the years where people know we're coming, they get the catalog ahead of time, but they don't look at it, they're not prepared. They're buying the products that will keep that store in business, and they haven't the faintest clue, and then all my work is for naught. Books & Co. doesn't take many children's books, just the cream of the crop, and I'm prepared to show them that. Again, you get to know the people, you don't waste their time, and you don't want your time wasted, either. I think of it as a taxi with the meter always running. You have other calls to make, and you don't want to waste anybody's time, but you want to make it as productive as you can. That's really your one shot, your one at bat. You really won't see them until the next season.   —ED SOLOWITZ

The reps tempted me with galleys of first novels or books about a bizarre tribe in the Amazon. They knew some of my steadfast interests. We ordered a certain number from the publisher; and six months later the publisher would send the books. If the store's on credit hold, you order from distributors, who were more expensive and demanded payment monthly. With the publisher, you have more time—the bookseller doesn't have to pay until thirty days after receiving the books—and you can return the unsold books. My father always thought it was so bizarre that you could return books—the unsold product—which doesn't happen in other industries. He thought the book business was old-fashioned.

> The return of books is something everyone agonizes over, and when things get bad, the first thing people say is, Hey, how come they can send it back; who else is allowed to send it back? I'm pro-returns. I've always said when returns drop, that means the salespeople aren't doing their job in putting out. It means we could have actually sold more, because the fact of the matter is, when the rep goes out to sell, this is a comparison I use, it's as if they were going out with a black-and-white photograph of the bottom hem of a skirt to clothes stores and said, We want you to plunk down your money and invest in our line of clothing based on this information. You've got a plot summary that has to do with what the editor saw in the book, an advertising and promotion and publicity campaign. You're oftentimes not even right about the page count, depending on where the book is in the season. Catalog copy and tip sheets are based on books that have not even been delivered. What the returns tell you is that you did your

job and put that book in as many places as it could have gone to. No one wants their returns dropping below 10–15 percent—that's scary; that means stores are not taking the book in the first place. If the returns drop below either 10 or 15 percent, what that means is, there were people out there who only bought what they absolutely knew they could sell, as opposed to buying more and taking a position on it.   —ELIZABETH BOGNER

We don't even want to talk about returns. I tell people, I don't even watch election results because they say, "We're going to the returns." I get very nervous. Returns, I get very nervous.   —ED SOLOWITZ

That's been argued about: one, it shouldn't be allowed, and two, give a higher discount and sometimes don't allow it. Now against that you have this: if you don't allow return privilege, you are of a certainty determining that the buyers will be cutting way down in their selections. They just can't afford to cover the very wide range of published books decently and not have a right to return.

—THEODORE WILENTZ

Location, location, location. That's what retail is, and this is all about retail. Which publisher is going to get the location with the independent? There's more of a dance of courtship with the independents, which means whose galleys the booksellers are going to read, which determines what books they notice and talk about when a customer comes in and asks, What should I read? Or what the store puts up front, which is what people are going to look at first. Ultimately the bookseller also bears the burden of all this power, and they also bear the burden of the financial risk. Of course, the publisher takes the risk of buying the book, publishing it, the financial commitment, but they're writing things off. Bookstores are buying and paying the freight for fifty books, because they were told that it was a great book, that the publisher was going to advertise, that there was support. The stores pay somebody to unpack them, put them out, and the books take up space. Then when they don't sell, the stores pay somebody to take them off the shelf, pack them up, and pay the freight back to the publisher. Returnability is not a gift. It's the publisher saying, We understand the burden you're taking on taking our book, and this is how we support what we're selling to you. They're saying, Send it back if you don't like it, if it doesn't work for you. Sometimes it doesn't work, everyone did their part, and you just have to say, That's part of life.   —ELIZABETH BOGNER

Many customers entered the store with expectant, indefinable expressions on their faces. They were the ones who wanted our help. We greeted them, and, if we knew their names, we used them. I greeted many people by name for years, but usually addressed them formally, Mr., Mrs., Ms. Many asked me to call them by their first names, like Robert Benton, the director and screenwriter. But my habitual reaction was, Hello, Mr. Benton. I couldn't stop myself.

I never understood. Nobody in this world calls me Mr. Benton. I had discussions with her about why she insisted on doing that. I felt so old. The only thing I hated about going to that store is that she would always call me that.
            —ROBERT BENTON

You go into the store, they might even recommend something. The people who work in the bookstore actually read books. They like books, or they hate books, or they hate a particular book, but they have opinions. Jeannette let them recommend to her, so you got a much more diverse stock. Even if you look avidly, as I do, for things to read, get book catalogs, publisher's catalogs, you miss stuff. I'll walk in the store, and maybe one of the people who works there will say, I think you would like this. I think that's a service worth preserving.

—FRAN LEBOWITZ

One of my favorite customers, Max Kaplan, asked me to call him Max, but it was hard to do. Mr. Kaplan came in periodically to bring chocolate cookies to us. He'd say, I'm sorry I haven't seen you, I'm so busy. He was a marvelous, lively ninety-two-year-old man, who sent me his stories and poems. He wrote some plays, and some may be produced. Mr. Kaplan once told me that when he died, he wanted to leave money for the bookstore; he even sent me an agreement about it.

When I moved to Manhattan, in 1985, the first thing I wanted to do was go to one of their readings. Jeannette and I took to each other quickly. She put my picture on the wall later. I used to go there every week. I met Harold Brodkey, Susan Cheever, and Susan Cheever's mother, Mary, who became my editor. I write poetry and stories. I have one letter from her that's so moving, it moves me to tears. My wife, May, went with me to Books & Co., too, before she passed away in 1991. I heard the well-known writers there—Fuentes, Susan Cheever, Susan Minot. In one of Minot's short stories, she buries the remains of her father or mother, and then after that, she has sex with about twenty-five, thirty people. After the reading, I rushed to her and said, "You've upset me very, very much with the names of the people you had sex with. You lay in bed with about thirty people. I write a short story and have trouble naming my characters, and I only have two or three or four. How do you name them? You're in bed with thirty, forty people?" "Oh," she says, "no problem at all."

—MAX KAPLAN

Another faithful customer and friend, Bud Pomeranz, who once worked for IBM, had a passion for fiction. He read enormously and came in every week. Books & Co. was part of his weekly ritual. It became a ritual for many, a place to stop in.

Stephen Dixon came into the store one day, and they had a pile of his latest book, *Frog.* It's a fatty, with a soft cover. I saw him with a pen. I thought he was autographing them, so I turned to Francis Cash, who worked there then, and said, "Stephen Dixon must be autographing." He said he's not here to autograph books. I said, "What's he doing?" Francis said, "Why don't you go over there and see what's going on." It turned out that Dixon had picked up a copy of his book and found typos in it. He was going around correcting them. I asked him, "How many bookstores are you going to go to?" He said, "I've been to about five or six already." I have one he corrected.   —BUD POMERANZ

Daily life was constructed from all the people who entered the store. James Falkin was writing his dissertation on Chinese political theory, but we encouraged him to read some fiction. He was hilarious, very smart, and he and I had a great time talking and laughing.

One day I was walking down Madison Avenue. I looked in Books & Co.'s window, and it reminded me of Blackwell's in Oxford, with the wood paneling. So I thought, This is a very excellent bookstore. I have my doctorate in Chinese politics from the School of Oriental and African Studies, which is part of the University of London. I also translate Chinese to English, English to Chinese. What I used it for initially was for the philosophy section, which I always thought was the best in New York. They weren't very strong in Chinese politics, but what I needed, as I was writing my dissertation, were books on contemporary issues in political philosophy, in Western political philosophy, like issues of nationalism, what political philosophy is, all those kinds of philosophical questions, to put my thesis in a broader context. I'd sit on the couch and look at the books quickly to see what was going on. I could spend hours doing that without realizing it. When I'd be home, writing, I'd think, Maybe I should think about the East Germans. Then it was always in my mind not to go any-place else but Books & Co. to get whatever they had on Christa Wolf. For years, I had tea with Jeannette. I criti-cized her when she went to Alaska. I was very frightened she was going to come back wearing big L. L. Bean boots and lose her whole style. It's true. I think she's terrific and I love it when she's chic, but when she said she was going to Alaska, I got frightened. I thought she was going to come back eating bear meat. I said, "You must come back wearing dark sunglasses and go to Paris immediately, and go back into an Audrey Hepburn look, because I will not understand this." Jeannette was my adviser on nineteenth-century English novelists. She got me to read *Vanity Fair.* I was very suspicious of it. She said, "You'll really like it, I assure you." She was right.   —JAMES FALKIN

Running a bookstore was occasionally like doing social work. Some of the people who came in were lonely and just needed to talk, and sometimes genuinely crazy people wandered in. We had to dis-tinguish fast between good talking and insane talking. A few people who ensconced themselves in the philosophy section were unbal-anced. They'd start violent arguments about philosophers, the way sports fans fight about their teams. Two, especially, came in often, simultaneously, as if they'd timed it, and argued ferociously about Hegel. But of course our philosophy section attracted mostly sane people. It was in many ways the jewel in our crown.

> I think of Books & Co. as a curated space, and that second floor in particular felt the pressure of the hand of the buyer or the mind of the buyer, because there was a particular emphasis during particular stretches of time on continental philosophy or phenomenology, or there would be more conservative angles. It gave the bookstore its own quirkiness. I have a personal library of over eight thousand volumes—I read a tremendous amount. It's my research and inspiration from reading that's a major motor for projects and the way I work. I look at a network of bookstores in New York on a regular basis. I live a block away from the Strand, so I always get a lot of new books half-price and then I have my network. What with the shrinking bookselling situation in New York, I work with half-a-dozen bookstores in New York, plus I'm a member of the Seminary Co-op Bookstore of the University of Chicago.
> —JOHN G. HANHARDT

Some people just wanted to be around books as much as they could, the way I did. Seeing these people regularly, I'd become interested in their lives: What did they do in the world outside the bookstore? What were their lives like? Often they were men, and why, I wondered, did more men visit us more regularly than women? There were some women who were regular, weekly visitors. One bought many philosophy books. She was obviously very smart, never asked for any help, and was very beautiful. She was a little mysterious. We all tried to imagine a life for her, yet I didn't even know her name. One day I determined I'd talk with her, and I found out she was a physician and that her father was very sick and in the hospital. She talked about his troubled health care. So, in addition to providing the books, it became part of what I did—I offered myself as a person to talk to. I had people to talk to. It wasn't in any way a one-way street. I wanted the staff to be friendly, too.

> The only way I ever buy books—I hate to say—is just by reading the reviews or ads in the *New York Times*, because how else do you know about books except when somebody says at a party, Have you read this?—word of mouth. But at parties you run into a lot of people who like different kinds of books from what you like. So it's terribly hard to know except from reviews and ads, and anything that hasn't been advertised or reviewed, which is probably 75 percent of the books, you don't know about. But if you have somebody you trust who says this is a wonderful book . . .
> —LEILA HADLEY

> I remember Alistair Cooke thought I was a fool to put his book in a bag, grumpy, I guess, that day. I remember Jackie Onassis was very gracious and nice, and I remember Woody Allen was secretive. I remember Gene Wilder floating by. The early eighties. I remember seeing the first Walkman, hot off of the boat, some guy coming in with it. I always thought that was impressive, suddenly here was this new thing.
> —ANDREW BERGEN

Our events—sometimes two a week—became more and more popular. Books & Co. was forging the community I wanted. My knowledge of books and my friendships expanded. I was leading the life I wanted, with my family, my books, with my writers, with my customers, some of whom I saw every day. The writers and the readers became a virtual family.

> I'm from Georgia and moved to New York in 1968, which, in a way, also enabled me to remember the South

the way it was when I left, so I don't have to keep up. Certainly one reason to come to the North is that there are a lot better bookstores, though Atlanta has a couple of good bookstores now. But when I was growing up in the Atlanta area, there were no good bookstores. Both times I read at Books & Co., they were a very responsive audience. It was a nice space to read in, because you're reading surrounded by books, and there's an odd collection of books, great philosophers, an abnormal psychology shelf, then there's a shelf full of Tacitus and Epictetus. It's nice to read where you have browsed. It's good to browse in. It's laid out by the human hand. I loved going in there, and the people at the desk—the employees—all knew more about books than I do, which is almost too much. I became interested in writing when I was a sophomore in high school. I had an English teacher named Anne Lewis who was a great influence on me. She suggested that I write for the school paper and also gave me Thurber, Perelman, Benchley, and E. B. White to read. I decided I could do that. I was always bored with the assigned topic. Still am. I've been rebelling against it so long I'm rebelling against rebelling against it now.   —ROY BLOUNT JR.

When Marian Seldes read from *The Bright Lights*, about her life in the theater, one of her fans brought her a long-stemmed yellow rose. She gracefully accepted the rose, then held it in her hand as she read. I remember her perched on the ladder—we didn't yet have our podium, just a microphone and a moving ladder—and as she spoke into the microphone, she clutched the rose in a genuine piece of theater.

My father was a wonderful kind of actor manqué. He was a textile merchant and not very good at it. He was one of that generation, born in 1901, who was too young for the

First World War, too old for the Second World War, and had a lot of friends who went into theater, impresarios and producers, and some of his friends actually went into very early television in England. They all came out of the Jewish East End. My father was part of a big Turkish-Jewish family. Thirteen kids, and he was the first of the children who was born in London, so he grew up in the East End, like the Lower East Side. He just didn't have the gumption, or he was bullied by his father or his brothers, who were all in ties, in the garment trade: "What kind of life is acting for a Jewish boy?" Actually, in fact, it was a rich tradition in London, from vaudeville on, from Chaplin's days onwards, of going into theater, but he never did it. He became a kind of amateur, an amateur charity theater producer, of quite brilliant, I thought, talent. But he was always very sad. So, he made up for it, really. He made me memorize Shakespeare when I was about seven, took me to Shakespeare very early on. We'd have little Dickens readings on Friday nights, after the Sabbath meal. He'd pick up *Great Expectations*, or Balzac sometimes, English translations of Balzac. He was a larger-than-life sort of Dickensian figure. All that got me into storytelling at an early age. —SIMON SCHAMA

Cynthia Ozick first read at Books & Co. in 1983. Later, after she had just won a MacArthur Prize—one of the first MacArthur recipients—she was late for her reading. We waited and waited, and finally she arrived. She'd lost her way, taking public transportation. Cynthia never changed, and I liked that about her. Fran Lebowitz came, and she and Cynthia decided to change places. Cynthia would wear sweaters and be witty, and Fran would have a Guggenheim and a daughter at Bryn Mawr. Cynthia's Sunday salon with Virgil Thomson and J. D. McClatchy was a unique literary event. Virgil Thomson read a great selection about Gertrude Stein, and Cynthia read an extremely violent story, in her calm, little voice. Virgil Thomson, who was quite old at the time, slept through her reading.

I remember meeting Margaux and Mariel Hemingway, who came in to buy a Françoise Sagan novel. I told Donald Keene and William Weaver how much I admired their translations. And one day I saw James Baldwin looking into the window of the bookstore. All of his books were in the window, and I said, Isn't that great? He was standing there and he smiled and said yes and then I walked away. I remember seeing John Lennon and Yoko Ono walking their two Great Danes down the street around 10:30 or 11. Someone said, They do that all the time, and then later when Lennon was killed, I remember thinking, someone like him in New York can't have a routine.

—JOHN YAU

We ran screenwriting panels and panels on the state of American fiction or on the contemporary novel—where have we been, where are we going? Bruce Bawer was a panelist on one, and we placed his memoir, *A Place at the Table*, in the window. His mother climbed into the window, with her camera. The devotion of mothers was a wonder to behold.

The most unhappy people I've ever met are screenwriters. If what you're interested in is movies, then it's fine to be a screenwriter, but if what you're interested in is writing, it's absurd to be a screenwriter. It's not a writer's medium, you have no control, and, as I always say, Why do you think they give you all that money? I remember being on a panel at Books & Co., because I haven't very frequently been on panels—maybe two dozen times in my life. I remember all of them to some extent, because I dislike being on panels. I don't like other people being allowed to talk.

A panel always means that I'm going to be with six people who don't agree with me. I suppose an audience of two thousand people won't agree with you—but they're not allowed to talk. I expect people to disagree with me, but I don't expect them to be allowed to talk. That's why I don't like being on panels. —FRAN LEBOWITZ

If stores have hearts, then at our heart was writing, the love of books, and friendship. Friendship was the center, dictating, leading, encouraging my adventures, our ventures.

I'd had a friendship in London with Jonathan Miller and had tremendous admiration for him and then lost touch with him entirely. I knew he was in New York doing an opera and found him. Then he phoned me, we had lunch, maybe at the Carlyle, and he was bemoaning the fact that he couldn't find any of the books he needed. I said, "Jonathan, do you know Books & Co.?" He said no, and I said, "Come with me." I took him upstairs, where all of this incredible philosophical, critical, psychological work was, and he bought a whole slew of books. I was able to get my book and give it to him, too, which was very nice. I felt very proud that I was able to give him this gift, the bookstore. —ANN LAUTERBACH

My friend Jane Stanton Hitchcock was a friend of the Baron Guy de Rothschild, who'd written a memoir. She organized his reading, and it was incredibly chic, all the women dressed up, the men in well-tailored suits. Jackie Onassis and Maurice Tempelsman attended, and I sat next to him at dinner. An extremely charming man. There were many titled nobility in attendance for the baron, not our usual crowd.

I introduced Jane to her first husband, Billy Hitchcock. In the 1960s Billy was famous for owning the house in Millbrook in which

Timothy Leary took LSD. In those days Billy was working as a stockbroker by day, leading a wild life by night. Leary and others stayed in his house for a while, dropped acid all the time, ran around naked. Jane and I have known each other so long and have gone through so much, though we did not run around naked together. Later, when her books came out, it gave me tremendous personal pleasure to have her read at Books & Co.

When you watch a friend through the years, you begin to get their measure. You begin to see them in a different light, because everything that they do kind of reflects on everything that they've done. I began to see Jeannette evolve not only as a bookstore owner, but as a person. One kind of fed the other. This store became part of her, it was like a confluence, and each helped the other grow up and grow out, and finally blossom into this full, full thing that is inseparable. —JANE STANTON HITCHCOCK

Unlike Frances Steloff or Sylvia Beach, I had my own real children—Ralph, Andrew, and Matthew. Every day, I raced from home to store and back, because of the boys. When I was pregnant, I remember leaving, feeling so tired, and saying, I'll be back, then getting home and falling asleep on the bed, exhausted. After the boys were born, I breast-fed, so then I'd come to the bookstore for about four hours. I was rushing, rushing everywhere, and I'd become ferociously hungry. The baby would be hungry, too, and I'd devour peanut butter sandwiches while I fed him.

You used to have to get there before three o'clock because after she got married and decided to have kids, that was another thing, but she was there earlier, and if I wanted to see her, I'd just go in and wave or just say something every now and then. I'd be coming up Madison, get off the bus, and look at my watch to see, because she might still be there, and she was upstairs, sitting in her window. I would have to just check my watch to see if she's there.

—ALBERT MURRAY

My two younger boys grew up with the store and liked it, especially when pop stars made appearances—Iggy Pop, David Byrne. I got to do crowd control. The lines for them were enormous. Pearl Jam's Eddie Vedder came in and bought a book. Goldie Hawn came in, and Bill Murray bought a book and gave me candy. My little boys loved hearing about these celebrities.

Iggy Pop's *I Need More* was a good window, cliché but effective. It was basically a layout of a hotel room with book and chairs. I bought lots of bottles of Cremora and dumped everything out, stuffed rolled-up newspapers, dollar bills, razor blades. Then his publicist came in, right before the signing, and said it was really inappropriate, and I said, "Why is it inappropriate?" He said, "That's not the kind of image we're looking for," and I said, "Look at the book." I also said I can't change it now. But I think I took out a few of the dollar bills. It was quite a scene, though, all these people who had never been to Books & Co. and would never come again. The line wrapped around the block for this book. Iggy Pop just signed the book, said a few words. It was published by this guy, who made his money in the scrap metal business. Andrew would remember this guy.   —PETER PHILBROOK

The signing happened because there was this funny guy I was friendly with, Sanford Cole, who'd been a scrap metal dealer and a sort of mover of money. He'd made a lot of money and started a small publishing house. He had real interests in the history of the Left and in the National Socialist movement in Germany. He produced some very fine books, and he also published an Iggy Pop book, at a certain moment, when he needed some cash. I think there's a Michigan connection, too. Iggy Pop's from Michigan. I think that's how it ended up at Books & Co., because that's not the normal place Iggy Pop would have shown up. I think we had another pop star who did a book, Andy Summers, from The Police, and he did a signing, too. We sold a lot of those books. I was more interested when David Hockney came in or Larry Rivers, if we could get Jasper Johns to sign some books, which we did, or Brice Marden. They were more interesting to me.

—ANDREW BERGEN

I wanted to do everything, and in a way, like many women, I tried to. But I often felt guilty that I wasn't at home all the time or at the bookstore all the time. I was Mom to the store, to my three sons, and wife to Alex. I was also involved in different foundations and groups, and on various boards, including the Academy of American Poets. I was committed to it. I'm a dedicated poetry reader.

You can often tell how great a bookstore is going to be by how much poetry it has in it, and there was a really serious poetry section at Books & Co.   —SIMON SCHAMA

I've spent about fifteen years in the field of poetry. I'm not a poet, but I've always cared very much about poetry. I'm chairman of the Academy of American Poets, and to strengthen the Academy, I persuaded Jeannette to join the Academy board. Books & Co. was practically the only bookstore in New York that carried a big poetry selection. Poetry is so important, and I feel I have been very lucky to be able to do this job, which I inherited from the principal founder of the Academy, Mrs. Hugh Bullock, an extraordinary woman. Marie Bullock was raised in France, where painters, writers, and poets were held in great regard and where they were part of the social fabric and much admired and listened to, and there were readings. When she married an American—she herself was an American, but her childhood was in France—she came to the United States and enrolled in literature classes at Columbia. She was quite amazed that nothing was going on with poetry in New York—no poetry readings at all. So she decided to do something about this, and she, her husband, and her professors at Columbia started the Academy of American Poets, which was inspired by the model of the French Academy—the Académie Française. That was in the 1930s. She herself was not a highly educated person— she hadn't been to college—but she was a very cultivated woman. It was quite extraordinary that an amateur enthusiasm would persist without pause, during her entire lifetime, and she never gave up on it. She found people who couldn't care less about poetry to support the Academy financially. Nobody ever gave that much money in those days, except Mr. Bullock, who, when there was a deficit, would get out the checkbook. I saw it as my task to broaden the board of directors. Jeannette was one of those. I saw Books & Co. also as an opportunity for poetry, for the publishing of poetry: poetry mattered to Jeannette and therefore to the bookstore. Jeannette has been a major supporter of contemporary American poetry.

—LYN CHASE

A range of small presses, such as the Fiction Collective and Ecco Press, had readings and parties at Books & Co. I was friendly with Dan Halperin, Ecco's founder, and we always carried his list.

Often, we were asked to provide space for the awarding of prizes: the O. Henry Award, the General Electric Awards for Younger Writers, the Pushcart Prize. We hoped to get more attention and a wider audience for smaller presses and new writers.

The small presses have a greater ability to brand. Graywolf generally means good fiction from the heartland. Sun & Moon generally means modernist or a particular European aesthetic, generally a somewhat modernist aesthetic, but also difficult works of lost foreign fiction. High Risk generally meant edgier, more urban, ultracontemporary work—cutting-edge work. Milkweed is like Graywolf, Seal means quality women's, City Lights means it probably has a relationship to the past, the hippie past, the beatnik past of City Lights. It's probably left of center politically. But it's very hard to give these qualifications now to large houses. Pantheon may have been one of the last houses that had a particular aesthetic, at least with regard to its intellectual and political connections to the old Left and particularly to a kind of older European sensibility which once existed in New York. That's not Pantheon's list anymore.   —IRA SILVERBERG

Like a cultural magnet, our location and reputation attracted fascinating people. We were cosmopolitan and international. Working in the store was like sitting in Les Deux Magots or La Coupole—after a while you'd see everyone, you'd meet everyone.

I was friends with Frank O'Hara, Kenneth Koch, John Ashbery—and my great friend was John Bernard Myers, who loved the bookstore. He was like my maiden aunt, he taught me everything, taught me to cook, to read, and I used to spend a lot of time going to Books & Co. with him. He loved Jeannette. He particularly loved Books &

Co. because he had started out in Buffalo working in a bookstore. In his book, *Tracking the Marvelous*, you learn that, suddenly, sales in this bookstore rocketed because John Myers at age eighteen was running around giving people copies of poetry books that he loved—very esoteric books—and people were buying them madly, and the bookstore sales just went through the roof. It was all connected. He began to read all the little magazines from New York City in that bookstore, and then he came to New York as the managing editor of *View* magazine. Johnny had been publishing a little magazine called *Upstate* or something, and he sent one to Charles Henri Ford. Then Charles Henri Ford said OK, get on the train, come on down. Then Johnny worked for TiBor de Nagy Gallery. TiBor de Nagy was one of his boyfriends. They worked together for a long, long time. Then John, very briefly, had his own gallery.

—ALEXANDRA ANDERSON-SPIVY

Like me, John Bernard Myers always wanted to live in New York. When he first arrived in the forties, he was a puppeteer, and then he became part of both the literary and art worlds. In 1982, he moderated a panel on art for us. He also published and edited *Parenthèse*, a magazine which first published Paul Auster and also published John Yau, James Schuyler, Barbara Guest, Niccolo Tucci, David Rieff, J. D. McClatchy, James Merrill, many writers first or before they were well known. He also included photography and art, all well printed. *Parenthèse*'s covers were lovely colors—lime green, lavender pink, orangey gold. Every month John would stop in and collect his money.

John Bernard Myers came to New York, and I hired him for *View*. Nobody was getting much salary. Our office was at Fifth Avenue and Fifty-third Street for which we paid fifty dollars a month. I was taking ten dollars a week for my salary, and I think the others were getting about the same. It was a labor of love; Parker Tyler was doing layouts and Betty Cage was secretary—after *View* stopped, Lincoln Kirsten picked her up, and she was one of the managers of the New York City Ballet Company for a long time. Johnny was very enthusiastic about *View*. He arrived with all his enthusiasm, so he really kept *View* going by soliciting ads. André Breton wanted me to stop *View* and become the editor of *VVV*. I said, Thank you, André, I think I'll continue with *View*. They had about three issues, and I had about eight years. Breton used to call me Le Poète Archétypique. But then some of his associates would say Le Pédérastie Internationale, a play on Amnesty International. There was a total prejudice against homosexuality. I was the big exception and René Crevel, naturally, he was one of the Surrealists. I was in Verona with Salvador Dalí when the news of Crevel's suicide came. But it was only after Aragon's death that I knew *he* was homosexual. I knew somebody in Paris who had a magazine, and his friend was interviewing me, so to one of them I said, I wonder who the heir of Aragon will be. Who was he close enough with to leave everything to? The young gentleman interviewing me said, I am. He was Aragon's lover. Breton didn't know it, nobody. He kept it hidden that he was homosexual. But it was not the first shock Breton had. He was bred on shock treatments, figuratively speaking.

—CHARLES HENRI FORD

I'd studied with Barbara Rose at Sarah Lawrence, and we interviewed a great many people for the Archives of American Art. We interviewed John Bernard Myers. He'd been involved with the Surrealists when they came over during the war. He started talking about the forties, Jackson

Pollock peeing in people's fireplaces, Dorothea Tanning showing up with cutouts in her blouse, Dalí going to parties without his shirt on. I thought, This is just great, and no one had done a book on New York in the forties from the point of view of the Surrealists in exile. That's what I started to write, but then it hit me that I needed a focus, and that the focus should be a woman. Peggy Guggenheim came leaping out. She was still alive, and I had her complete support—she used to introduce me as her bio-graph-er. She loved it.   —JACQUELINE WELD

John Bernard Myers was full of stories and gossip, much like Truman Capote. He was always telling me which famous writers had turned gay, or straight, or gay again, which I loved hearing about and quickly passed on. I often wondered where he got all of his information. He was knowledgeable, always amusing, and entertaining, the bearer of scandalous literary gossip and such fun. He loved to laugh.

John was not a businessman. Perish the thought. I think he felt great affinity with Jeannette. They had a similar kind of catholic attitude about culture and enthusiasm. Also he inspired many writers. Whenever he had any money he would publish something, have another little magazine. I think he published about six in his lifetime, and he did poetry chapbooks. He introduced her to people like Kenneth Koch, I'm sure she already knew John Ashbery, but Tony Towle and that whole group of poets, if she knows them, it's through him.   —ALEXANDRA ANDERSON-SPIVY

We were constantly reorganizing the bookstore, trying to be more efficient. It was always a team effort to make things work better. During this time, there were excellent sales, but I always worried—maybe we had spent too much.

When I was in college, I worked in a bookstore. It was one of the greatest jobs I ever had. My life's ambition was always to run a bookstore. You really have to have much more courage to have a bookstore than I have. How Jeannette did it, I don't know. The people who run these small bookstores, it's heroic. Directing films, you have a whole battery of people around you, and it's not your money!

—ROBERT BENTON

Steven Aronson visited often. He can imitate anyone impeccably, and I often wondered what his version of me was. He'd helped the bookstore so much, but he never wanted to give a reading. I persisted, and finally he succumbed. Steven read from his first book, *Hype.*

I don't like readings, although I'm told I'm good at them. Jimmy Merrill was great at them, and Brendan Gill can certainly rivet an audience, but most writers are pretty flat. It's not a matter of reading—we can all read, right?—it's a matter of drama really. Now, when you give a reading, you usually have to set up the passages, but in the case of *Hype* I actually had to set up the title, because at that time nobody had a clue what the word meant. In fact, the first time I went on TV the announcer mispronounced it—he said, "And now Steven Aronson will tell us all about his new book, *Hippie.*" —STEVEN M. L. ARONSON

The signings and publishing parties, unlike the readings, were paid for by the publishers. The parties spread, overflowed, onto both floors. Everyone couldn't fit, even walk, upstairs. There was usually a waiter or two serving wine and some food. For some reason, food and drink spilling on the books was never a problem. People met people all the time. I loved introducing people to each other. It sometimes felt like the fairy tales I read as a child. Fortunes could change, something magical could happen: a love affair might start or an unpublished writer might suddenly find an editor.

To have successful readings and fun parties took a lot of energy and attention to detail of every sort. I spent a whole day with American surrealist Charles Henri Ford, planning his publication party. In the morning, when *Avenue* magazine took photographs of him in his apartment at the Dakota, I saw the Tchelitchev paintings he and his sister, the actress Ruth Ford, owned. Tchelitchev and Ford had lived together for many years. We decided to make a window dedicated to the Surrealists, Ford's contemporaries.

> I must have read at the party they gave for *Om Krishna*. I was still connected with the Robert Samuel Gallery then and had a show about the same period. The night of the book party, I was very happy to see James Purdy and Glenway Westcott. Glenway was a novelist, too. He was at one time in a ménage à trois with George Platt Lynes and Monroe Wheeler. Wheeler was one of the top men at the Museum of Modern Art; George Platt Lynes was a very gifted photographer. One of Glenway's books was *Apartment in Athens;* another was *Good-Bye, Wisconsin,* where he was born. I remember what Gertrude Stein said about him in her *Autobiography of Alice B. Toklas*: "Glenway has a certain syrup, but it doesn't flow."
>
> —CHARLES HENRI FORD

> One of the tensions at a publication party was a lot of people came thinking that they should be given the book, and our view was, *sell* them the book. We tried to discourage authors from giving away books, because it led to a lot of confusion—people walking out, thinking they should have been given the book. I always said, Good friends of the writer should buy the book.   —PETER PHILBROOK

Sometimes our parties were wild, but usually, unfortunately, after I had gone home. Rumor had it, during the roaring eighties, that cocaine was snorted in our small bathroom. I never witnessed it, and it was certainly not the rule. Usually a bathroom was a bathroom, which was what I liked it to be.

> There was a reading where somebody OD'd in the bathroom. I don't know if Jeannette ever heard about that one. Maybe she did. It wasn't something I reported the next morning. —PETER PHILBROOK

In 1984, Roy Blount Jr. headed the cast for a 939 Foundation fund-raiser, a reading from *The Best of Modern Humor*, with George Plimpton. Roy had signed his book *Crackers* to me. "This is my favorite copy. I sewed the binding myself." In fact, he signed twenty-five copies for Books & Co., all differently. "Help support an author and buy this book." It was a great selling device. Customers went through every book, trying to decide which inscription was best, and bought the one they liked most.

> I'm pleased to be able to make a living writing, but when I tell people I've been working on a movie, they suddenly perk up and it sort of pisses me off—it's more impressive to me that I've written a book, but movies have a lot more glamour. To me, the gratification is putting something on the page that will stay there and sort of shimmer a little bit and will be readable for a long time, trying to write something that sort of reads itself. It's not a message from one person to another, but it's something to stick there on the page, and a lot of different people may be interested in it, just for the sake of the words on the page. When you work in the movies, it's not about working on the page. It's not about words. —ROY BLOUNT JR.

I wasn't happy charging admission for readings, even though there were additional expenses—food, drink, extra sound equipment, printing, mailings, waiters. Waiters were the biggest expense, about

$125 each. Then there was the alcohol. I'd buy wine for about five or six dollars a bottle, not terrible, passable, and the reading would wind up costing about $1,200. When I decided to run the reading series myself, I ended the foundation. I had fewer readings, only those I personally cared about, and they were free. If I threw a dinner afterwards, I looked on it as public relations. I should have printed on the invitations: Buy the book, or you can't eat. But I never did.

I love my work. I feel, in some ways, lucky like Jeannette in the sense that I'm in this wonderful company. I've got a great job and wonderful authors. It's a struggle, but anything worthwhile, worth doing, is a struggle. I feel that in spite of the direction the culture is going in, there's still a huge interest in real literature, and her bookstore is a testament to that. You just have to find ways of getting it across. The trouble is that the media are ever more mass-oriented so that making use of media becomes more and more complicated. Readers or media consumers are so bombarded with information now, getting their attention is—it's just like when you come home and you open your mailbox and the first thing you do is throw out 90 percent of what you've got that day. That's just the same as surfing the Net; you're bombarded. Getting someone to realize that this book is what she really wants is a very difficult task.

—JONATHAN GALASSI

We were always thinking of ways to get people into the store to buy books. The reading series was a prime draw, developed with a specific shape: a first novelist, introduced by a better known writer, or the editor, or we joined an unknown with one or two famous writers. Over the years I worked with several editors and publicists regularly, and they often introduced their writers.

Publicity is pre-exposure for books in the media, which includes reviews in newspapers and magazines, profiles of writers, arranging for them to be interviewed on television, radio, and also, more and more, setting up tours to bookstores. When I got started in publishing, there was very little of that. It was kind of haphazard. A handful of stores in New York would occasionally call up a publisher and say, Do you think this author would like to read here? There was no organized attempt at a marketing meeting to propose, Let's send this author on an eight-city reading tour. I think it was probably in the mid-eighties with my then-boss Victoria Meyer that we thought we should start organizing them. At that time a lot of publishers started to think about sending authors to do readings. This coincided with bookstores realizing that they wanted to expand their services, be more like a community center. Readings were a great way to increase traffic in the store.

—PAUL SLOVAK

Jane Stanton Hitchcock and Wendy Gimbel were very interested in Edith Wharton, and we set up two Wharton salons, in 1985 and 1989. Cynthia Ozick participated in the 1985 salon. Salons were on a Sunday afternoon. I served muffins and cookies, with coffee afterward. It was a very different atmosphere on Sundays. People were more relaxed and willing to sit around longer than on a Tuesday night. When Edith Wharton's letters were published, revealing her affair with Morton Fullerton, Wendy, Jane, and Jean-Claude van Itallic, a playwright and great friend of Wendy's, put on a play based on them. We all dressed up, and I remember Jane looked very pretty in a white Whartonian dress. They read excerpts from the letters, giving the story of the affair from the beginning to its sad end. Wharton had asked Fullerton to return her letters. She'd had a very brief flowering; her first and only orgasm was, as far as I could tell, when she was close to fifty, with him.

It was wonderful because, for one thing, there was R. W. B. Lewis, who'd written a biography of Edith Wharton. My dissertation, *Edith Wharton: Orphancy and Survival*, was published by Praeger in its series, Landmark Dissertations in Women's Studies. Here we were in this little world, reading the love letters Edith Wharton wrote to Morton Fullerton. The bookstore was jammed on a Sunday afternoon, and I thought, There really is a special world. The letters said things like, "I have been warmed by the wine of life at last, never to grow quite cold again." Wharton writes to him when he hasn't written back to her, and she knows it's over. It clicked into the heart of everyone who had ever had a romantic moment and a fear of its ending.

—WENDY GIMBEL

Books & Co. loved romantic books, and it also loved erotic literature. Peter ordered many erotic books from Germany and we always had a good selection, mostly from Taschen. I liked the nude photography books—human sexuality in all its forms fascinates me. *Submission* had pictures of dogs and people—interspecies love, my favorite unusual coupling. One dog was photographed with the most intriguing, enigmatic expression on its face. A dog in ecstasy. The book's publisher wanted to have its party at the store, and we set an appointment to meet. But I was afraid to be alone with them in my office. I insisted that Andrew sit in with me. After everything I'd seen in the book—a lot of defecation, too—I thought they might destroy the bookstore. There was only one erotic book I wouldn't carry. It had a photograph of a man having sex with what looked to me like a baby. I played censor then, but we had everything else.

Is it fetishistic to love books? I remember when my mother brought me a bizarre volume called *Selected Poems* by Witter Bynner. And I still long for the hardcover copy of Roethke's "The Lost Son" I memorized for years. I even want a book just for its cover: a Bosch on the front of

Bly's and Wright's translations of Trakl. The translations I have; it's the book's physical beauty I truly want and am still looking for. —DAVID SHAPIRO

What was special to me at Books & Co.—you could find books in the Bollingen Series. A fine book I treasure is *Symbolism in Greek Mythology*. Romie [Bearden] and I had been looking for it, and they had it, and he bought two copies and gave me one, and it's right on my desk. It's a book I keep out, along with the dictionaries I have on my desk, and other books, like Joyce, mine, Malraux, Hemingway, plus fairy tales and fables. The book from Romie is right beside Joseph Campbell's book, *The King and the Corpse*, from the Bollingen Series. —ALBERT MURRAY

It was Christmas again. I loved this time of year at the store so much, everyone doing their Christmas shopping. Poet James Merrill did all his shopping with us. He told me he sent books to fat friends and food to everyone else. James and I discussed Peggy Guggenheim and how cheap she was. He described a party she gave at which she served no food.

Every day held the possibility of excitement, and it's no secret: I'm a closet thrill addict. An author's arrival was very important, and I wanted to be told whenever one arrived. When John Cheever came in and signed his books, he was with Hope Lange, the actress, and I remember how very beautiful she was. When Gregor Von Rezzori came in, back in 1981, Peter knew his work and admired it. I hadn't read him yet, but we both made a big fuss over him and put his book in the window. He spent about twenty minutes signing my book, creating a little medal for me. "*Pour le mari*," it said. "This newly created order has been given for the first time to lovely Jeannette Watson, gratefully, by Gregor Von Rezzori." Peter was furious. He was the one who had loved the writing, knew it, and I was the hanger on, awarded a special medal.

121

We're on vacation. I'm out with the kids, I'm waterskiing, I'm windsurfing, I'm with the kids on the beach. So is she, with the kids on the beach, but she doesn't like the sun that much. So she's under an umbrella; she's reading. We're in our bedroom; she's reading. She's not reading at meals, but close. I'm scuba diving with Ralph, and she's polished off all of Proust, on a six-day vacation.

—ALEXANDER SANGER

Though I can concentrate completely when I'm reading, all my life I've liked to jump around, move from one activity and thought to another. Working in the bookstore necessitated it. I switched from one task to the next, one thought to another, one kind of demand to another. The store turned my nervous vice into a solid virtue. I was forced to adjust, interrupted by a visitor or phone call, to rush to meet an editor, go downstairs to work on the floor, greet people, sell books. I leaped from role to role and adored it. A bookstore must change, not exactly leap about as I did, but change, or it becomes a dead bookstore. The culture's continually shifting and changing, and a bookstore reflects that.

After Christmas, business was a little slower, as it always was, but basically it was still good. For me, the big literary excitement was the publication of the unabridged version of Richardson's *Clarissa*. The store received two copies, which I thought wouldn't sell, but a faithful customer bought one. Then I practically had a fight with another customer over the other copy. Later, he called to complain to the manager about "a blond woman who took his book away from him." My love of books sometimes surpassed my love of selling books.

Peter became very interested in African literature, and we began an African section. Introducing the section, we became acquainted with some of the writers, and once that presence was established, the books were integrated into the Wall. We kept changing and adding to the Wall.

Books & Co.'s limitations are its power—the fact that its philosophy section was a particular kind and changed; its books were a particular kind. Again, it has to do with the fact that Jeannette always had quirky buyers. That's why there's no one bookstore that answers everything. It's like you put together a set of bookstores to find what you want.　　　　　　　　　　　　　　　　　—JOHN G. HANHARDT

One day a man walked in and said, "You don't have your fly-fishing section anymore." I explained that the person who'd been interested in it had left. We knew nothing about it and couldn't sell it for the same reason. He said, "I guess there wasn't a big call for it, anyway." Another customer asked for a book "with a beginning, middle, and end." A hard request, I thought, these days.

We changed sections or added them—a gender section—or subtracted them—fly-fishing. We attempted different approaches over the years, maintaining a consistent focus on art, literature, poetry, and philosophy.

I remember when Candice Bergen was coming in looking for books on Borges. The staff got together and they started suggesting where to start with Borges. I can remember standing in there when things like that happened. It was like a college bookstore, but like a graduate school bookstore. Because you've got the ultimate professionals, and you might run across them any day. Carlos Fuentes—you could see him there any day. John Cheever. He signed five hundred copies of a book. Once you signed all of those books, the store couldn't return them.

　　　　　　　　　　　　　　　　　　　—ALBERT MURRAY

In every conceivable way we showcased books and writers, the windows being our first line, and occasionally, to some, the line was offensive. When Arthur Paul was working as the buyer, he placed about ten goldfish in bowls in the window. The goldfish kept dying, and animal rights people kept calling, How can you do this, live goldfish in your window?

Peter and I had a running joke about the suicide window we were going to do. So many writers had committed suicide, we were going to pull out Hemingway and hundreds of others, and feature books by writers who'd done themselves in. Peter volunteered to hang in the window, but he said he could do it only once.

Our windows and readings were generally upbeat, though, and timely, timed to new books coming out. I tried to be at all the readings, if I could, especially first novelists whose cause I took up. Sometimes the readings were nerve-racking events, not only for the writers.

When Bernard Malamud was reading, we began hearing extremely strange and inexplicable noises. Andrew had been there adjusting the microphone and all the sound equipment—and the sound equipment was just held together with Band-Aids. It barely functioned. There was only one person usually who knew how to paste it together so it would work. Andrew thought he had it all set. Then we started hearing a bizarre noise, a noise never heard before, one Andrew didn't know how to deal with. I looked at Malamud and said, "My god, it's his pacemaker." Andrew had to run upstairs and take the mike away from his chest, move it farther up toward his face, so it wouldn't pick up the noise. —SUSAN SCOTT

Though our reputation was good and growing, I constantly worried that we wouldn't get an audience for our readings. Or that something might go wrong. I knew that authors worried, too, and were anxious about other issues as well. But the fear of no one showing up was usually all of ours.

Curiously, one of our best readings had almost no one in the audience. Anne Porter, painter Fairfield Porter's lovely widow, read her beautiful, religious poems to about five people. It was a quiet and reverent hour. She was like a little saint—afterwards I hung a picture of her on my wall. Though Mrs. Porter's friend had insisted months before that invites would go out, nothing was done. People were continually promising they'd do the work, but they didn't understand the problems. I'd said to her friend, I'll do it because you like her, I like her, but it's terrible to make an eighty-three-year-old woman read if no one's there. Don't worry, I'll get an audience, she said. Still, it turned out to be a magical evening.

I particularly loved introducing Anne Porter. Anne was publishing her first book at age eighty-three, *An Altogether Different Language*, and receiving just a little but true public attention. I was pleased with the intensity of her reading, like the intensity of a Fairfield Porter watercolor. She is a great Catholic poet. I remember being particularly pleased when Jeannette gave me a book of prayers as a gift. —DAVID SHAPIRO

In the mid-1980s, I spoke at the Colony Club about how I started the bookstore. I told the audience that I'd had to borrow half of the money from my father. Daddy was in the audience, and at the end of my talk, he raised his hand and asked, "Did you ever pay your father back?" I said, "Yes, I did, I paid my father back." Everyone knew he was my father, and as usual all the women were in love with him.

The store's life was a mix of everything, from silly and annoying to fun and the sublime. When Benita Eisler dropped by, I decided to play a vintage fifties Elvis tape for her. But suddenly, we lost electricity. Then the sidewalk in front of the store was being repaired, and in order to get into the store, everyone had to walk on planks. It was hard to know how many customers were chased away by having to walk a plank.

Though we were doing all right, and I'd paid my father back, the Whitney Museum of American Art had bought the row of buildings we were in; and in 1986, they were considering expanding. The architect Michael Graves made a design, and if it were adopted and approved, 939 Madison would be torn down. I was on the Landlord's Conservancy Board, and we had to vote on it. I explained, I'm totally biased, so you shouldn't listen to me, but I don't think it's a good idea. The townhouses were in keeping with the neighborhood, which was zoned for small buildings. The Graves design would do away with an entire Upper East Side historic district. Nobody voted for it, but for a couple of years, there was great controversy and the beginning of unfortunate public arguments between the Whitney and Books & Co. People rallied around the bookstore, and there was a lot of press about the situation. I remember one article's rather gothic title: "Literary Tenants in Museum's Dark Shadow." Flora Biddle, who's on the Whitney board, took me out to lunch at Pleiade. She asked how I felt about the Graves addition. I burst into tears. Several people I knew were in the restaurant, too. They couldn't figure out why I was sitting with Flora and weeping. Ultimately, the Whitney ended its attempt to build an extension.

> At the end of the day, it had been watered down by two or three versions of Michael's work, from what was originally in fact a very tough and brilliant idea, and by the third iteration I don't think it had what the initial one had, although it made certain people happier. It's the process you go through. But I think the biggest issue was not Michael or his design, or even the community, although that was looming big. It was that it wasn't really affordable.
>
> —DAVID ROSS

Some days were more difficult than others. Customer relations were important and occasionally delicate. I had an unpleasant encounter with actor/writer Andre Gregory. He'd been complaining about how cold the atmosphere was in the store, so I explained, in what I thought was a tactful way, that we had become exhausted suggesting books to him that he never bought. I hoped I had been diplomatic. But when singer Pearl Bailey came in, she said she loved the bookstore. She said she "wanted to join up." Pearl Bailey felt what I wanted people to experience—that Books & Co. was a club open to anyone who loved books.

> It was like a place to have an intelligent conversation. I realize that you feel this sort of magic about some bookstores, where simply because the people who are working there are there, you feel you could sort of get into a conversation about the particular type of book you were looking for. —SIMON SCHAMA

To much acclaim, Jacqueline Weld's book, *Peggy: The Wayward Guggenheim*, was published in 1986. Jackie grew up in Uruguay and Venezuela. She was the great-granddaughter of Juan Idiarte Borda, the martyred Uruguayan president, about whom the extraordinary Jorge Luis Borges wrote in *The Book of Sand*.

> It took me a very long time to write *Peggy*—biographies are very draining. I think only because I hadn't done a biography, I thought I should write a biography. It took me about eight years—two years of research, four years of writing and research, then another two years editing it and vetting everything, every single footnote. I have a reverence for the arts, I have a great reverence for the pictorial arts—I knew a lot about it—I always studied it. When I was a kid I would go through art books—that was my idea of a fun thing to do. But I was unprepared for the trauma of publication, because you work for years in your little garret—if you will—happily playing with your material,

involved with every nuance of your character to the point where you know them better than they ever knew themselves, and you have this strange sensation that you're now the keeper of the flame. Often even her grandchildren would come see me to ask me about this, that, or the other, because they also had the intuition I knew more than they did. So you're working on that level, then all of a sudden you're out there. I got thirty-two rave reviews, but I didn't like the process of publication. At the beginning you're very tender, by the end of the experience, I couldn't care less. Johnny Myers used to say, You know how you take the measure of a review? With a ruler. At the end, all I'd look for was: do they have my picture, do I look beautiful, how big a spread is it? But that's something, as a first-time writer, you're not prepared for, and somebody should prepare you. Jeannette was extremely helpful—supportive emotionally—and she was very good at telling me what I should do to promote the book. Even though it wasn't necessarily in her interest, she told me I should go visit all of the booksellers, introduce myself before the book came out, and thank them for everything they had done. She showed me the way to get out there more than I would have known how to do. It wouldn't have occurred to me.

—JACQUELINE WELD

When Paul Auster read from *The New York Trilogy*, I gave a dinner for him after the reading. My apartment was filled with Paul's friends.

Bill Zavatsky's press, Sun, was the original publisher of *The Invention of Solitude*. A party was held at Books & Co. for my book as well as several other recent Sun titles— three or four writers in all—and I remember it as a crowded, boisterous, and altogether pleasant evening. A couple of years later, around the time that *City of Glass* was published, Jeannette and Peter invited me to give a reading. That was lovely, but on top of that, Jeannette threw a party for me at her house. It was an exceptional act of generosity, and I'll never forget it. This big, splendid party with dozens of people and an atmosphere of such incredible warmth. There was no particular reason for Jeannette to do it—she just wanted to. I look back on it as one of the best evenings of my life, as one of the kindest things anyone has ever done for me.   —PAUL AUSTER

These initial parties, these readings around the beginning of a book, do have some of the classical, social value of exactly that sort of declaration of something going into the world. Go dumb book into the world! So you gather its immediate family around, but really what you're doing is saying, I'm releasing you now into the world, and then the bookstore becomes an idealization of that idea of the world.   —ANN LAUTERBACH

I have always loved having book parties at the store, as when *Lateness* came out and David Hockney came and wasn't fazed that Overlook had printed his cover in red with white lines rather than white with black lines. He looked at it with a tolerant smile and enjoyed the party. I also loved my party for a Jasper Johns drawings book that I felt was not good enough for that artist. I had dreamed of a book that would have a text as beautiful as his drawings, and a book that would be as beautiful, as if each reproduction were an original. Jasper came, and I was amazed that he so leniently signed copies.

          —DAVID SHAPIRO

Things were going well, but I worried about what would happen when our lease was up. Ted Wilentz's rule of thumb was: Your rent should not be more than 12 percent of your gross. After the first few years, we were making over $1 million a year. One year—our high point—we made $1.4 million. Profits went into bigger salaries or bonuses. For a while, I took home $2,000 a month, which was thrilling. Though my father's loan had been $150,000 to start, we both had had to put more in. It cost much more to build the space originally. Finally, too, that money was paid back.

But I had wretched financial advice around this time from an adviser who proposed "special situations," all specially bad situations. My father had said, "The only way you're going to make it in this business is if you own your building." By the time I could have bought 939 Madison—early on I thought why buy it for a bankrupt bookstore?—the Whitney had.

> Her father advised her to buy 939. At the time she thought, "I'm not sure . . ." I think that was the timidity factor. Jeannette, in a funny way, like all of us, didn't know who she was when she was starting out. It's one step in front of the other. It's contradictory, a paradox. She should have listened to her father, but that's probably a case where she wanted to do it alone and her way.
>
> —JANE STANTON HITCHCOCK

On the advice of my adviser, I decided to buy a building, to give me a little security about the future of Books & Co. But I bought the building at the height of the market, in the neighborhood, Seventy-fourth Street and Lexington Avenue. Investing in real estate, if you're not a professional, is treacherous. When the market crashed, we couldn't lease it out. We started a costly renovation, but, it turned out, no mechanical engineer had evaluated it. After the building was painted, a great gash appeared down the facade. The building had collapsed. I tried to rescue the building for Books & Co., but it drained me financially. My business adviser kept telling me everything was fine, when, in fact, I was in serious debt. In a way I became a character in an old story, the one about women who are born into money, but are never trained to manage it. Many lose it all. I nearly did. I felt I'd endangered my family, too, because, in theory, my inheritance would pass on to them.

Traditionally, my father would never talk about money—it was a dirty secret, one didn't get involved with it. I hadn't been great about watching it. Anxiously I told him about the disastrous building. But he didn't rescue me. Instead he recommended his financial adviser, Ted Ladd, and through him I used the money I had left, invested it wisely, and slowly, slowly, was able to crawl out of debt. I sold the building finally.

I'm an eternal optimist, but Peter's suicide window was occasionally appealing. After I'd saved myself, I declared, like Scarlet O'Hara, I'll never be hungry again! Why does it always have to be the hard way? I asked Brendan Gill. Brendan said, Everybody learns the hard way. That's the only way you can learn anything in life. In a way, though, Brendan had a charmed life. He once told me he tried to act a bit like an idiot with his children, because he felt it must be so hard for them to have him as a father, a man with a perfect life. When we presented his book, *Many Masks: A Life of Frank Lloyd Wright*, in 1987, it was another fulfillment for Brendan. His great hero was Frank Lloyd Wright.

Architecture was my boyhood-childhood-infant passion. Designing I think is just in one's head—it's a talent. Actually it's in one's hand and not under the aegis of architecture or anything else. At three or four, I was always building. I was seven when my mother died. But I was already a confirmed amateur architect. I used to turn over the chairs in the house and put sheets and blankets over them and make long endless houses. One of the maids— one had maids in those days—complained, because this was the period, in 1920, when hygienic housekeeping, written about in the *Ladies' Home Journal*, held sway. The maids were supposed to take off all of the bedclothes and pile them all up and open the windows and air the bedroom, then make the bedroom up in the afternoon. That treatment has long since died—people throw their bedclothes on as fast as they can—so no more airing of the bedsheets. But in any event, that had given me the opportunity to take the bedsheets, put them on the furniture— and the maids were furious. And then my mother uttered the wonderful words, "Let Brendan do whatever he wants to do." I've always thought that that was what everybody in the world should do because my mother said so. It sounded like a sound doctrine to me. We had an exceptional family, and I may say that the family that my wife and I created is exceptional, too—seven children and they all love each other and stay together, and they all have different gifts. The secret I think was the fact that my wife loved them and spoiled them as my mother did me from birth. We said, You are absolute perfection, to all of them, and they just were bathed in love. You get them past the dangerous point—this is around three or four—and that degree of self-confidence of having got enough love, endless quantities of love, is the protection you need to make the next step, because every step is perilous, and you have to have been loved an awful lot to draw that capital down as you need it.   —BRENDAN GILL

No matter what transpired in my private, financial life, the life customers and writers weren't exposed to, I relished Books & Co. It was such a good place.

Not since college had I had the joy of standing around and getting really scrappy about literature. Around those tables in her store, love affairs began, great enmity grew. . . . I remember that we would go out on intellectual, literary limbs we would never dare do anyplace else because we were safe, with lovely, benevolent Mama Jeannette watching us squabble like siblings at a dining room table, listening to us say things like, "What in the world did you see in that book? What could you possibly see in that book?!!" Just getting into fights or great passionate agreements with other readers. Not necessarily writers, although they were often writers, but other readers. To be passionately caught up in conversation about literature, do you know what a rare treat that is in this day and age? I always left feeling exhilarated. —BARBARA LAZEAR ASCHER

Bruce Chatwin dropped by whenever he was in New York. I loved *The Songlines* and *In Patagonia*, his first book. Bruce would sweep into the bookstore, very handsome in his green loden cape. Each time he appeared it was as if he'd just flown in from some distant, exotic place. He'd run into people he knew, and then he'd run upstairs, sit on the couch, and read. His *On the Black Hill* was one of the last nineteenth-century novels written in the twentieth, almost a Thomas Hardy novel. I can still see Bruce sitting on the couch and reading, his silky blond hair light against the dark green leather.

Now when Andre Gregory came in, he was very friendly, even though, or because, I had chastised him about not buying books from us. A new approach to customer relations? Though Isaac Bashevis Singer never visited the bookstore—he was a very old man by the time we opened and we weren't in his neighborhood—we went to his home, where he signed books for us. But Niccolo Tucci came in almost every day for a long time, and, of course, I always addressed him as Mr. Tucci. We were fortunate that, in 1991, his daughter, Maria, read from his work, with Mr. Tucci in attendance. (Around this time we started taping the readings, so I have an archive of writers reading from about 1990.)

Two amazing women, Mai-Mai Sze and Irene Sharaff, who lived together, frequently stopped by and brought us their stories and intriguing lives. Mai-Mai Sze was an artist, lecturer, and author of *The Tao of Painting—A Study of the Ritual Disposition of Chinese Painting*. She was raised in the Imperial City in China and emigrated to the U.S. in the 1920s. Irene Sharaff was a celebrated stage and movie costume designer, of *The King and I, Oklahoma!*, and *West Side Story* fame. Book lovers they were, too, and they loved English authors especially. Mai-Mai and Irene often told me about English bookstores I should visit.

We had a huge crowd for Walker Percy. Everyone tried to get upstairs to get closer to him. I felt like the bouncer at Studio 54. Percy was truly charming, gracious. He remembered everyone's names—and signed each book individually. His publisher Robert Giroux said in his introduction that to speak of Percy as a Southern writer was ridiculous.

The extraordinary Italian author Alberto Moravia came in to sign *The Voyeur*. He was a good-looking, elderly man, with a cane. Moravia was not at all interested in conversation, though, only in signing his books efficiently. It was around this time that I received very sad news from John Bernard Myers. Bruce Chatwin had AIDS, he told me. I hoped it wasn't true. He was such a brilliant writer and attractive man.

Over the years, Books & Co. did very well in the love and meeting department, a virtual section in bookstores. Richard Price met his wife there, and Jessica Lange and Sam Shepard were seen kissing in the back of the store. Peter Philbrook met his wife, Danielle, there. Countless friendships and love affairs blossomed and, I suppose, wilted.

It was a home on Madison Avenue. You could be doing your errands and stop by. Jeannette watched the world from that window, and luckily Jeannette is a discreet, nice person. I can assure you that the assignations that were going on. . . . I thought a great book, a novel, would be what she saw from her window, which nobody was supposed to see.   —JANE STANTON HITCHCOCK

When I was a lawyer, one of my clients, a very beautiful, wealthy woman, very well read, came to see me one day at the firm, and said, "I got picked up in the philosophy section of Books & Co." She was sort of half-smiling, half-offended, half-thrilled. I think she continued to go back to the philosophy section, and she probably told all of her friends.   —ALEXANDER SANGER

Sometimes a favorite customer became a favorite writer, like Jeannette Haien. When her first novel, *The All of It*, was coming out, Jeannette asked if she could have a reading. I told her I had to read the book first. I have my principles. It became one of my special books, with a place on my table.

She believed in it, and said yes. After that, one becomes confident. I was known as a pianist, touring all over the world, and on tour, I used to write short stories for myself. One or two—three—four were published randomly, because other writers and other people read them and saw to that. I began *The All of It* as a short story, and then it became a book. It's an Irish phrase: "Sit down and I will tell you the all of it." Mark Strand introduced me and also wrote marvelously for the jacket, and that was thrilling for me. Mark referred to my musical life, my life in music, but he said that I had always been a good teller of stories. When I tell a joke, I tell it with musician's ears, so I can tell it in many accents, and I'm a good storyteller. He spoke of how that had been translated, that capacity had translated itself—only he did it so much better than that and so adroitly and cleanly. It was wonderful the way Jeannette introduced him, the way her remarks about him laced into his remarks about me. None of this had been planned—it was all spontaneous, but it was, for me, coming from those sources, very exciting, and it was a full house, gratifying, too. I stood up without any notion of how this was going to read. But I started in, and I read the usual length of time, and there was festive wine afterwards, and I went home euphoric, walking on air, like my editor Robert Jones's title, *Walking on Air*, because it appeared to be listenable to. I don't try and affect an Irish form, of sentence structure or anything like that. I tried very hard only to get the lilt in the language. So that I didn't have to be Irish, yet I think you'd know it's an Irish speaker, an Irish reminiscer. I went home euphoric about the whole evening, and then rose to the wonder of it.

—JEANNETTE HAIEN

The window was absolutely appropriate to the book, perfect. I had brought in Alex's big fishing waders and other fishing gear, to evoke the priest who fishes. Cleaning up the store, ten years later, I discovered the waders still there in a closet.

The denouement of the novel involves a priest's thinking, as he salmon fishes, about a confession he had heard, not from the lips of the dying, but from the lips of the living. He had tried to wrest the confession from the dying man, but had heard it from the living, left alone. And there he is, on a terrible day, casting in strong wind, in unspeakable conditions, on the wide and roiling river, thinking about that confession. And there is the window—and guys going home from work, macho guys, lawyers, stockbrokers, walking up the avenue, all sorts—men, transfixed, standing in front of this window she'd created with a great pair of waders suspended and fishing gear. Right away, you entered into the world of the book, from Madison Avenue, and as I entered the store that first time, with that window, a man had gone in before me, hadn't held the door open for me; he couldn't get in fast enough to buy the fishing book. There wasn't an angler who walked up Madison Avenue for the next two weeks, who wasn't arrested. *The All of It* has been a steady underground best-seller, read and studied by book clubs. I receive telephone calls, questions: Was I an alcoholic, am I a lapsed Catholic? They're thinking the riddle of the text will be clarified by some biographical knowledge of myself.

—JEANNETTE HAIEN

In 1987, I introduced Hugh Nissenson, who read from *The Tree of Life*, about life in a frontier settlement in Ohio. It included detailed descriptions of torture Indians practiced on settlers, while their families watched. Gruesome, but to me fascinating, and Nissenson read exactly those pages at the store. I was thrilled, though I don't know how some in the audience felt. The book asked questions about the existence of God in a brutal world. Before the reading, Hugh brought in some pieces from his Native American collection, and Peter and I decorated the window with the book, a skull, and an Indian headdress. Peter dressed up in the leather outfit and wore the headdress, too, all day.

I remember I dressed as an Indian for a day, because Hugh Nissenson's book had something to do with Indians, and he brought this outfit in for the window, and I put it on. I remember another favorite window, for Todd Colby, a writer and musician. Todd worked in the basement for years. We knew it was going to be his birthday so I talked to his girlfriend, and we got a photo of him we then blew up, for the Todd window. It had nothing to do with books. This giant picture—and Todd loved Pepperidge Farm cheese fish crackers—so I filled the window three feet deep with goldfish and his picture. Some boats too with some of the funny things he said, which I liked, because they had nothing to do with books. People walked by and didn't understand what it meant, who this person was. No one said, what is this? Who is Todd, do you have his book? Todd worked in the basement, for a while, did the shipping. There's usually one person in charge of the basement. He wrote weird Dada-esque things all over the basement—and later painted it all over, unfortunately. I wish he hadn't. You'd go downstairs, and you'd always see something new. —PETER PHILBROOK

A favorite Books & Co. writer, Andre Dubus, had a terrible accident—he stopped his car to aid another driver, who was trying to change a flat tire. Andre got out of his car to help and was hit by another car. One of his legs had to be amputated, and he and his wife had just had a baby. A fund was started, and Books & Co. tried to raise money. Peter's idea was to send a free, signed copy of Andre's book *Dancing after Hours* to all of our house charge customers and ask them to send money to the fund.

I broke up with a lover of a long time, fifteen years, and decided that that signaled a good time to go to a therapist. I found one through the recommendation of a friend, on Seventy-ninth Street between Madison and Fifth. I would dutifully show up once a week for a year, but I do remember that after every session, I would walk down and stop by the store. And in retrospect I can't really decide which had the more beneficial effect and pulled me out of my slump, the shrink or the store. I tend to feel the store did. I probably looked for books that I thought would answer some particularly obscure need that was just surfacing then. I found that it was much cheaper and I think much more useful, finally, than psychotherapy. The books I found there and the atmosphere of the store, it was an image of the way I wished my mind were. Neatly ordered ranks of ideas and feelings, instead of the sort of sloppy mess that it was at the time. It was a very bracing, tonic image of what I was hoping to achieve for myself.　　　　—J. D. MCCLATCHY

One friend brought in others, so the intimate circle kept expanding. Jackie Weld took Gordon Lish's writing class, and because of that, Amy Hempel started coming in.

In 1985, when my first book came out, *Reasons to Live*, my editor, Gordon Lish, engineered a reading at Books & Co. It was my very first reading. I was absolutely undone by it, even though it's an intimate setting, and there were many friends and Jeannette is, of course, the most welcoming person imaginable. I remember being unbelievably nervous, calmed by Jeannette, and went through with it. My big decision was to take a tranquilizer or not. You weigh the pros and cons—I wanted an edge, the nervous edge, and I didn't know who was going to be there. The stakes were so high to me. I kept saying, through my terror, this is not a situation that is actually dangerous. I'm terrified of flying—which is actually dangerous—it could kill you. Probably giving a reading won't kill me. I just don't want to make a fool of myself. I remember sitting in Gordon's office at Knopf, while he spoke with Jeannette, arranging this, and when he got off the phone, I begged him not to make me do it. He said, You have to do this, there just was no equivocating. I think I was most afraid of fainting, from sheer terror. I thought later, I'm glad the first—as if you're talking about your first lover—was Jeannette, in that place.　　　　—AMY HEMPEL

Tom Wolfe came in and signed *Bonfire of the Vanities*. The novel took off like a rocket—one hundred copies in a week, which was phenomenal. And what a relief to have a novel I really liked to sell.

There were, along with pleasure and fun, the everyday niggling problems, including ones with our landlord, the Whitney. The scaffolding they had erected, which had spoiled the facade of the store for so long, obscuring our all-important window, was finally taken down. But when it came down, it ripped our canopy. So I had to write the Whitney to get them to pay for the canopy's repair. There was a flood in the basement, because of the holes in our roof, and the basement was where our overstock was stored. Luckily, there wasn't much damage. A Whitney employee, John Murray, was very helpful, and he became my new knight in shining armor. When we had a terrible pigeon problem, John helped with that, too. He told Peter that the Whitney planned to trap the pigeons and drive them to New Jersey. Then there was the day a fireman came in and warned us we had too many books in the basement. It was a fire hazard, in addition to everything else.

Amy Hempel and Jackie Weld introduced me to writer Anderson Ferrell. It was through Andy, later on, that we had an Agnes de Mille evening. Andy was great friends with de Mille—he and his boyfriend Dirk Lombard met her when they were young dancers.

During the time that I was setting up a reading for Agnes de Mille, I was pregnant with my third son, Matthew. Irene and Mai-Mai treated me to lunch. Irene told me, "There was a time when Agnes choreographed everything on Broadway, and I did the costumes." When de Mille read from her memoir, *Portrait Gallery*, in 1990, she loaned us her portrait for the window, as well as photographs of herself dancing in *Oklahoma!* I love musicals, and *Oklahoma!* and *Carousel* were my favorites. To me, presenting de Mille, a larger-than-life figure, was another dream come true. By then, de Mille was in a wheelchair and had to be carried upstairs by Andy and Dirk. Her publisher had had her hair and makeup done for the event. Her white hair was drawn back and tied in a big, floppy bow, and she was flushed and happy, like an excited, young girl.

Amy Hempel also introduced me to Christopher Coe. He'd studied with Gordon Lish, too.

In 1980, Christopher and I met in Gordon's workshop. A lot of the people who studied with him and who went on to publish books ended up at Jeannette's, for example, Anderson Ferrell and Mark Richard. She devoted an evening of readings from *The Quarterly*, which was Gordon's lit magazine, so Gordon definitely was tied into Books & Co. for a long time. I remember saying to Jeannette, You should know about Christopher Coe. He's an extraordinary writer and character, a real strong character. He was a very dear friend, and I think I sent his first novel to Jeannette, which was called *I Look Divine*. She liked it as much as I did, arranged for him to read there, and I introduced him. I remember asking him, "What would you most like the person introducing you to mention about your work?" He said, "Could you work in the word *breathtaking*?" So I did.

—AMY HEMPEL

I told Christopher that I had wanted to see Plato's Retreat, the sex club, and had gone with one of my old boyfriends. I told him how much I enjoyed it. Christopher was horrified. I, the mother of three, had been there and enjoyed it. He incorporated that into his last book, *Such Times*, and read it at Books & Co., his last reading. I was honored.

For a few years, in the late seventies, it became a place for men and women. They came to the Continental, renamed, to cavort in public, pretty much as the fags did, I imagine. I wouldn't know. I suspect it was pretty much the same thing. Last week a woman told me she had been there once or twice. She is not a woman I would have expected to have gone there. She is a married woman, a mother, runs a top photography gallery, is a social figure, always beautifully dressed, impeccably manicured, a woman with a polish. Really, she is the last woman I would have expected to go there, so I took her at her word that she had gone only to watch.

"It's hard to believe there used to be such times," she said.

Jasper was much more than tasty.

"Yes," I said. "It is hard to believe, isn't it?"

I didn't say this merely to agree with her. I really do find it hard to believe that there used to be such times.

—from *Such Times*

When he read from *Such Times*, he was dying of AIDS. He was very, very ill. That reading was something he had to get himself up for. He had to go to some lengths to be able to do it and showed up looking terribly ill, but dressed in a floor-length Japanese ceremonial robe.

—AMY HEMPEL

Christopher was so very thin, he thought that if he wore a beautiful robe, it would distract people from his appearance. Cork Smith, his editor, introduced him. After Christopher died, we held a memorial at Books & Co.

Jeannette offered the bookstore, and his editor and his friends read from his work, had wine, and there were flowers. It was so awful. He was quite young, under forty. It was just the right place. It wasn't just a bookstore then, and we were there to talk about Christopher and read. Jeannette had gotten together photographs of him and had someone put together a photograph album. It was gracefully done.   —AMY HEMPEL

It was a fond, sometimes poignant or sad pleasure, paying tribute to writers, introducing readers to writers, and of course meeting writers.

One of the authors I was eager to meet was Tobias Schneebaum. He was an artist and an anthropologist—an ideal combination—and had lived with tribes in the South Pacific, in New Guinea,
where Michael Rockefeller was possibly eaten. Schneebaum participated in a cannibal tribe's rituals, wrote about his life with them, and
described killing people and eating them. He was so much a part of
the life of the tribe, so involved, he was able to think as they did. He
explained how through eating their enemy, they believe they receive
their enemy's bravery. Eating his heart, I take on his qualities, which
will make me stronger.

> She has this weakness or fondness, if you will, for inter-
> species love affairs and cannibalism. I'm not quite sure
> how the two are related. But the scheme kind of goes
> throughout the bookstore. How you relate cannibalism to
> interspecies love affairs, where these two literary genres
> meet, is probably only in Jeannette's mind.
>   —ALEXANDER SANGER

When Tobias's next book, *Where the Spirits Dwell*, was sched-
uled to come out in 1988, I called his publisher, announced myself as
one of his biggest fans, and set up a reading. Tobias Schneebaum arrived carrying a long, narrow object, which turned out to be two
spears from New Guinea. He then proceeded to pull two skulls out
of his bag and some necklaces. Now, he told me, he was working on
a cruise ship as a lecturer, and had been researching the sex lives of
Tahitians. He read in Captain Bligh's description of Tahitian practices that women inserted coconut in their vaginas and let their dogs
lick it out. Others stuck ants in their vaginas, to swell the lips, so that
intercourse would be tighter.

At the party afterwards, some of my friends were a little wicked.
Everyone had had a few glasses of wine, and people asked Tobias
questions like, Which part of the body tastes best—the knees? Who
ate Michael Rockefeller? Tobias wasn't offended and went along

with it. He was able to adapt, obviously, to all kinds of societies and customs. Shirley Hazzard was at the party—she's a great friend of his—and Hortense Calisher, Curt Harnack, and Hilma Wolitzer.

> The eighties were such a boom time in more ways than just real estate and Wall Street. It was a time when popular culture was discovering its own power, becoming conscious of it. It was no longer naive. Now we can look at old clips of Dick Cavett on VH-1, at girls screaming in the sixties, those days which I would characterize as pop culture being unaware of itself, still innocent in a way. By the eighties they knew what they had, they knew what it could make, they knew what it could portray and the influence it had, so that became a very powerful thing. I was sending my children to school in New York in the eighties, which was the capital of that kind of influence. I wanted them to be intellectually bilingual. I wanted them to know all the pop culture, but to be independent, intellectually, not to be of it. This is where Books & Co. really played a role, because there was the choice of books, of having people there who loved thoughts and ideas, and it was independent. It wasn't academic, you weren't going to get graded, it wasn't something you had to apply to get into, it was there for anybody. It encompassed art, photography, poetry, philosophy, and erotic books. I always told my children, "There's all of this, too." They were influenced by my being influenced. There is another way, there's another approach, there are other voices you can listen to, and I attribute that to my own upbringing, to my own wonderful teachers, but also to the fact that Books & Co. *manifested* it.   —CLARA DALE

I introduced Tobias to Charles Ryskamp, the director of the Frick Museum. Tobias had two books in print then, but they kept going out of print. We found them for Charles, who then ordered four or five a week to send to his friends. It was what happened when people loved books, loved their friends. They wanted their friends to read what they loved. I tried always to keep his books in stock.

I would go there and load up. I never walked out of Books & Co. without a hundred dollars' worth of books. I just couldn't find those books anywhere else—and I just snapped them up the way I do anything I know I'm not going to see anywhere else. Books are sort of like a garage sale of Western culture. You have to snap them up when you see them, or they're not going to be there again.

—RICHARD HOWARD

Big drinker, big eater, big enjoyer of life, Jim Harrison became a bookstore favorite. His novel *Dalva*, published in 1988, was one of the cherished, and it returned to my special table constantly.

I really don't care for public appearances, but my several readings at Books & Co. are as pleasant as they get.

—JIM HARRISON

Do I like going to readings? Not especially. I tend to steer clear of them—except as a show of support for friends, people whose work I care about. Generally speaking, I like to read books, not listen to them. But it's astonishing how popular readings are, isn't it? Every day in every city across the country, dozens of writers are standing up and reading their work to audiences. I suppose that's a good thing. At the same time, many people go to hear an author read—and then don't bother to read his book. I find that a little disturbing. And very strange.   —PAUL AUSTER

Dalva was written from the point of view of a woman whose family consisted of very strong women. Her grandfather had been great friends with the Indians in the region, and the book presented a great deal of Indian lore and history. Jim was from Michigan and was part Indian. Dalva was such a strong character, someone I'd like to be like. Bravely she would set off on her horse, ride across the desert, throw down her sleeping bag, and sleep under the stars. I would be riddled with anxiety—I couldn't even sleep in the family house in Stowe unless other people were there. No bathroom for Dalva, too. But she was my idea of perfection, a role model whose role I could never play. I loved the writing and also Jim's poetry, his collection of haiku.

Readings were not my cup of tea. Usually it was an overexposure to the author's ego. It was as often as not a disappointment to meet an author—you'd have read wonderful prose for a long time only to find out that the author was sort of a jerk. The readings were often difficult from the standpoint of watching the hungry arrive. Everybody involved was hungry. The author involved had such a hungry ego, and a certain segment of the public was so hungry for the author, for the fame and all of that stuff, that it was hard to watch after a while.

—SUSAN SCOTT

You always feel like a fraud as a writer. It's such an ephemeral art. You never feel quite real. It helps to make you feel real and part of a community and part of an ancient tradition when you're reading aloud.

—BARBARA LAZEAR ASCHER

I'm not very good with readings, because I tend to lose consciousness. I tend to start to drift away and look at certain people. And I'm a terrible snob. I look at how people are dressed. I notice how the women are dressed and think, Now why is she wearing that sort of funny scarf?

—JAMES FALKIN

Books & Co. shopping bag
designed by Ed Koren

Jeannette Watson and Brendan Gill

Jeannette's parents,
Olive and Thomas
Watson, Jr., at the
Stork Club (1942)

Fran Lebowitz

Barbara Lazear Ascher

(Left to right) Paul Auster
and Peter Philbrook

Jeannette Watson and Walker Percy; in background, Dorothea Straus

Bicky Kellner

Jeannette Watson

Calvin Trillin

Salman Rushdie and Jeannette Wat

Amy Hempel

Larry Kra

Brendan Larson

Susan Sontag

(Left to right) Anderson Ferrell, Amy Hempel, Jeannette Watson, Christopher Coe, Sunny Rogers

Joyce Ravid

Jeannette Watson

Richard Howard

The second floor of Books & Co.

Roy Blount Jr.

Albert Murray

I've been staying at the Carlyle, compliments of show business, for nearly twenty years, and I met Jeannette the first trip. Ray's Pizza is one of the salvations of that neighborhood, along with Books & Co. and the Carlyle. I felt it my sacred duty to take Jeannette to Ray's for lunch rather than low-rent hash houses like Bernardin. Many of the local stores are so sophisticated, you can't tell what they're selling by looking in the window. I brought Art Garfunkel in, and he thought Jeannette looked nifty in her gray gabardine skirt, and I readily agreed.   —JIM HARRISON

One rainy afternoon, Jim said he was going to go see *Henry & June* and invited me to go with him. We ran away to the movies, which I love doing. I had such fun with him.

I took Jeannette to the Anaïs Nin movie. It was a tad erotic, and I was a little embarrassed to have taken her, but then Henry Miller is one of the most persistent heroes of my life.   —JIM HARRISON

One of our all-time greatest parties was for Montana's Clark City Press. Hundreds showed up, including Dan Rather. There were huge tubs filled with beer, and it was a bacchanalian affair. Artist Russell Chatham had started Clark City, which published Jim and Dan Gerber, and then he stopped it. It didn't make enough money, the too usual story.

Clark City Press is a raw point as we simply got too ambitious and self-indulgent, not looking at the bottom line. The reason we did as well as we did was due to independent bookstores with ultraliterate owners like Jeannette. I normally don't spend much time in bookstores as I feel a natural anxiety in them, like "what's it all about?" Have "I fragmented heart and mind to fall into the service of words," as Ungaretti said? I met Susan Sontag at Books & Co., but couldn't think of anything to say because of a youthful crush I had from her photos twenty-five years before. Luckily, I'm dark complected, and my blushes aren't noticeable.   —JIM HARRISON

By 1988, we were nearing our tenth year and flying high. Peter and I decided to go all out for the tenth anniversary. Steven Aronson suggested we publish a book and write our customers and ask for their memories and anecdotes. Some great anecdotes and memories were written up and came in the mail. Saul Steinberg wrote for it, and many others. I was touched by how many people responded to our request. And, we received no hate mail.

Peter and Annabelle Levitt edited the small, green book, which was printed by Stinehour Press in Vermont.

Annabelle and I worked on that book really hard. We sent out a form letter to everybody on the house charge list, and then we had a letter downstairs on the horseshoe counter, which requested anecdotes, memories, dreams, reflections. Then we got them and we edited them. Jeannette thought we would be flooded with all of these great epistles, and there were some really nice things, and, given what we had, we put together a really attractive book, for not a huge amount of money.   —PETER PHILBROOK

I wanted the staff to make a concerted effort for the whole year, to make the tenth year special all-year round.

Jeannette's Notes to Staff
10th Anniversary Year September 1988
Now 'til end of Dec. Most Fun—Busy Time

1. Demeanor—consider yourself on stage, customers audience.
2. Eating and drinking at register in general is discouraged.

3. Don't discuss personal problems. If you need to take a break, take one.
4. Don't criticize customers.
5. Answer phone: Books & Company.
6. Don't point—whenever possible, walk customer to the section. Put book in their hands.
7. You are at desk, so be alert—don't read catalogs. Can't do both.

The tenth anniversary was designed as a three-pronged celebration and required a lot of preparation. The bookstore paid for everything by saving $1,000 each month for a year. We planned a book, a party at the store, at which the book was a literary party favor, and also a reading on October 20, 1988. Three of the readers who had read in the first official reading would read again: John Hollander, Richard Howard, and James Merrill, and again, Harold Brodkey introduced and read.

The party was absolutely fabulous. Cynthia Ozick, Grace Paley, and the Watson family: my mother, Olive (my father was climbing the Matterhorn), my brother Tom III, my four sisters, Olive, Lucinda, Susan, and Helen; Fran Lebowitz, Roy Blount Jr., Hortense Calisher, Jeannette Haien, Steven Aronson, Brendan Gill, Paul Auster, John Yau, Jackie Weld, Joyce Ravid, Lionel Tiger, Philip Lopate, Ted Mooney, Mr. Kaplan, and his beloved wife, May, Martha Wilson, Albert Murray, all of the regulars, Hugh Nissenson, Ally Anderson Spivy, Tammy Grimes, Patrick McGrath, Bradford Morrow, among many, many guests, the staff. We took the books off the central island downstairs and off all the central tables. I hired a caterer, and we served lavish platters of food and a cake from Greenberg, decorated with a picture of the bookstore. There was music, music everywhere, and they were dancing in the street.

James Merrill showed up very late. The night was almost over, and suddenly he appeared. I knew he'd had a reading that same night and told him how happy I was that he'd been able to make it.

Many people knew James Merrill a lot better than I ever did. He was an extremely elegant, refined, delicate I think, personage, but without affectation, really belonging to a kind of world we don't find anymore. There was a demeanor of gladness, which certain people have that is neither egotistical nor self-effacing. It's sort of between those two states. I'm trying to think what it was like to have looked at this man's face. You see his amused interest, and it's something that artists of a certain caliber often have. It's not the look of, Do you know who I am, have you read what I've written; it's much more outgoing, and actually has attached to it almost a kind of naïveté, a kind of openness. He had that. —ANN LAUTERBACH

James Merrill was a sweetie. Always, always very polite. Soft-spoken, really nice to me. He didn't seem to buy a lot of books. He would come in often with J. D. McClatchy. —PETER PHILBROOK

Brendan Gill was shocked when I told him, "I enjoyed your two short stories: 'Truth and Consequences,' and 'The Fat Girl.'" He was shocked that I knew and remembered them. They're awfully good. When she had the tenth anniversary party, I told him. I knew the stories, probably he wouldn't want to remember, but I had to tell him I enjoyed them. He was so shocked.

—MAX KAPLAN

I started writing short stories for the *New Yorker*, so I started out as a fiction writer. But I couldn't make any money, and then slipped more and more, as people do with age, into writing factual pieces and criticism, and so it has gone. If Bill Maxwell and Shawn didn't think it was a good story, I never tried to sell it anywhere else. Surely they were right. When Shawn had to hand me back something, he would try, standing in the doorway—tiny little man—to think of something to say. I was, like, Don't say anything, go away, go away, because I'll start crying. I used to say, We're all six years old, we won't be able to bear it. It would be too much. But he knew that didn't mean that I disagreed with him in any way, or I didn't want to hear an explanation, because something obviously was the matter with it, but I had lost interest. I would try again, but not for a moment suppose that they were wrong and I was right. There are only two or three people I've met that I ever—you ever—felt like that about in my lifetime. That's why I stayed at the *New Yorker* for sixty years, because there was that kind of trust.   —BRENDAN GILL

Harold Brodkey's introducing the tenth anniversary reading signified his continued, strong presence at Books & Co. He'd often stop by and flirt with Peter and me, equally charming to both of us. One of our many employees, Sharone Einhorn, was a talented cartoonist, and though her cartoons were based primarily on Peter, in a series titled "Lifestyles of the Poor and Intellectual," she drew one based on Harold. It read: "Harold Brodkey was convinced that his depression sprang from the time of maternal deprivation." Harold had told me, when I was sitting next to him at dinner one night, that he became depressed every day at two o'clock, because that was the hour his mother had died. We became a kind of second home to him. He even had his hair cut at Books & Co.

In full swing, the bookstore was making a community around books. It's not only that a bookstore serves literature, it can also forge a community, one that hadn't existed before. It can actually engender it.

Books & Co. gives you that sense that you exist as a writer, because writers aren't necessarily recognized. They're not movie stars. You get your book published, and if you don't know any bookstores in New York City, and you don't know any of the people running them, you might not even know if your book is there. But with Books & Co., you could actually say to somebody, My book is out. Then have some kind of formal moment when they order the book and ask you to sign it.   —JOHN YAU

We were a profit-making business. This was before the impact of the Barnes & Noble superstores and before the stock market crash of 1987, which had a debilitating effect. I had the nagging worry, though—the lease. We had five more years on it.

We couldn't stock the bookstore fast enough between 1983 and 1986. People walked out with more than they could carry in those years. I had one woman, who was really awful, an irritating customer, and she got very indignant one day. She spent a hundred dollars whenever she came to the store and couldn't figure out why she didn't get better service. I felt like putting my hand on my hip and saying, Honey, I got a customer who spends hundreds once an hour in here. Come up with a better figure.

—SUSAN SCOTT

We'd done well enough to raise $20,000 for our tenth anniversary celebration. I'd also had two children within that time and entered my forties. But now my hip condition cried out for more attention— more surgery. The doctors hadn't wanted to replace the hips earlier, because once the hips are replaced, one's not supposed to gain weight. The more weight, the more quickly replacements wear out, so pregnancy is not a good idea. The theory was, don't undergo this major surgery until the pain was so great, you can't even walk. There came a time when Alex and I could hardly go to the theater together. We had to strategize—for one thing, the restaurant would have to be right across the street from the theater. One night, our theater seats were high up in the back row. For me, getting there was like climbing Mount Everest. When we went to Disney World with the children, I'd have to be in a wheelchair. The children loved pushing me in it, running all over, and just pushing Mommy around.

The pain became unbearable. It had been barely bearable, but I walked with a limp. People would often ask, What's wrong? I hated the fact that there was something wrong. In our family it was important to be perfect, to look good, to be fit. I hated limping. People asked out of concern, What have you done to yourself, Are you in pain? But it was hard to handle.

The surgeon did the first hip, and we hoped the other hip would be all right for a while. I'd had the choice of having both hips replaced at once, which is very strenuous and painful. I thought I'd go the route of one at a time and perhaps have a year or two between. But once one hip was replaced, I had to put all my weight on the other. Then I had to do both within about four months. During my convalescence, I was depressed. I couldn't read, which was the first time this had ever happened. I had no concentration. I was able to do needlepoint. I didn't have to think to do that, and it was a kind of therapy for my hands. I watched *I Love Lucy* every morning. Peter came over some afternoons. We both loved *I Love Lucy*, and we'd discuss the day's episode, then he'd tell me which episode would be on the next day. He had the entire rerun sequence memorized. I read the paper, waited for the mail, but incapacitated for six weeks, for two periods of six weeks, I became stir crazy. I was lucky to have three or four friends who visited every week. Susan Cheever and I became very close then. She came over every week.

Look what she had done for me, not that I am only nice when people do things for me, but Jeannette's given tremendous service to the literary community, more than anybody I know. She's been very generous to me and I think she's been very generous to a whole generation. Particularly of women writers, although she's also been generous to a lot of men.   —SUSAN CHEEVER

Writing is such a lonely thing. You can't help feeling isolated, and early on, before anyone knows that you exist, a little sign of encouragement can help a great deal. When you get older, you tend to remember those people who were there for you when you were young. The others don't really matter. They found you when you were already on your feet. But the ones who discovered you when you were still crawling, still struggling to get up off the ground—those are the ones you don't forget, the ones who make all the difference in a writer's life.

—PAUL AUSTER

I hated being sick and forced to stay home. All the time I was away from the bookstore, in touch but away, I tried to be philosophical. I thought, the first ten years of the store I had two children, the second ten years I'll have two hips replaced. I imagined I was moving into the next phase of my life, replacing body parts.

My biggest regret about Jeannette is that when she had her hips replaced, I sent her a postcard to the hospital saying, Hip, hip, hooray! She never got it. I don't know what happened, I was so pleased with it.   —ROY BLOUNT JR.

Peter was attentive and concerned. I was lucky, too, that when I had my children, Susan Scott and he were around. I was able to take time off. I relied completely on Peter—especially his unfailing memory. His mind was like a computer. People often teased me, Jeannette "IBM" Watson wasn't computerized. She couldn't work a computer. I've always appreciated the irony.

I have a good memory certain days. Some days I can't remember my own phone number. I could always remember the stock really well, how many copies we had. This is why people—now that computers came in—can't really understand how people could keep all this information in their head. It was always pretty easy. I knew every book we had in the store. I think it was almost a visual memory. I remembered what a book looked like, what the spine looked like, and all that. —PETER PHILBROOK

Barnes & Noble's a computer-driven point of view, but it does feel a certain obligation to represent certain kinds of books because of its vast size. It's a kind of mall experience. The experience they're trying to create is a kind of Disney-fication of the bookstore, a malling of the bookstore. In other words, you make this thing big. You have escalators; you can watch yourself and watch other people reading and hear the music. It doesn't bother you too much, and there's the smell of coffee coming from off in the distance, and it's cozy. Last time I went to the one at Union Square I was afraid of falling over people lying on the floor and doing work, which I found really interesting. Jammed with younger people—it's not an older audience there at all. It's obviously appealing to a generation that comes out of college, in high school, or going into college. —JOHN G. HANHARDT

Bookstores began using and relying on computers, but there were many flaws in the early system. Ted Wilentz said for the amount of money we were making, considering all their flaws then, computers wouldn't make that much difference to our business. Later, by the early 1990s, it didn't make sense to invest in computer-izing when business was so much worse. We've also always felt that we wanted to have very good staff; we wanted them to look on the shelves for the books, to know the inventory. There are negative aspects to relying on computers, and as the store becomes computer-driven, the staff might not need to remember the stock, to be able to talk about it. How does one sell books, really?

Computers seemed very complicated, and it struck me that—and I know from talking to other people, this is true to some extent—after a certain point your sense of the inventory gets driven by what the computer tells you. You start to look at things and say, Oh, well that hasn't sold since such and such, and that hasn't sold since such and such, that kind of thing. There's a way of doing inventories I think that are useful and probably for that they're very good. I always wanted staff to do inventories by hand, because I felt that was the way they'd learn stock. The ignorance—they were great kids—but people didn't know who Euripides was. I felt it was the way people learned what was in the store. They'd have to look at the book and have a tactile grasp of it, because my own way of remembering was so tactile, visual. Jeannette's father gave us a computer system, but it never worked properly. It was just another expense to have somebody program it properly. But if you have a situation where you have more staff turnover, which happened after I left, people can't be expected to have the historical reference that goes back fifteen years. But the computer replaces human memory.

—PETER PHILBROOK

Peter not only remembered the books he liked, he also remembered the books I liked. I'd say, What was the book about so-and-so's daughter who has an affair with a whale—he'd remember. He'd remember what color the book was, what it smelled like, everything. So, I'd always say, Why do I need a computer, when I have Peter? He knows every single book in the store. He also backed me up in a sweet way. If someone came in and asked me a question, and Peter saw a furrow in my brow, he knew I was struggling to answer it well. Then he'd ease up behind me, enter the conversation, and help me out. He was a terrific support, very generous. For the bookstore to look good, he felt, I should look good, too. Steven Varni, our last buyer, felt that, too.

One of the funny things I remember was when a book came out on Umberto Eco, on his *The Name of the Rose*. It was a small scholarly study. We'd ordered a couple of copies. One was buried in a pile, you couldn't really see the book—it was in a pile on the stairs. Eco came in, headed right up the stairs, because he always headed up the stairs to the philosophy books, and I watched. He turned, bent down, reached down, and pulled out this book about himself. How he knew it was there—it was an amazing thing. The ability of authors to find something, if it concerns them, was amazing.   —PETER PHILBROOK

The staff changed in a big way after both Susan and Andrew left. It was hard losing two of the three originals. It would be harder still when somewhat later Peter decided to leave—but it was change and adjust, or wither and die. We were constantly adjusting. Around 1986, Lisa Bernhard became the manager of the bookstore.

I was hired as part-time Christmas help. I came to Books & Co. from Scribner's on Fifth Avenue. Scribner's had decided that all the booksellers had to wear blue polyester smocks. Nothing subtle like the little "B's" worn at Bloomingdale's, to identify salespeople as different from the customers. There was something antithetical to me about putting on this suffocating garment, so I quit and found Books & Co. and worked there until 1990. Selling books is about asking somebody questions, like what you do when you're trying to elicit a story. You're finding out what their story is, what their interests are, what excites them in books and in life. Because that's really what books are about. Usually I would say, "What's the last thing that you read that you really loved? Are you interested in books that have a very clear sort of story line, or are you interested in a more dreamy kind of book? How do you feel? What do you feel like reading?" Sometimes you'd get an "I don't know. I don't know what I feel like reading." A lot of times I don't know what I feel like reading, either, so I can understand. But I was a kid in a candy shop. I'd open a book and go, This sounds wonderful. Then I'd take it home. Jeannette always encouraged you to read. She felt you can't sell what you don't know, and I think that's true.

—LISA BERNHARD

John Burnham Schwartz started to work for us, too. His mother, Paula, was married to William Merwin, and he was the god-son of Anne Arensberg. The family were great friends of Dennis Hopper's and James Merrill's. We had hired this young kid, yet suddenly he knew more people in the bookstore than I did. I'd walk downstairs, and people would be greeting him. He was writing his first novel, *Bicycle Days*. In 1989, when it was published, John read from it at the store. I brought my son Andrew's bicycle in for the window. We had a party at the bookstore, too. Some time later David Halberstam came in and told me he had thought of a new title for John Burnham Schwartz—that well-connected bookseller.

Books & Co. tried to support young writers in a variety of ways. John Burnham Schwartz and I wrote a letter to the *New York Times Book Review* after Ethan Canin's first book, *Emperor of the Air*, was reviewed harshly by David Leavitt. Leavitt had worked at Books & Co. for a short time. John and I thought *Emperor of the Air* was a wonderful story collection. Our letter was never published. I had not yet met Ethan, but sometime later I did. He came into the store to sign his book. He was dark-haired and good-looking, and he was very appreciative of what we'd done for his book. Then later he read at the store from his next book, *Blue River*, and I had a dinner for him, too, as a way to make up for that first bad review. Ethan was handsome, young, and single, and many women showed up for his reading. At readings, often it was either all men or all women. His was definitely on the all-women side of the equation.

Indifference is probably the worst kind of response. Nice job, people say, and then they pat you on the back and forget all about it. Controversy is probably better, even

158

though it can be hard. At least it's a sign that people are wrestling with the work, that you've touched a nerve. No one likes to be attacked, but if you believe in what you're doing, you just have to shrug it off. The same thing with praise. You have to ignore that, too. How many times have we seen writers go to hell because they started believing their own good reviews? Block it all out is what I say. Block it out and stick to your guns.   —PAUL AUSTER

Terry McMillan worked very hard at the beginning of her career, doing her own publicity. I was one of many bookstore owners who received sample chapters from her first novel, *Mama*, and a letter from her asking for a reading.

Jeannette gave McMillan a reading and a momentum gathered after that. It was certainly a pivotal time in Terry McMillan's career, and it probably was not the reading itself that did the trick, but I think if nothing else, Jeannette was certainly one of the early contributors.

                                        —SUSAN SCOTT

I worked with Terry McMillan on all three of the books we've done here. She had gotten very upset because the publisher of her first novel, Houghton Mifflin, said they weren't going to put her on tour, so Terry sat down and gathered all these lists of bookstores and personally wrote to hundreds of bookstores saying that she was available to come and give a reading. I think that's how she ended up at Books & Co.   —PAUL SLOVAK

In general, my customer Bud Pomeranz and I were concerned about the general state of fiction criticism, its lack of complexity.

I once worked as a reporter for two Newhouse newspapers, the *Long Island Daily Press*, which was put out of business by *Newsday*, and the *New York Star Ledger*, also gone. My beat was New York City, and I did cultural reporting. I covered Khrushchev's famous shoe thumping at the U.N. for the *Long Island Daily Press*. Part of my interest in literature is in what literature does—it alters the way that you see things, it changes you. It is a self-examination as well as information. There's a lot of information in literature. Interestingly there are a number of great fiction writers and poets, who have had important positions in foreign affairs, Carlos Fuentes, Mexico's ambassador to France; Octavio Paz, Mexico's ambassador to India; Lawrence Durrell was in the British Foreign Service; Washington Irving was the American ambassador to Spain; Ben Franklin, France. A serious problem, as far as I'm concerned, is that in the *New York Times Book Review* and the *New York Review of Books*, the number of works of fiction reviewed is very small compared with nonfiction. I wrote about this to Charles McGrath, the editor of the *New York Times Book Review*. He replied that he appreciated my concerns, but he said there were problems with the dearth of American writing—part may be the publishers' fault, part may be the writers' fault. He took issue with my "assumption that there was a rich harvest of literature available right now." He thought American fiction was in a rut, but if I followed what he was doing, I'd see they were giving American fiction its due. What bothered Jeannette and me most was his focus on American fiction. He was ignoring all sorts of books.   —BUD POMERANZ

Some of the editors I worked with over the years were integral to the store. Ilene Smith worked at Summit Books, which no longer exists, and had been John Burnham Schwartz's and Howard Norman's editor. Howard sent me his book *Northern Lights*, which I loved. Atheneum was another strong imprint, but by now it was also gone. By the late eighties, that was the fate of many imprints. They disappeared.

The fewer owners there are, the less product there is. If an owner owns ten lines of books, and they all have five literary titles per season, and only 30 percent of those titles are working, it's likely that the owner is either going to cut some of the lines entirely, or say, Look, you just do three books a season instead of the five you're doing. It's denied up and down by the heads of conglomerates, but think about the number of imprints that aren't here anymore. Poseidon, Summit, Linden—three at Simon & Schuster—Turtle Bay at Random. Most publishing houses can't survive strictly on literary publishing—that's why there's been a proliferation of nonprofit presses beginning in the 1970s. There just wasn't enough money to be made in literature, poetry, even belles lettres. Some of the corporations have existed for a hundred years, like Doubleday which turned a hundred in 1997, or fifty years in the case of Farrar. But for the conglomerates, publishing is a part of an entire approach to entertainment. There's a synergy in certain companies. HarperCollins is owned by Murdoch—Murdoch owns the Fox network—the Simpsons are on Fox, the product in the bookstores comes through HarperCollins. The same is happening at Viacom. MTV, owned by Viacom, has its own imprint at Simon & Schuster. Nickelodeon, owned by Viacom, is doing its books through Simon & Schuster. Now again, if you're a media conglomerate, you need to cross-collateratize your product across all product lines, you need to look for syndication, you need to look for books, you need to look for mugs, the mugs are probably licensed.   —IRA SILVERBERG

Sometimes customers had very strange requests. One day, there were two. A man walked in with a package from the Metropolitan Museum of Art. "Do you gift wrap?" he asked. "Yes, I do," I said. "Well, will you wrap this?" It was highly unusual to be asked to wrap a book from another shop. But I did it, and he tipped me one dollar.

Then a woman walked in asking me to let her xerox an Andy Warhol book. I had to say no. On another day, Michael Thomas asked for William Boyd's bound galley, and Susanna Moore for pornography. She told me she was writing love scenes and wanted to see how other writers had handled it in modern fiction. Peter suggested Bataille's *The Story of the Eye.*

> Writing fiction is the creation of character—characters, really. Voices. I lend parts of myself to all the principal characters in my novels. Maybe I mean, I identify with all the voices.   —SUSAN SONTAG

Editors worked with me in different ways. Some sent letters extolling a first novelist, encouraging me to look hard at a new book. The astute ones were aware I wanted the thrill of discovery. Paul Slovak, the director of publicity at Viking, also worked as an editor.

> Whenever I walk into Books & Co., the first thing I do is cruise around the front of the store and look at all the books that are face out on the tables. Most books are displayed spine out, and if you can get a store to put the books face out, it can make a difference. It can catch somebody's eye. Then I go to that long table farther back where they have the new releases—they have a very tasteful way of selecting books. It's not like Barnes & Noble where the publisher actually has to pay money to get their books displayed in the front of the store for two weeks. In that way every independent bookstore is different—there is a different philosophy, a different aesthetic operating in terms of the people who are stocking the shelves, in terms of what they're going to display. They become very personal.
>   —PAUL SLOVAK

Sam Lawrence, another editor in Books & Co.'s life, was an enormous presence in American writing and publishing. He always kept in touch with us. When he died in 1994, we held a series of readings by his authors. Practically all of Sam's authors had books coming out that spring from which they read in a powerful tribute to him.

Shortly after Mary McCarthy died, her brother, actor Kevin McCarthy, came in and wanted to know why we didn't have more Mary McCarthy on our shelves. I told him I was sorry, but since she died, there had been a huge demand. We had sold out and so had the distributors.

Another spectacular reading was by Robertson Davies, who read from *The Lyre of Orpheus*. It was a huge success, packed. Everybody wanted me to save them seats, but that was impossible. Davies had the most wonderful face, like a combination of God and Santa Clause. Mrs. Davies told me they had met in the theater, where she used to direct his plays. He was one of the best readers we ever had.

Robertson Davies had a glorious reading. He was in all his splendor—he looked like God, he sounded like God, he was God. I noticed in the back of the room all these people with piles of books, and they were reverently coming up to Robertson Davies to ask him to sign them. I said, "Jeannette, look, isn't that wonderful, all these lovers of Robertson Davies's writing." She looked at me and said, "Those aren't people who love Robertson Davies's writing, those are book dealers, and they're getting copies signed so they can sell them for more money." I said, "Oh no, oh Jeannette, another myth shattered. I thought lovely students have been collecting these books for years and finally their writer has appeared." "No no," she said, "I used to think that, too."

—ALEXANDRA ANDERSON-SPIVY

Nineteen eighty-nine was the year of Salman Rushdie, *The Satanic Verses*, and the *fatwa*. Rushdie's plight electrified the industry. All of us became involved whether we wanted to be or not. Peter was heroic. The minute the *fatwa* was declared, Peter made a window for

163

The Satanic Verses, which was up for about two weeks. Customers would say, You're courageous, or you're foolish. You're brave, or you're crazy to put the book there. Haven't you heard about the bookstore that was bombed? It's sobering and instructive now to remember how dangerous it was, that people were killed over the book. The store also held a writers' speak-out for Rushdie. Susan Sontag was very much involved in his defense. She told me she had to change her phone number because of bomb threats. But she felt, basically, that the bomb threats were empty threats. A B. Dalton store had closed its doors, though, because it received one. No one could afford to take the chance it wasn't real.

James Merrill came in to buy "that controversial book" in a plain brown wrapper. The controversy inspired Andre Gregory, who came in impersonating an Arab. I thought for a long time about how I might repay his little practical joke.

Everyone in the business was forced to examine their beliefs and how far one was willing to go to defend the freedom of speech. Editors' homes were being bombed. We were receiving telephone threats: Why are you carrying this book? Then the person would hang up. I hadn't appreciated the full significance initially. Did I want to be killed over a book? But Peter understood its importance immediately. I, too, soon understood how important the issue was, and I was glad we responded as we did, though I didn't immediately have the courage of Dalva.

> Jeannette received death threats, not only for herself, but for her children, a few very ugly phone calls. I happened to call her one day, and she said, "Janie, I don't know what to do. I'm in a real bind. I can take my life and do what I want to with it. But now they're threatening my children, and I don't know whether I should take the book out of the window. I really don't know what to do." I told her I couldn't answer that for her. Later I went by, and the book was still in the window. We were in her office. I said, "You didn't take the book out of the window." She said, "No,

because I realize that principles are something I believe people have to have. I feel it's important for my children to grow up in a world where people fight for what they believe in. I feel that this is an issue that is bigger than all of us. I had to keep it in." —JANE STANTON HITCHCOCK

During that period, I was asked to speak about the window at my son Andrew's school and about our decision to sell and prominently display *The Satanic Verses.* The ninth-grade class was very interested. One of the kids asked, "Did you ask your employees how they felt?" I hadn't. I should have made it optional for my employees to come to work.

I don't think initially we had that many copies of the book, because it wasn't selling. But we filled the window with them. I remember Jeannette at first wanted to take it out, then we talked her out of it. She was nervous, but then she felt good. We sold a ton of the books, tons. It hadn't been selling, then BOOM, we sold out, and then we couldn't get them. —PETER PHILBROOK

We sold one hundred copies a day. Arthur Penn warned me about the window and told me that Pennewick Publishers was confused with Penguin, and had been threatened with bombing. I had another long moment of panic.

Several bookstores have put statements in their window, either supporting the book and author or noting that the book is unavailable. Books & Co. on Madison Avenue and 74th Street posted a sign outside the door reading: "Rushdie's *Satanic Verses* is sold out." The store sold its stock of 250 copies by noon last Thursday, although it kept one copy. "So if anybody wants to read it, they can come in and read it," said Peter Philbrook, the manager. —*The New York Times*, February 1989

After Rushdie decided to leave his seclusion occasionally to test the *fatwa*, one day he walked into the store. "Do you mind if we take your picture?" I asked. No, he didn't. The customers were tremendously excited and lined up to get their books signed. Then he disappeared just as quickly, in and out like a flash.

> Somebody at Random House would always set me, Jeannette, and Steven up with the good stuff. We got into the Salman Rushdie reading at the public library. They'd always send us the limited edition signed galley, which I have of Rushdie. I don't know if it was before or after his reading at the library, but he was still in New York, and he walked in one day. I sort of smiled to him, and he was looking at some stuff. Then other people started to notice him, so he had to end up signing books and didn't really get to see the store. We sold our entire Rushdie stock really quickly. —FRANCIS CASH

My father was proud of the bookstore, but he didn't entirely understand its philosophy. He wondered why we didn't carry more best-sellers. One day David Halberstam, a longtime customer, asked for Daddy's number. He was doing a book on the fifties and wanted to interview him. My father expressed his perplexity about the bookstore to Halberstam. He called me afterward and said, I didn't really understand your bookstore philosophy, but after talking to David Halberstam, now I think I do. That's nice, I thought. I wished it had come from me. Still, he finally got it.

An exceptionally significant night for me was my father's signing his memoir, *Father, Son, and Co.: My Life at IBM and Beyond* on May 23, 1990. I wanted the event to be perfect, from beginning to end. It was very complicated to get everything right. I had never worked so hard just to put out an invitation.

Daddy had said, "I think I'd like to be downstairs next to the cash register." I suggested he'd be more comfortable seated at a desk on the second floor. He had been concerned that people would leave without paying for their books. Finally I persuaded him he should sign upstairs at a table. But he felt the best place was next to the cash register, reminding me again of what a terrific salesman he'd been.

The day of the signing the telephone rang every three minutes, with inquiries about it. I was petrified. What if hundreds showed up? The night was completely nerve-racking. Daddy and I had agreed he was going to sign only one copy per person. We knew hundreds of people would attend; people who had worked for IBM would be coming from all over. Russell, the man who had run the elevator, showed up. Russell used to take me in the elevator when I was a little girl, and it was very touching to see him again. People stood in line for a long time, carrying five and ten copies. I couldn't move the line along fast enough, but eventually, everyone had their books signed.

Just as I did some years back, Daddy lectured at the Colony Club, but this time I introduced him and talked about my selling of *Father, Son, and Co.*

I took pictures, and our kids were there. I think he read about the early part of his life, where he was a really rotten kid, getting into trouble. He read the story about putting skunk juice in the heating system of the day school out in Jersey, where he was a third grader. This juice went all over the school, and they had to close the school. Our then nine- or eight-year-old, Andrew, was there, hearing this, and he just got inspired. God knows what he did; he did something naughty at school within about a week. Her father revealed much more in his book than he ever thought he did. It was weird.   —ALEXANDER SANGER

In his book Daddy stated his father's and his three principles for managing a business: "Give full consideration to the individual employee; spend a lot of time making customers happy; go the last mile to do a thing right." His influence had been great, in my life and in this country's, and I was happy to be able to sell his book in my store. Once he brought Jimmy Carter into the store to visit. We rushed around hiding or removing the pornography, not wanting to cause any lust in President Carter's heart.

It must have been by osmosis or by example that I had absorbed my father's and grandfather's three business principles and made them my own. I often had had the sensation walking past the Loeb Classics near the green couch—passing by, just being in proximity to these wonderful books—that I might absorb their teachings. I loved walking past them, feeling knowledge was being transmitted ineffably, and that I was a better person because I walked past them. Tibetans walk past their religious texts and feel knowledge comes to them, somehow, and even before I became interested in Tibet and Buddhist teachings, I felt that way. Be considerate to each employee and make customers happy, do whatever I could to make it work.

> Books are going out, and writers are going the way of all flesh, and soon it's all going to be visual and everything is going to be interactive. Jeannette is like a monk guarding the sacred texts. I think she's come to symbolize a kind of safety that we all once knew.
>
> —JANE STANTON HITCHCOCK

There was a dramatic shift between the tenth and fifteenth years. Peter made a momentous decision—to leave us and take a job in rare books. We'd been together such a long time, the mom-and-pop, in a way, or mom-and-son, of Books & Co. It was extremely hard losing him.

> I met Danielle at Books & Co. Our wedding was the 21st of December 1989. I think it was also the same day as Jeannette's wedding anniversary. When I told Jeannette I was getting married, she wanted to have the ceremony in the store. We had no specific plans about getting married in any format or anybody's family being involved. We were married upstairs and went back to work. It was Christmas season, so back down to the cash register.
>
> —PETER PHILBROOK

Leaving Books & Co. was in many ways the best thing for him. He could make a new start. Business had, by the thirteenth year, worsened, and, in a way, Peter had seen the writing on the wall.

The book business never was a high-profit business on the producing side, either. It was a small business. Early on, it was usually gentlemen publishers who wanted to do something worthwhile, and all that has changed. Farrar, Straus was sold two years ago to Holtzbrink, so we're not independent anymore, but the way we publish has not been changed by our new owners. But I think a lot of publishers were forced to try to come up with the same kind of profit margins that other businesses do. Independent bookstores are best equipped to sell our kind of books, because the staff knows the customers and the stock, and they can put the two together in various ways, which the big stores can't. We've lost something, because the independents are in such a weak position, are such a small part of the market now. But I think the independent bookstores will make a resurgence eventually. I don't think the superstores are going to quite do it for a whole segment of the readership, but a lot of people are going to be hurt in the meantime. —JONATHAN GALASSI

There was always some flux in the staff—a classic problem, maintaining staff—but it became more unpredictable. We had too many temporary employees. Still, I kept my optimism and sense of humor. Our fifteenth birthday was approaching, and so was our lease renewal. But party lovers, we celebrated our fifteenth with verve and flair, with a great party and a Greenberg cake. All our friends and regulars were there.

There was a sense that, not quite that I belonged there, but that I was attached to it in this fundamental way, to the space of it. I could wander around and pick up books, and the whole sense was of a certain kind of intimacy that seems to me one of the most valuable things one can have in a public space. You could be there literally hours— without all the window dressing of cups of coffee and all of the rest of it that people are thinking have to be part of the experience of finding books. —ANN LAUTERBACH

Our sales were being affected by Barnes & Noble's superstores. Before, we could sell many more copies of a novel, and after the advent of the superstore, we'd sell maybe a quarter of that number. Even my loyal clients would purchase the new Seamus Heaney at a discount rather than buying it at Books & Co. But I can get this at a discount, they'd say, and that felt terrible. There were many more books being published, too, but they were novelty or how-to books— how to write a how-to, package deals.

There are many more books being published in many more fields than just literary fiction and intellectual nonfiction. Twenty years ago there was no need for as many computer books; five years ago there weren't as many books on the World Wide Web or HTML or Java. As we grow as a culture, the categories of publishing grow. We have more books because we have more things to learn. Category books have nothing to do with short stories, poetry, fiction, belles lettres. The marketplace is a very peculiar marketplace. I think it was Nan Talese who said there are four thousand people in America who genuinely care about literature. That's probably the number most of us shoot for on an initial print run, at least to make a book stick. We want to get at least four thousand copies into the hands of people. Everything on top of that you have to work for.
—IRA SILVERBERG

These chains have changed the publishing business. They are now the engine instead of publishing being the engine.

They drive the publishing business, which means the publishing business has adapted to them. I went on a book tour about a year and a half ago when I published my children's book. It was my first encounter on a book tour with the chains. I was in Chicago, and there's a gigantic Barnes & Noble the size of the Library of Congress, and across the street a Borders was going up. Now this is just pure crazy boy stuff. Are there enough people in Chicago to support these two bookstores? No. This is territorial stuff, like we're going to put this store up to kill you, to move you out. If you look at the pattern of where they open up, it is not inadvertent that the little stores go out of business. It's the point. This is Agent Orange, the point being to put the other out of business. I wish I lived in a country where there were that many customers for books, but we know there aren't. I'm not saying they're not profitable. They are, though they can't all be profitable. They're places to hang out, like a kind of singles bar. They sell coffee. This will pass, I think, but by then they will have put smaller bookstores—some of which were really institutions—out of business.   —FRAN LEBOWITZ

Our European, Mexican, Australian, and Japanese customers still spent a lot of money, but I began to wonder if Americans were reading, especially the young. Sometimes I speculated that my readers were aging and dying off, and there weren't enough younger ones interested to take their place.

We don't get very many young people. I think it has so much to do with location. If you're going to the Whitney, you'll come in, but I don't think there's that much you can do about it. Also if the store stayed open and was on the World Wide Web, that would help. Because some people know what Books & Co. is; it definitely has an identity.

—PENELOPE BLOODWORTH

I don't think books are as vital to the culture as they were in the sixties. It's a generational issue. Younger generations are coming along and books aren't as significant in terms of what's being communicated. Now you don't have novels that seem to appeal to everybody, that everybody feels compelled to read. That era is over, I think. Video, film are much more vital to people. What books represent is the life of the mind, and I'm not saying that's gone, but it's finding different forms. I think that the aspect of technology that has diminished the book is also a phase. Books are the perfect technology; they're portable. An old argument. I don't really have any doubt that there will be books. Young bright people will always be interested in writing books because that's how you express what's on your mind. —BOB CONTANT

There was a customer, Agnes Gund, I thought she was great. She's well known in the art world and did something terrific. She'd often give parties and would come in before one, and say, "I'd like a book for everyone. I'd like you to pick a paperback I can put on every plate. This is how many people there will be." I might run over the titles with her, after I had chosen them, but it sometimes fell to me to choose. She would also give art books as Christmas gifts. It was wonderful to see somebody so keen, who felt it was such a worthy thing and do it, and do it. The party favors were especially great because they're a surprise. A book could open somebody's life in a completely different way. —LISA BERNHARD

People were finding information in different ways. Books were viewed as commodities, product, as content-delivery systems. Publishers allocated a disproportionate amount of their budgets to the few and focused on their ten best-selling authors. Most authors received little attention from their publisher.

You have to convince people through good reviews, author tours, advertising, word of mouth, buzz, but we don't have that many people who are going into bookstores looking for entertainment, looking for a new experience with literature in quite the way we have people looking at TV or at the screen, so we need to create demand in bookstores. The way you do that is to respond to things that are happening in the culture: a book on the Internet, on cybersex, on rap music, independent film. Nowadays you're going to find audiobooks—something you hardly saw ten years ago—literary T-shirts, literary mugs, blank books, greeting cards, leather bookmarks. The bookstore has become more than just a place to buy a book to read, it's become a place to buy gifts. If you go into a lot of children's sections, you'll find stuffed animals, Beatrix Potter pottery, dishes. There is not enough money in books to allow the retailer to survive. Thus the proliferation of the superstore, publicly held companies which can afford to go into very large spaces at very high-ticket rent with a diversity of product that a small store can't have.   —IRA SILVERBERG

It's very hard, and I always feel bad. I say to writers, "I know your blood, sweat, and tears went into this book, and now what I'm going to tell you is, that much energy has to go into promotion. It doesn't seem fair, because your talent is writing, other people's talent is promotion, but wake up and smell the coffee. This is America. If you don't understand how stuff works here, it has nothing to do with the value of the book, the worth of you, or your talent. Try and understand that. Nothing." I've gotten so frank, because I've done it for so many years. I just come right out and tell them. "If you don't go out and do it . . ." "But," they say, "that's your job." No, it's not. My job is keeping the store alive so I can offer this place for you.

                                        —MARGIE GHIZ

I'm of the generation, or the persuasion, who wanted to read and to own books. In New York, along with books getting more expensive, rents rose higher and higher. People began living in smaller spaces or sharing space—there was less room to keep books even if you wanted them. Yet, paradoxically, and unfortunately, public libraries' hours shrank when the city's budget was cut.

> It's a disaster. There are no libraries. In fact the bookstore is the only place for children, and anybody can get a comfortable place to look at books and to think about admiring them. I don't know any children who go to public libraries and live there as I did. I used to go with my father, in Denver. That's where I had my greatest library experience. In places like Denver or Dallas, there is no downtown, just an isolated hulk of a big library. That's where you would go from doing your simple reading and on into a research mode. What would be really interesting to do is one of those studies where you go through every book and look for a reference to libraries. Like Jamaica Kincaid's *Annie John*, where so much of that story is about stealing books from her school library and taking them home, reading and devouring them. The beginning of her self-education started in the library. If you looked at older memoirs you'd see a lot of stories about libraries, and I wonder where writers are going to be twenty years from now. I think they're going to remember bookstores more than libraries.　　　　　　　　　　　—MAY CASTLEBERRY

Even I became less optimistic. The conditions were tentative and tense. One day the Whitney was doing some maintenance work. Workers cut a tree down in their backyard, and the tree crashed through our back window. One of the staff, Brendan Larson, and I were in the store by ourselves. No one was in the back room, luckily, because someone could have been killed. All the glass shattered, it was terrifying. I didn't think it was symbolic, but the conditions were threatening.

> The good old days weren't so great, either. Let's go back thirty, forty years. It's not that there was a huge literary audience; the literary audience is bigger today than it was forty years ago. There's just so much else competing with it. When I was a kid, aspiring to literature was more the main thing. Now there are films, television, and other more passive media that people are much more attracted to, and easier to give yourself over to. In some ways, things are better for writers. I think they make more money than they did— they have more readers—but they generally have a more marginal position in the culture.   —JONATHAN GALASSI

> People who love books, who read and own them, have always been in the minority. True, for most of the nineteenth century great novelists, Dickens, Balzac, and so on, as well as lots of terrible novelists, were mass entertainment—like television. Before then there wasn't a large audience for good books, any more than there is now, in our own era of near universal literacy. The audience for literature is small, as for the most part it has always been. But it's still there. It's absolutely still there. —SUSAN SONTAG

Contemporary life seemed almost to oppose sitting down and reading a thoughtful novel. Books were slow, while computer games, TV, MTV, everything else was fast. Movies were edited differently, faster, than they were years ago. Where was the place—the slow track—for Books & Co. and others like us? We'd begun idealistically, as had most other independents.

Lawrence Ferlinghetti had the idea with Peter Martin, in 1953, to make City Lights an exclusively paperback bookshop. At that time there were a lot of independent booksellers in San Francisco, but bookstores were so different then; most were what we'd call today "carriage trade" stores. All the people working there were very tweedy, and scruffy writers coming in would feel unwelcome. And they carried only hardbacks. Lawrence saw the need. Paperbacks in those days were considered beneath most bookstores. Ian Ballantine and Alan Lane had the Penguins going; Jason Epstein was starting to get Anchor going. Many good books were becoming available in paperback. Alan started Penguin in England, and then Alan and Ian became partners for what became Penguin USA. Ian formed Bantam Books and then went on to form Ballantine Books. He was someone I consider an incredibly important person in the history of the industry. Peter's and Lawrence's initial investment was $500 each. North Beach in those days was a writers' and artists' community, a working-class community—they opened the doors, and it was an immediate success. Lawrence's first few years, all they had was a cigar box. No cash register. We're still in the same location, but now have the whole building, though we're still small—only about 2,100 square feet of retail space. I do the buying, and Richard Berman is the manager. We've worked together for almost a quarter century. He and I have been forced to become decent businesspeople, if not good ones. We've stayed as much as possible to Lawrence and Peter's intention: to show the best of contemporary literature and publishing, and with us, that's all the work which has a strong left-wing bent. We look at independent presses, university presses, what's good that comes out of the big New York houses, but we have the privilege of not being driven by whatever megabook is coming out of the corner of publishing in New York. Basically, we're here to serve the backlist of good

writing. People know if it's at City Lights, it's here because we as a crew feel that it's an important book.

—PAUL YAMIZAKI

No book was discounted when I started. If books were important to people, they bought them and didn't complain about the
price. Now, everyone wanted a discount. It was not coincidental that
books cost more, too. Discounts became a way of life.

If you're only in the new book business, and Borders opens
up across the street, what are you going to do? You can either discount more than they do, but if you're only making
5 percent, it's not hard to imagine that discounting's not
very attractive. You can go into specialization or believe
that somehow customer service is going to carry the day.
Powell's Bookstore had the strength of the used-book
world; we can keep focusing on used and out of print, and
that's something that Borders and Barnes & Noble don't
have, and that gives us the strength. When people ask what
are the keys to the success of the company, why is it unlike
all other bookstores, the answers I think are twofold, at
least. At heart, it was letting the customers decide how big
a store they wanted, and the other was mixing the new and
used together. I would say the third was, we have kind of a
motto, "Any book for anybody." We were not prejudiced
against any class of books   we don't sell pornography
but we were not prejudiced against pop fiction, romances,
history. We wanted to treat all customers, all readers, as serious people.   —MICHAEL POWELL

I believe that prices have to be protected. Price controls
are the only thing that can save independent bookstores.
No discounts. No underselling to drive the little guy out of
business. One standard, fixed price for every book—period.

Some other countries have done this, and it works. We've done it with milk. Why can't we do it with books?

—PAUL AUSTER

The way it works is that they discount off the *New York Times* best-seller list. They discount most books at Barnes & Noble's, I think, but they give a bigger discount off the best-sellers. So what does this mean? Take a look at the best-seller list. What this means is that there will be huge print orders. The publishers know the books that are likely to make the list. They're not always right, obviously; if they were, they'd all be rich. They start producing for that. The best-sellers are the ones that bring the majority of the people into the store. An independent bookstore can't afford to discount. And there's no backlist at the chains. You get money off books that came out two seconds ago. The independent bookstore performs other functions which add advantages to the city that you can't see by how many people walk into the store, how much sales tax is being rung up on the machine.

—FRAN LEBOWITZ

In tandem with tough times, good times were with us, too, the brightness and the bright lights always. A belief in the bookstore, and in the necessity of independent bookstores generally, was often restorative to me.

When we got into financial trouble, it was the publisher and entrepreneur Robert Rodale who came to our aid, out of the blue. The *Wall Street Journal* had written an article on us—it's the textbook case of a small business that expands without taking into consideration the cost of expansion. Rodale read it and called us. He asked, What could he do to help St. Marks Bookshop. It was the classic angel, a theatrical angel, story. There were many factors, which were personal for him. His father had come from the Lower East Side and founded a theater there. Rodale wanted to make a contribution in the family name, to the Lower East Side, where we're located.

—BOB CONTANT/TERRY MCCOY

Bookstore life was often lighthearted, full of humor and amusing banter. When Mark Strand read from *The Continuous Life*, I threw a small dinner for him beforehand in the store. I don't know how we started talking about sex, but in the middle of dinner, he asked, "How many times a day do you think about sex?" I said, "All the time. I think about it all the time." I also exaggerate, because obviously I was able to think about the bookstore. When Madonna's book, *Sex*, was published, Peter did a huge window. He hung black fabric over it, so that you had to peek in to see the silver book. *Sex* sold very well for a while. Everyone thinks about it.

I suggested to Jeannette, "Let's give a Valentine's Day party for the Academy of American Poets. Let's get people to come in and read love poems. . . . And nobody has to pay anything. People just come and listen to love poetry. You and I will buy the food." We listened to wonderful poets reading their poetry, and we bought little heart-shaped candies, and all sorts of good Valentine's Day food.

—BARBARA LAZEAR ASCHER

It was very typical of her to want to do these light thematic readings. I read a children's story that I'd written called "Sybilla and the Valentine Girls," which I never published and which no one had ever seen. What was so wonderful, again, was that there was this thing I could do that was completely unlike my serious poetry. It was a different kind of work I could expose there, and I think that was part of the pleasure of the place, that you felt comfortable enough to dare to do something that you might not elsewhere—you know, when you are trying to prove you are a real poet.   —ANN LAUTERBACH

Every Valentine's Day we did a romantic, sexy window. I kept a bed at the bookstore—doesn't every bookseller?—and each year I brought in pink satin sheets and wicked underwear Alex gave me as presents, which I never wore. A beautiful purple garter belt with black lace on it, red satin underpants. I'd make up the bed with the pink satin sheets, throw the red satin underpants and purple garter belt onto it, wantonly strew books like *Jane Eyre* or *Pride and Prejudice* around it, anything I found romantic.

The sex window. One year we got a bed for Valentine's Day, and we put a cognac bottle in, falling over, and probably pills, too. Jeannette wanted to do it every year, so every year we'd drag out the bed. And every year, she'd worry that we didn't have enough books, and I'd forget about it until the day before.   —PETER PHILBROOK

We included erotic books, and sometimes I'd select strange titles like *The Bordello Cookbook* or Bataille's *Story of the Eye*, a rather perverse book. One day, a poetic-looking man came to the bookstore, studied the window, walked in just a bit, and then reached into the window, picked up a pair of my underpants by the crotch, put them to his nose, and breathed in deeply. One of the amusing interludes brought on by our windows. People are so strange and interesting.

Watching for shoplifters was one of my favorite things. The way the shop was constructed, if there were people standing around the front of the horseshoe, you couldn't see when people were browsing in the art books, because your view was obscured. People would take advantage of this quite frequently, especially when we had the art books on the lower shelves, just on the front along the wall. I remember once, it was not that crowded, but there were people standing around, and some guy came in and headed very subtly toward that wall. He was a skinny little guy wearing a coat. Then I realized that I hadn't seen him for a while, and I hadn't seen him walk out, either. So I left the horseshoe and went round, and there he was, on his knees, stuffing books down his pants. He was wearing great big pants, and he was stuffing books down his pants. I said, "I think perhaps you have something that you'd like to give back to us." He started taking these books out of his pants. Of course, you want to drop the books and boil them in water before you touch them, but there was just so much you could do. The law didn't permit you to prevent somebody from leaving the store. Once they're outside you could get your hands on them, but at that point you're dealing with a crazy, maybe, somebody with a knife, so you just try to solve the situation as quietly as possible in the shop. But this was unbelievable, he was on his knees, and he was shoving books down the front of his pants, which were obviously extra large, to accommodate his profession. Big art books.

—LISA BERNHARD

There's the petty kind of shoplifting, someone stealing a paperback that you can't worry about. But in the mid-eighties, it had gotten really bad with people who made a living out of stealing art books. So you'd have constant pep talks with the staff about observing, watching what was going on. They would grab a bunch, put them under their coats, and run out the door. It was a tremendous problem. I'm sure the store lost a lot of stock that way. You get kids for staff who are nice kids, not cops, and they don't want to deal with shoplifting, so it's not that anyone ever looked away, but I think it was very hard to get people to zero in on it. Because you then have to take the next step, which is to confront the person or go outside and confront. I chased people to the park quite a number of times. They would usually just hand the books to me and laugh. —PETER PHILBROOK

One evening Dutch writer Cees Nooteboom read with Paul Auster, who introduced him. Lisa Bernhard admired Nooteboom's writing and was the force behind setting it up. Cees was a delight, witty and amusing. It was a great reading, with a good audience that included novelist Patrick McGrath. Cees inscribed my copy of his book, "I enjoyed being in your place." Most ambiguous, I thought.

Authors reading always seemed to me a very difficult thing to do. I'm somebody who doesn't like to get up in front of people and speak. Also it seemed to me difficult from the viewpoint of, here you are, a book is something to be read. I can't get past that idea. It's a relationship, an intimate relationship, and then here's somebody who's come in, the author, and they're going to read it in a voice that isn't yours. There's always a kind of shock. You're so used to your own voice reading those words, your own intonations, and there's somebody else who's doing it, and they're the authority, because they wrote it.

—LISA BERNHARD

When you imagine that the world of books is a kind of mental neighborhood, you get to talk about the other people even though they're not there. There's been a lot of conversation in that bookstore about other writers, other people—have you seen so-and-so, what's going on. I will not have seen my old friend Paul Auster for a while, but Jeannette will have just seen him, which I think is very valuable and consoling in the kind of atomization that we experience. It doesn't have to be made sentimental, but there is a way in which we have so few spaces available to us in the urban world that mediate, the way literature mediates, between the private and the public disposition, and the balance there is exactly that, it seems to me. It's a public space. People come in off the street, it's available to everybody, it's not private. That to me seems to be the most invaluable thing—a public invitation to the private act of reading. —ANN LAUTERBACH

I took time writing the introductions. They weren't just a quick line or two. Sometimes I'd introduce the person who introduced the reader, if that person were closer to the work or the writer than I. When Gary Snyder read, in a tribute to North Point Press, Allen Ginsberg introduced him. During the reading, little white things flew across the room. I thought, What are they? I looked around. Ginsberg was sitting next to me, using a Swiss Army knife to clip his nails. Very peculiar. When Ginsberg spoke about Snyder, he referred to him as "an antenna of his race" and then eloquently quoted Shelley, who called poets "the unacknowledged legislators."

North Point was a distinguished press and folded after eleven years. Jack Shoemaker, the editor in chief, sent a letter to booksellers around the country, thanking us for spreading the word and selling their books. "Good work, it is said, is its own reward," he wrote, "and we should take pride spending our days as members of the smallest minority in America, the literary community."

One of the wonderful things about being in the used-book business is that you're constantly putting out odd things. You watch how quickly the odd thing sells, and you always say, "Jesus, I never would have thought there would have been a market in Portland for a book on Cleveland, or a book on nuclear physics." We were much more willing to broaden the selection, because we had the experience of what could sell as a used book. We didn't go into it with a prejudice that Americans are dumb and stupid.

—MICHAEL POWELL

At her reading for *The Stories of Eva Luna*, Isabel Allende was gregarious and unusually frank. She talked about how she met her husband, how they married quickly, how she had a difficult relationship with her stepson. Then she told us about a dog that shat all over the floor. She was hilarious. Allende was introduced by her editor, the late Lee Goerner.

I first read Isabel Allende eight years ago in rather extraordinary circumstances. I was working at another publishing house at the time, and we received the Spanish language edition of the book you know as *The House of the Spirits*. No one knew anything about this writer, the agent didn't explain much about this writer, and all we had was the book and a rather charming photograph of this very attractive young woman. Since I was the only person at that house who read Spanish, it fell to me to read the book. And I took it over on a Friday afternoon to Carl Schurz Park and read the first chapter over a couple of hours—my Spanish was rustier then than it is now—and I thought, This is OK. I then went home and proceeded to do some more homework over the weekend. As the week went by—I can tell this now, I would never have told Isabel before—it took me a week to go back to the book. I read some more in Carl Schurz Park on a Saturday, and then I stayed home all day Sunday; and I'd begun to get drawn into the story, all the magical events. Then I stayed home Monday—I didn't go into the office until I finished the book—my Spanish was getting better all the time— and I went to Bob Gottlieb, who was then head of the distinguished house of Knopf, and I said, "I don't know anything about her, you don't know anything about her, but this is the book we have to publish." He looked at me and blinked. He said, "Well, OK." We were extremely lucky in this regard because as we found out later, three other North American houses had turned down this book. And as I said, that book was *The House of the Spirits*, and I'm sure that's where you first heard about Isabel Allende.

—LEE GOERNER

I'm always terrified in these events that no one will show up, except my publisher, who is forced to come, he has no choice. I didn't know that story that my book had been refused by so many publishing houses. I mean, that really affects my ego, my self-esteem. Actually, it was refused also in Spanish, and after everybody rejected it, I always thought that it was not because the book was bad, but because the manuscript was filthy. I had a very small typewriter and I corrected with Typex. So some of the pages were so stiff that they looked like cardboard. And they were full of coffee stains—you know, with children, I was working in the dining room. So I thought that my eventual or potential publishers had refused the book because it looked so dirty. I didn't know it was because it was a bad book. I mean, I never thought about it.

—ISABEL ALLENDE

A wonderful night was when Michael Cunningham read from his first novel, *A Home at the End of the World*.

It may have been the moment when I felt most viscerally like an adult and a writer. I felt like Janis Joplin going back to the Panhandle. You write all your life, and I find I hardly ever feel like a *real* writer, like I'm actually doing what I set out to do. I still feel I'm sort of bluffing my way

185

through and hacking away at it, some kind of hopeless amateur. I've come to realize that I'll probably carry that feeling around with me all of my life. I went back some time after the reading and saw that Jeannette had my picture from the reading on the wall, where all the pictures are. I still think about that sometimes, I still think about how my picture is up there at Books & Co. On the wall. It feels like a profound kind of inclusion, the only kind of inclusion, the only kind of group that could possibly mean anything to me. —MICHAEL CUNNINGHAM

Michael was introduced by the inimitable Harold Brodkey.

Being the introducer is one of the truly useless things. It's a great luxury. . . . I think reading is a genuinely intimate act, head to head with a few ghosts, and maybe a few commentators and critics hanging around, but essentially it's two people alone with a certain kind of narration going on, in a way between them, although the reader isn't directly involved unless he or she chooses to involve himself or herself. And this makes for a very peculiar relationship, because the reader is there physically and the writer is not, which may be one reason why people come to readings, in order to see what the writers are like physically. But this peculiar relationship between a writer and a reader is something that Forster deals in, and Hemingway deals with. I mean, Hemingway proposes himself as a kind of intimate buddy or a lover, and Forster proposes himself as someone deeply courteous but not closed off. And it's very hard to finish a Forster novel without caring a little bit, perhaps even deeply about Forster. It's a little harder with perhaps somebody like Tolstoy, who plays with and in and around this whole relationship between the writer and the reader. —HAROLD BRODKEY

Sometime later Michael Cunningham came into the store, searching for a title for his next novel. Together we pored over all of the poetry books.

My next book was done, except I just couldn't come up with a title. Nothing felt right, and time was running out. The thing was going to have to go to the printer—it was to be published by Farrar, Straus, and it needed to be called something. I just couldn't think of anything. I went up to Books & Co. I live downtown, and I went up thinking, Maybe if I just look through the books up there and sit on the magic sofa, something will come to me. I told Jeannette what I was doing, and she spent a couple of hours with me, looking through the poetry, kind of looking all over the store, leafing through books and coming up with lines or phrases that seemed like possible titles. . . . There were some great titles, but they weren't right for this book. Finally, I was walking through Washington Square Park—a few days after I'd been up at Books & Co. with Jeannette—and I ran into Larry Kramer walking his dog. He asked how I was, and I said, "I'm OK, but I can't think of a title for this book, and I have to have one today." He said, "What's it about?" I told him a little bit about it, and he said, "You can have one of the chapter titles from my book, it's called *Flesh and Blood*." I thought, All right. If the title goddess chooses to disguise herself as Larry Kramer and walk through Washington Square Park and deliver something like that with such force and conviction, what can you do but just yield?

—MICHAEL CUNNINGHAM

I loved looking for a title with Michael, an unexpected pleasure in my day. I was able to do work that meant something to me, that mattered to me, that I enjoyed, which was a blessing. I met people who mattered to me, like Martha Wilson. Martha was making a unique contribution to artists' books and art at Franklin Furnace Archive.

Jeannette was introduced to me by Ally Anderson, who was the first lady in a mink coat to come into Franklin Furnace. She was working for *Art in America* and interviewed me for an article. I scarfed her up immediately. Ally was bookish, but she was also interested in art. She saw Franklin Furnace as a place where books and art came together. She introduced me to her bookish friends, especially the ones she thought would relate to the art end of things. Jeannette at that time was on the Council of Fellows of the Morgan Library. But she took substantial time out to help me with the benefit we did for an avant-garde exhibition, "The Avant-garde Book: 1900–1945." Janoslav Andel was the curator and the editor of the catalog. The premise of the show was that the book has been an art medium since Laurence Sterne wrote *Tristram Shandy.* Andel traced the history of the book as art form through the symbolists, the Cubists, the surrealists, the futurists. The benefit was on February 27, 1989, which was my due date. I was pregnant with my son, Comly, and luckily, I didn't have him that night. I had the benefit instead, and Jeannette was the chairperson of the event. We reconstructed Dada performances. She had put together the committee and worked really hard.   —MARTHA WILSON

It was a fine day when poet J. D. McClatchy came in. We discussed how to spell *spury.* And then another poet, Bill Wadsworth, arrived, and then Philip Roth. I'd written Roth, because Michael Herr had told me Roth was hurt that no one greeted him at Books & Co. Years ago, Stan Lewis had told me that Roth didn't like to be recognized. We learned that wasn't true and changed our behavior.

Harold Brodkey's much-awaited and long-anticipated novel, *The Runaway Soul,* had at last appeared. His reading was important to

Books & Co., given the seat he had at our table, and it went well. The place was packed. Harold kept saying how shy he was, which was very touching. The audience was mostly men, and all of them appeared to be quite familiar with his work.

I remember the first good conversation I ever had with Harold. It was about Thomas Bernhard. Harold compulsively seduced everyone. He had that kind of insecurity. He was very charming. We were quite friendly for a while. Then there were years and years and years of a buildup. Harold was working on his masterwork, and it was going to come out, *The Runaway Soul*. I read some of it, but I didn't care for it; and I sometimes wonder if it's one of those books that fifteen years from now I'll pick up and see that there was a lot there I didn't see at the time. But that was personally difficult—one of those experiences where, when he came in and the book was published, he was expecting something from me. I was extremely supportive of the book in the sense of displaying it, but again, not in the sense of really liking it. So it was very difficult. It was painful, too, because it got such a negative and lukewarm response. Those are the situations when it becomes really painful to know a writer that well, if you're trying to sell books, and where the writer expects some kind of response or support, and you find it very difficult to do that, to separate the book from the person. I was on the floor a lot, and I probably had a harder time than some other people might. I think it's good that Jeannette could unself-consciously say to someone, "I loved your book. Your book is wonderful. We have your book." I couldn't do that. I didn't know how to do that.   —PETER PHILBROOK

Books & Co. loved Thomas Bernhard, and after he died, we had a Thomas Bernhard reading, hosted by Mark Rudman. Harold read, along with Stephen Dixon and Katherine Washburn.

One of the things that started to make itself manifest was I never read novels, except on summer vacations maybe I'd take one great novel. I would talk to the staff and say, "What do you recommend?" For a long time I wouldn't read women authors, wouldn't read this and that. I won't read anything depressing, and I have changed in all these things, but I gave them a long list of my criteria, which narrowed it down to two books. But they would always find it. Somebody would say, "Have you ever tried Queneau? Have you ever tried these French writers?" I would say, "No, I've never even heard of these guys." They'd say, "You might like it." It opened up a lot of things. I still will ask, and if it's a novel, unless it's someone like Hermann Broch, someone I really know, I'll say, "Does anybody know who this person is?" Then they'll up and say, "Yes, she specializes in Russian literature." There's no other place you can do that. Peter had a penchant for very serious German novelists. That's redundant. I mean, very depressing German novelists, which is also redundant. I mean, seriously, bag-over-your-head kinds of things. In fact, Thomas Bernhard, oddly enough. I once said to them, "I want a happy novel." They said, "Have you read *Wittgenstein's Nephew,* by Thomas Bernhard?" I said no. They said, "Oh you're going to love this. This is so hilarious." I said, "Are you sure? It doesn't look hilarious." They said, "No-no-no. You take this home, it's going to be incredible." I read it. I couldn't believe it. I said, "You think this is a comic novel?" She said, "Didn't you just laugh and laugh?" I said, "NO! Of course I didn't laugh." There was a girl who used to work there, she had the strangest taste. But I did actually come to love Tommy Bernhard after that. Almost everything other than *Concrete,* I thought that was a bit too much.   —JAMES FALKIN

I became a historian rather than a novelist, but I was very torn. It's this meticulous way in which you're brought up in England. You're forced to make these ludicrously, sort of exclusive choices. Think of A levels, which in those days was the high school exam: You're obliged to take just three subjects, and I took history, English, and French. I had an incredibly brilliant, charismatic English teacher, who I think did want me to spend my life in literature. But it was the late fifties, early sixties, the world was opening up, and, if you were living in England, it was sort of the excessively slow death of Tory England. You felt a new England was about to emerge from under the carapace of traditional England. So, if you were in love with Freud, Marx, and nuclear disarmament, you needed to be out there, in the political world. I, at any rate, was like that. I was also crazy about early Mailer, *The Naked and the Dead* and *The Armies of the Night*. Without writing a kind of reportage, I thought, if you do history, but do it as a kind of literature, then you get the best of both. If you go after the life of a novelist, then you're always going to be kind of one-brained. It was sort of ridiculous. I've spent the rest of my life trying to bring these things back into play together. So even though I thought I had made the choice, I really hadn't in some way. But it was always very hard, and it remains very hard. There were siren songs, and some of my friends, at the *New Yorker* in particular, are always saying, "Time you stopped all this crap and wrote your novel." Bill Buford says that to me all the time.

—SIMON SCHAMA

Harold Brodkey's death from AIDS was a great personal loss. We relied on his presence from the beginning of our existence. Part of our history, our life, it struck me, was observing the inevitable losses and absences from the literary community. Harold left the world, I must note, in spectacularly Harold fashion. Uncannily, the very week he died, an essay he wrote about his illness and dying appeared in the *New Yorker.*

A particularly moving occasion was Barbara Ascher's reading from *Landscape without Gravity: A Memoir of Grief.*

I wrote two books of essays, the first one called *Playing after Dark*, the second called *The Habit of Loving*. I was one of the original "Hers" columnists in the *New York Times*, in the good old days when "Hers" was on Thursdays, and people would have their six or eight weeks. The two books grew out of my columns. I got offers to do a collection of essays based on those essays. Those were in the good old days when you could actually be paid to do collections of essays. My third book was *Landscape without Gravity: A Memoir of Grief*, a completely different kind of book, not essays, but again, inspired by something I wrote in the *Times*. It was a short piece about my brother's funeral in New Orleans after he died of AIDS. I wrote a book about that experience after I wrote the *Times* piece. My reading at Books & Co. was very, very interesting. It was my first reading of this, and because this is such an intense subject, much to my amazement, at a certain point in the reading, I started to cry. I looked up, and there was Jeannette. I thought, It's OK, I'm safe here.

—BARBARA LAZEAR ASCHER

Our events kept pace with what we thought was culturally and aesthetically significant: Fernanda Eberstadt, a talented young writer, read from *Isaac and His Devils* in 1991. Literary critic and brilliant theorist Edward Said read from *Musical Elaborations*. The next year we held a Trollope afternoon and a modern painters panel, hosted by Jed Perl. We had readings by novelists Caryl Phillips and Graham Swift. In 1993, Peter Straub read from *The Throat*, introduced by Ann Lauterbach. It was an especially warm and familial Books & Co. night.

When Susan Sontag read from *The Volcano Lover*, her editor, Roger Straus, glowingly introduced her. Susan was very gracious, saying "there aren't many people like Jeannette or stores like Books & Co." She was a loyal customer right from the beginning. She was also loyal to her publisher, Farrar, Straus & Giroux, and it to her.

I've always been published by Farrar, Straus. This was the first publisher to whom I submitted my first book, and, to my astonishment and delight, I didn't have to look further. The book was a novel, *The Benefactor*, which I'd begun in 1960 and finished in 1962. Knowing nothing about how an unpublished writer gets published, I'd made a list of ten New York trade houses I liked (meaning I owned a fair number of books they published), and prepared to submit the novel to each in turn, daring to think that somewhere around the seventh or eighth I would get an acceptance. Farrar, Straus was my first choice because they published Nathanael West and Djuna Barnes; my second choice was New Directions; third was Knopf; and so on. I was living in my first apartment in New York, in the West Seventies, and I remember putting the manuscript of *The Benefactor* in the cardboard box that Sphinx typing paper used to come in, tying the box with a string, taking it down on the subway to the Farrar, Straus office on Union Square, and depositing it with the receptionist. There was an envelope under the string addressed to The Fiction Editor—I knew there had to be a fiction editor, which mutated into the idea that this was somebody's title. The letter inside went something like: "Dear Sir or Madam, I am submitting this novel for your consideration . . . My address and my phone number are . . . Yours sincerely . . ." Two weeks later I got a phone call from the senior editor, Robert Giroux, who invited me to lunch and offered me a contract with an advance of $500. And Farrar, Straus & Giroux, as the firm eventually came to be called, has published every book I've written since.   —SUSAN SONTAG

In the early 1990s, Andrew Harvey entered my life and the store's, and Harvey mania was let loose. I was riveted by him. Andrew was a spiritual writer, and he changed my life. I met him through Leila Hadley.

In 1982, when I saw the bookstore, I went in. I had Crisco on my face, all covered and shiny. I'd heard it was a magical moisturizer. Jeannette was on a cane or a crutch. With Crisco on my face, I felt anonymous, invisible, the way you can talk to anybody when you feel totally anonymous, like getting into a taxi. We talked and talked about books. Once I got into the store, you couldn't pull me away—I wanted to go from one book to the other exclaiming how wonderful everything was. I knew my favorite books were there. I had this tremendous exhilaration when you find that somebody else shares an interest in the same sort of authors you do, who likes an author other people don't know about. This wonderful feeling of companionship or comradeship—I went skipping around, or as Andrew would say, dancing on one toe with delight.

—LEILA HADLEY

"Darling, darling, you've got to meet Andrew Harvey," Leila exclaimed. "He's too wonderful." He was the youngest professor ever at Oxford and could easily recite Pope, Dryden, and Donne. At lunch, he spoke about the Dalai Lama.

At that point I think Andrew Harvey was doing a magazine called *Normal*, with Gini Alhadeff, and we started talking about him. He'd been written up in the *New York Times* as the "merry mystic" and had written three novels—he'd won the Booker Prize for *Journey in Ladakh*, which was about how he became influenced by Buddhist thinking.

—LEILA HADLEY

I didn't know anything about Buddhism, but Andrew said the Dalai Lama was coming to Ithaca, where Andrew taught. He entreated, Come with me, you'll meet his Holiness. It will change your life. That night I told Alex I had to go to Ithaca, to meet the Dalai Lama. And it did change my life. It was an amazing adventure, seeing the Dalai Lama. I felt I was in the presence of true greatness. I was genuinely and deeply moved. I started reading about Tibet and became involved in Tibet's plight. We also started a Tibetan section in the store.

In the late seventies, I'd talked with people about the Dalai Lama, but nobody had ever heard of him, or they'd say, When you go to India ask him if he thinks life is a birdcage, or What would he do if he had a hundred-dollar credit card to Bloomingdale's? I think now of the horrors people said then. They really didn't know anything. Very, very well-known writers and editors who should have known much better. But then I knew nothing at all about it, either. I was just terrified. My daughter was in India in Dharamsala, where the Tibetan government lived in exile. I was a writer, at one point, but then I had gone back to what Capote used to call a typist. I was doing *Traveling with Children in Europe*, that sort of work. Then I met Andrew, when, I think, the Dalai Lama was coming to America, to do the Kalachakra ceremony in Wisconsin. Kalachakra Mandala is when they made a sand painting, meticulously— it takes about three days to make—and then they let the wind blow it all away, showing how temporary everything is in life. Jeannette was very interested in this trip.

—LEILA HADLEY

In *Hidden Journey*, Andrew described his own mystical experiences. The book was, in large part, about Mother Meera who was born in India and supposed to be enlightened. She was a beautiful

195

woman, with a figure like a curvaceous Indian statue. Mother Meera moved to Germany, and Andrew followed her. They lived there quietly, and people from around the world visited, to be blessed by her. Andrew and Mother Meera communicated through dreams and visions. Since childhood, I'd been drawn to mystical experiences, but I'd never read a truly accessible description. His was. When Andrew read at the store, it was a major Books & Co. event. Almost everyone in the audience was in thrall to him, men and women. Andrew had placed a picture of Mother Meera on the podium and looked at her as he read. He wept copiously as he talked about her, and his editor passed him tissues.

> We had the momentary—what I call—society Buddhist flirtation. We all were sort of smitten with him, briefly. I was the consultant on a magazine called *Normal*, and Andrew Harvey was involved with it, sort of this gorgeous society guru. He had a fabulous reading at Books & Co. Harvey was a brilliant man, but he was, in my opinion, a kind of intellectual gigolo.
> —ALEXANDRA ANDERSON-SPIVY

Andrew had a cataclysmic, public rift with Mother Meera. He claimed she was opposed to homosexuality, which caused a great split in the community. I wanted to stay out of this particular religious war, since I'd just gone through one in my own church.

> In 1990, Jeannette and I reconnected not in connection with literature, but in connection with our dashed ideals. We were both members of a church in Manhattan that we loved. It meant a great deal to us and our families. My daughter was married there, and her little boys loved Sunday school there, and Jeannette and Alex and my husband and I would go. . . . What really brought us together, which was very interesting for two rather reserved, shy

girls, was we became the leaders of a revolution. We both continue to look at each other in amazement that we had the nerve to do what we did. There was a terrible, terrible upset in the church, and let's just say that the way it was handled was less than honest, and Jeannette and I thought, This is so wrong, being lied to is wrong under any circumstances, but in the church, where we come to find "the truth"? This deviousness, this is wrong. Before we'd really thought about it, we were standing up saying this is wrong, and before we knew it, it was like the French Revolution, and we were at the barricades. So we really bonded in our disappointment and our sorrow, and then our determination, and then our disappointment again, because we had to leave the church. But it drew us together intensely.

—BARBARA LAZEAR ASCHER

Leila generously brought me into her rich circle of friends, and fifteen years later, in a wonderful circle of friendship and literary appreciation that the bookstore inspired, it happened that Jonathan Rabinowitz and I published her book, *A Journey with Elsa Cloud*, which was about her trip to India to see her daughter.

Robert Thurman, a distinguished professor and head of religious studies at Columbia University, was also a great advocate for Tibet. He wrote about Tibet often and had founded Tibet House. A monk for about five years, Bob was the Dalai Lama's official translator. He also translated *The Tibetan Book of Living and Dying*. We had an "Afternoon in Celebration of the Year of Tibet," with Thurman, Andrew Harvey, and Gelek Rinpoche. Sogyal Rinpoche himself was going to appear at the reading, and I was eager to meet this spiritual man. I kept looking out the window. Finally I saw a long, silver limousine pull up to the curb. Out he stepped, jolly and cute, not at all as I'd pictured him.

The bookstore constantly brought people or things my way, which led to other adventures, other journeys. Sometimes I took actual journeys—to Tibet, for one, because of Andrew Harvey and Bob Thurman. I had become so involved, I wanted to see it, to be there. I was extremely fortunate to have Bob Thurman as my knowledgeable guide.

> She had two hip operations, and then to show how she's all healed, she went to Lhasa with Bob Thurman, and she was climbing up in the Himalayas at 16,000-feet altitudes. Walking and climbing and you'd never notice anything's the matter. —LEILA HADLEY

Later I traveled to Medjugorje, Yugoslavia, because of the journal *Normal*. Its first issue carried a story about a town in Yugoslavia where young children were seeing apparitions of the Virgin. She was appearing at the same time every afternoon, and this phenomenon had transformed the village. People were being healed, too. I was fascinated. Would you mind if I went? I asked Alex. He said it was fine, as long as I didn't return a nun.

Books & Co. sponsored a fund-raiser for the Kogi, a pre-Columbian tribe who lived on top of a very high mountain in Venezuela. Basically untouched by the West, the Kogi were a spiritual people, not Christian, and somewhat mysterious about their practices. The priests were called "the mamas" and recognized in infancy, when the infant priest was removed from his mother's breast and taken into a cave. The mother entered only to breast-feed him. The infant priests were raised by other priests and not brought into the light of day again—only enough to keep them from going blind—until they were seven.

The Kogi had a message for the West and contacted Alan Ereira, a British journalist, who talked with their interpreters, some of whom had gone out into the world and returned. Their message was about the environment: Little Brother was destroying the world and must stop or much worse was to come. They took Ereira to the top of their mountain, where everything was withered and dying, evidence of the devastating effects of environmental destruction. Along with Nina Resnick and Leila Hadley, I tried to raise money for them, to buy their land back and keep their culture distinct. They needed access to the beach—shells are used as part of their rituals. The fundraiser was an event springing from my desire to merge different worlds into the bookstore—and to spread the word.

> Jeannette's got this charming what-do-you-call upper-class manner or style. One day she says to me, I'm going to take a week off, I want to see the Black Madonna in Europe. It was similar to her curiosity when she lived in Michigan— she told me she had attended witches covens not as a witch but to see what it was about. She became very involved in Tibet. People sometimes don't realize the depth of Jeannette's mind and the consistency of her interests.
>
> —THEODORE WILENTZ

One day Carlos Fuentes came in with his son and opened an account for his children. Carlos told me he needed information on the McCarthy hearings, and I was able to give him Patricia Bosworth's number, who was working on a book about that period. That was one of the real pleasures of my work, being able to help make those connections.

> We had long talks about Iceland. She has me trying to persuade my family to go to Iceland with me, but they won't go. They're not interested in rotten shark, or whatever is there. They're not interested in Icelandic sagas. I was introduced to the Icelandic sagas about twenty years ago, and they're great. I've always wanted to go there to see them and see that landscape, and Jeannette's the only human being I know besides me who's interested in it, and

also a friend of mine named Michael Chapman, a cinematographer in Los Angeles. But she's been there. She's terrific. I have a big crush on her.   —ROBERT BENTON

Brendan Gill's grandson, Brendan Larson, who joined the staff around this time, was a Buddhist and also involved in Tibet. He was with us for about five years and helped during the time of transition, after Peter left. Brendan was on the floor, talking to people, which was his forte. He had a knack, too, for discovering writers and was the first one at Books & Co. who recognized Cormac McCarthy, the first one to really sell him. Brendan was full of flair and came up with many great ideas for windows. He devoted a window of cow skulls to McCarthy's *The Crossing*. When we had Buddhist afternoons or Tibetan evenings, Brendan brought in his own small Buddha, prayer beads, and altar for the window.

Brendan Larson used to stand behind the counter, and I would amble through the bookstore and then put my books up on the counter. There are always interesting things on the counter that you end up adding to your stack. Brendan would take a great interest, and when I telephoned I would ask for him. He was so devoted to Books & Co. that he used to deliver books before the store had a delivery service—he'd leave them with my doorman on his way home. It was some time before he said to me, "I think you know my grandfather, Brendan Gill." I said, "Of course! He's a friend! I didn't realize you were his grandson." That cemented our friendship.

—LYN CHASE

Finally the day I'd been dreading came—our fifteen-year lease was up. It was renewed, thank God, but the Whitney doubled our rent, to about $120,000 a year. This was not much for Madison Avenue, but it was high for a struggling bookstore already hit by the superstores and discounting.

I hate to admit it, but the mall-based chains, B. Dalton and Walden, did broaden the interest and the base for books, and also then right on the heels of that was the rise in independent bookselling, beyond New York. I think the audience was built through the seventies and eighties in a lot of ways. The awareness of more people about books and about authors. I think that author appearances on media, for instance, was nothing in the fifties and sixties. Now, you can't turn on your television or your radio without seeing or hearing an author. When Clinton was campaigning the first time, I remember vividly when some reporter talked about, "He's in Atlanta on Monday, in Chicago on Tuesday and Texas on Wednesday." I said, "That's not a campaign, that's a book tour." Twenty-five years ago there wasn't such a thing.   —DAVID UNOWSKY

I would be in favor of the chains if they stayed out of cities. They are antiurban. There are many places in this country that have no bookstore. Because there are no places left in the country, there are just malls. So then you have a chain in a mall, and that makes sense. It's better than not having any bookstore. But in a city, you don't want this, because the point of a city to me is—why did we move here, did we move here because there weren't enough chain stores where we came from? We came from there. That's why we came here. We didn't come here because we had a burning desire to pay $8,000-a-month rent. We came here to get away from this. Now *this* is here. Now there's no place to go. The things that make a city are the opposite things that are exemplified by these chains. My anger at the chains is that they came here. Bookstores, coffee stores, whatever. We want all the little, junky, weird places, that's why we came here. It's like the smoking laws. What did New York have? Why do tourists come here? Now New York is full of tourists. It's all Mayor Giuliani talks about. He's turned New York into a tourist attraction. It means it's over. There's nothing to see. They come to see the remnants. They come to see the ruins. This is Ancient Greece. There's nothing here anymore. This isn't anymore a place to make books, it's a place to sell them. It's not a place to make paintings, it's a place to sell them. Always, writers and people sit around and drink and talk and smoke cigarettes. Now you make a place where they can't do that. This isn't supposed to be a health spa. No one ever moved here for their health. You want to be in a healthy environment? Think of anywhere else. Why did they have to turn New York City into a suburb when there are already plenty of them. Why this city had to be made comfortable for the middle-class American white tourist, I have no idea. There is never consideration of the native population. We are the indigenous population of this city. We deserve to be here, they don't. They knock down Times Square, so where do our hookers have to go? Where are our hookers? Where are our three-card-monte dealers? Giuliani says we're bringing in business. That Virgin record store? He's not even American, Mr. Giuliani. All this money, Hard Rock Café, all these theme restaurants, they don't live here—that money goes right out of the city. That isn't money put back into the city except in the form of taxes, and if they weren't there, there would be other stores here. Our stores were here. Bergdorf's, Tiffany's, that's what belongs uptown. Does Kmart belong here? No, it doesn't. We had a very nice Woolworth's.

—FRAN LEBOWITZ

Jeannette let me bring my dog into the store, so I could go get books while I'm walking the dog, which nobody else in town let me do.

—AMY HEMPEL

Sometimes the store was in total disarray, as when we worked to get our Christmas catalog together and mail out the invitations for our fifteenth anniversary party. There was so much to do, we never seemed to have enough staff to do it. Susan Sontag and Annie Liebowitz came in one day, and Susan asked why the store was such a mess. Then she suggested we have a good vacuuming.

When we were very busy, I wondered, dare I hope that things may be improving, really improving? We thrived, struggled, revived, hung on. We couldn't have kept going as long as we did without our staff knowing the customers. It was an essential piece of Books & Co. I remember Brendan Larson quickly learned customers' names, and it helped bring stability to the store. When customers didn't find what they had come to expect, there was havoc.

I'm Barbara now, the last vestige, the repository of all of its history, having bought the store in 1967 from Barbara Siegal, who started it in the heyday of the Chicago Old Town area, the Haight-Ashbury of Chicago. Barbara's was a radical left bookstore when it started in 1964, and feminist, such as it was then. We have nine stores now and are opening more. We tailor each bookstore to the needs of a particular community. The best example is one we recently opened in a primarily black area. Our interest is to operate a bookstore, which was missing in that area, which caters to the people who live there. In terms of stock, that store is substantially different from our others. What we're doing is responding to the changes and competitive circumstances of the business, which required us to find new niches, locations that were, competitively, more sensible than going head to head with superstores. Our customer philosophy is the same. We're interested in people used to coming into bookstores and demanding real service, demanding employees who know books. I just got a call a couple of days ago. "You're a chain, aren't you?" I said,

"No, we're not." "What's the difference?" I said, "I don't think that Mr. Borders or Mr. Barnes picks up the phone and asks why a shipment is missing, or why a particular book is not in stock or whatever." —DON BARLIANT

What Books & Co. offered, in the face of discounting, in place of discounting, was something more personal. The feeling was we knew who came into our shop and what they liked to read.

Sometimes we had peculiar customer relations problems. There was a daily browser who smelled terrible. I felt it was a moral dilemma. I felt badly about wanting to kick him out, which I should have done, but I couldn't. Then finally I couldn't stand the smell any longer and asked Brendan to tell him to leave. He wasn't happy, but he left. Then we received three very bizarre letters from him, sent overnight mail with his address. So he wasn't homeless, I thought. I was alarmed, though. I called William Zangwill, a cognitive thera-pist, who said he was harmless, but to save the letters, to show to our policeman. I never wanted to encourage a crazy again.

I get a huge number of résumés and inquiries all the time. I look for people who are interested in books, but I also look for personality, I look for character, I look for people who have some background in customer service. Knowing about books isn't enough. You have to be interested in dealing with the public. Retail is not always fun. It's eating shit sometimes, and you have to be able to do that.

—DAVID UNOWSKY

What builds a bookstore like Midnight Special, and I have a feeling most independent bookstores, is your customer base. But independents are kind of dinosaurs. What wor-ries me more than the future of bookstores is the future of any kind of free exchange of ideas, and that has already been so much under attack. People have accepted so much now that I don't even think we realize how much we've accepted the closed society we live in. It's so part of the norm. It's very scary. Because of that, I think people will let go of independent films, independent books, independent thinking. And if they'll let go of independent thinking, they'll let go of all the institutions that represent it. They already have. Chains have redefined what bookstores are. Bookstores used to be places where you would go and converse, learn new things, get ideas, find something you didn't know about before, they were community centers. Now, it's "The coffee's really good. You don't have to climb up to get a book." Nothing to do with the content of a bookstore. A bookstore now has sandwiches, wide aisles, forget what's in it. Forget the fact that there are books.

—MARGIE GHIZ

The window for Jim Harrison's book, *Julip*, produced another controversy. We had rented a stuffed coyote, or maybe it was a wolf, and put it in the window. The animal rights people were furious. How can you have dead animals in your window? It was clearly an area where I was not as spiritual as I might be.

We threw our last party for Jim Harrison, and Mark Strand came. He was then Poet Laureate. I'd ordered the special brand of whiskey Jim drank. He wanted some more, but someone had finished it. I looked at the empty bottle—Jim was standing next to me—and muttered, "Shit." Jim said, "I can't believe these words are coming out of your mouth." People probably imagine my armpits are located in the Upper East Side.

We held a Planned Parenthood reading with Ellen Chesler, at which we sold fifty books, and would have sold more if we'd had them. A bookseller's nightmare—running out of books.

When Ellen Chesler read from her biography of my grandmother, Margaret, *Woman of Valor*, I got to introduce Ellen. My grandmother had a flamboyant, randy, exotic personal life, to say the least. Boyfriends galore, sex life unbelievable. . . . Jeannette had up as her art exhibit du jour an exhibit of nude photographs, all over the second floor. There was one right behind the lectern. I remember getting up, Jeannette introduced me, and I was to introduce Ellen. We had a lot of our Planned Parenthood donors there, and I turned around, looked at the picture behind me, and said, "I'd like to thank Jeannette for having pictures of my grandmother on the wall."

—ALEXANDER SANGER

Keeping employees became harder than keeping a relationship going. Elizabeth Bogner was our buyer for about eight months and organized some great evenings. Susie Bright's night drew many people and was really fun. Elizabeth was like a daughter to me, a spunky girl with a lot of ambition. Her most lasting contribution was integrating the paperbacks with the hardcovers on the Wall, putting all the different editions and translations together.

Everyone is always desperate to feed their trade paperback line. It's an extremely lucrative business. You make more money than mass markets because they're more expensive, and you have the potential for building a backlist, and everyone knows that the financial health of a bookstore or a publishing company is based on the backlist. Remainders are now feeding a whole separate arm of retail that didn't exist before. Most publishers are judged by what bookstores they know, what booksellers they know, who they're friends with. But from a publisher's point of view, it's almost like having multiple children. You want to make sure that they all feel well loved and make sure that they know that you understand their role in making your life a good one, but the independent was always sort of the shining star, your special child. The exciting things about all the superstore openings—if you look at their inventory when they first open, they just have everything. It's amazing! Really obscure stuff. The real question is, what do they have after two years, once the store is settled into its location. What does end up being a part of their inventory? That inventory's going to be smaller than one would hope. Less deep, particularly in certain sections. They're all smart, computerized, they have the ability, to a certain extent, to adjust things to the individual store, but in fact, in order to be truly centralized, they can't, so there's a little tweaking. But ultimately we're going to end up with stores that aren't as great as they were to begin with, and then, and only then, will specialty stores be able to open up around them and take away their business on those sections which they've gone less deep on. Then essentially the cycle begins again. —ELIZABETH BOGNER

The fact that a television just sits in your house, and you can turn it on, I think, really has kept people from reading in a way that movies never did. I find among young people I know that almost no one reads anymore, and it's shocking that they don't read. Especially people in the movie business. I have to believe it will change. In some way I have to believe it will change, because it is appalling.

—ROBERT BENTON

One of the staff, Francis Cash, was dedicated to poetry, and to William Vollmann, so he set up a Vollmann reading. It drew a young audience. Vollmann was very intense. It seemed he'd practically killed himself writing some of his books.

A lot of the nice things are really simple, like getting to see all of the books. Shelving books, you come across things that are interesting, every day. Especially new books, but also old books. A difficult thing is if somebody comes in and asks for a health book, and you say, "We don't carry any health books." They'll say, "It's not a health book." Then you have to come up with another category of things you don't have, because you know you don't have the book. Somebody came in and asked for *Love, Medicine & Miracles.* So I said it's a health book as opposed to self-help, because to me that sounds better. "It's not a health book." OK, we don't have any books by doctors. You have to come up with something. Or just, "We don't have that book." "But why not?" they ask. It's stressful. I think in other bookstores they get more completely insane people, but people are extremely, extremely demanding. Everyone in the staff has gotten, "Can I talk to someone who knows about books?"   —PENELOPE BLOODWORTH

Arthur Paul was our buyer for about a year. Arthur was so enthusiastic about books, the sales reps adored him. He was an endearing character and young, only about twenty-seven. Arthur held that people shouldn't wear new clothes and bought all of his fifties-style clothes at thrift shops. As a practical joke Steven Varni circled one of the shirts advertised in a J. Crew catalog, which described the shirt as "Derridean," and wrote "Arthur." I hadn't actually gotten Arthur's philosophy straight yet and didn't know he loved Derrida. So I thought, Right, it's what I'll get him for Christmas, it looks just like him. Arthur politely wore it once.

The weirdest aspect of being a bookseller: you're standing behind a desk and a perfect stranger comes up to you and says things like, "I have to talk to my child about sex, and I need some help," and then the next person who walks up to you says something equally bizarre, like, "Do you have *The Anarchist Cookbook?*"—eyes open, you know—not planning on making a bomb or anything, just wants to read about it. Then the next person comes in and walks up to you clutching twelve books on incest, and you have no idea why they're clutching twelve books on incest, and it's really none of your damn business until they say what specifically happened. What's nice about being a bookseller is that people really do feel free to open up to you because you almost take on a shrinklike role. I do miss working in a bookstore. I go down to Three Lives and wander around, and sometimes they let me open up boxes. I help customers when they ask questions I know the answer to. And, of course, no bookstore person can walk through stores without realphabetizing, when they find mistakes or spining out books you don't like, facing out books that you do, surreptitiously.

—ELIZABETH BOGNER

Arthur left us to join the Peace Corps in Africa. Perhaps he thought the work would be easier. He told me what he wanted for a going-away present: a shower that caught rainwater and held it for later use. I said, "Arthur, you *want* to be someplace where there's no running water?" He said if there were running water, he would come back home. I told him we certainly look for different things when we travel.

I had a manual typewriter, an Olympia, and I gave it to Arthur as a gift for his trip to Africa because I heard he may not have electricity. Peter, Arthur, then Steven. That's the sequence of buyers. Peter brought a great passion to the bookstore, and of course when you're passionate about things, sometimes you can be difficult. But that's all part of, for me, the wonderfulness of the store, the short stories you can tell about the store. I can't really talk about many stores, even bookstores that I go to in New York, the way I'm talking about this one.

—JOHN G. HANHARDT

We tried to expand our business, with an improved newsletter. During Arthur's short, idiosyncratic reign, business did revive. But our business was basically poor for our last seven years, and I had to put in money each year.

The whole key to all this is still selling books, taking in more money than you are spending in order to stock more good books, pay the rent, employees, pay yourself. William Faulkner and Eudora Welty are not square feet, but one can display more books, more effectively, with more room to do it in. I started Prairie Lights in May 1978, with 1,000 square feet. In the 1970s the typical Dalton's or Waldenbooks store was 3,000 square feet, in a mall. During the 1980s, the more aggressive independents grew to double or triple that size (around 10,000 square feet), which enabled them and us to have more books. From the beginning, Prairie Lights had a strong literary image, which was due mainly to our customer base. Most but not all literary stores seemed to be located in cities or towns associated with large liberal arts universities. We've had five Nobel laureates here: Milosz, Morrison, Bellow, Walcott, and Heaney, but we've had many local authors who've written only one story or poem. And a hell of a lot of people who only read books. Our radio broadcasts work very well, but personally I would rather listen on my car radio than sit in an audience. My concentration is many times higher. Or stay at home on the couch under a blanket with hot tea or, better, buy the book on the next trip to town.   —JAMES HARRIS

Arranging to get our books, when we were on credit hold, was maddening. We juggled, the way many independents do, with publishers and distributors. Steven Varni would sit with our bookkeeper and figure out what distributor must be paid first, to have the books necessary for our readers. The bookstore had to appear normal, as if it could offer everything, as if nothing were wrong. Figuring out who to pay when was tricky, an acrobatic feat. We were enacting a form of bookstore triage.

We were under pressure. We couldn't always get what we wanted because of finances. It got really creative getting books. I was the third man for a while, after Arthur and Brendan, and did the backlist buying and would chime in on the front list stuff later with Steven Varni. Steven and I were really juggling, and if I wanted to place an order, we had to talk about it, go to the bookkeeper, and see what kind of money we had. Everything was on a pay schedule—you'd put the order in, and they would release it. We'd say, We'll get you the check by this date and try to have the books on time. Jeannette would have to dip into her own finances to cut a check. It was just a wreck. I'd say about 95 percent of the customers never noticed a hitch at all in terms of what we had or didn't have. That fact was amazing, but it was incredibly stressful. This pressure to try to keep up a bountiful image at all times with no real resources to do it was stressful. I'd walk out at the end of the night drained and exhausted. Though Jeannette was very generous by giving us four weeks' vacation—she did for two years and then stopped, we had to break it up— and I went away for a month one summer, which was beautiful. Full-time people got health insurance.

—FRANCIS CASH

Our windows continued to draw crowds. There was a particularly terrific one for William Wegman's book, which sold like hotcakes. His signing was also a smash hit, thanks to Amy Hempel, who helped organize and pull it together. We presold twenty-five books and sold about a hundred more at the event. We were also doing well with Alasdair Grey, Nancy Drew, and, like everyone else, *The Bridges of Madison County*. But, nevertheless, we found out even that month wasn't quite as good as we expected.

When Arthur left, Steven Varni stepped in or up, to become our buyer. Our buyers or employees usually emerged organically. Steven had been trained from our Dante's inferno, the basement, up through to the celestial harmony of the philosophy section on the second floor.

> I never really wanted to be the buyer, I just wanted to write. I was hired for six dollars an hour and put in the basement to do returns, which is a good job for a writer. I could hunt around and find the traces of an earlier Books & Co. I found a great little catalog of Giacometti drawings, the best I've seen of his drawings—there were three copies, the white covers really filthy. I bought them all. Returning books to the publisher when they haven't sold I guess should be depressing for a writer—it's like being Bartleby in the dead letter office. You're too self-involved to think about it too much. You do the work, go home, and don't have to worry about anything.   —STEVEN VARNI

> In 1970, when the civil rights movement was in pretty good full swing and the Vietnam War, Midnight Special started in Venice, California. There was a huge demand for information, and independent bookstores, political stores, were popping up all over the country. We were one of them, a collective. I started by volunteering at Midnight Special. My sister and I both did, and we had other jobs, but that's what people were doing, volunteering.
>
> —MARGIE GHIZ

If we made a profit, I could pay employees better salaries and give nice bonuses at Christmas. Obviously this helped keep people around.

Booksellers are in all kinds of dilemmas. One is the competitive pressure, the other is they're a minimum wage business, and nobody likes being in a minimum wage business. You want to pay your people more. The problem was, bookstores were very weak, so Barnes & Noble and Borders could knock them off like tenpins. All the wishful thinking in the world aside, from a business point of view, they were very vulnerable, had no cushion to absorb any of these shocks. A lot of bookstores, if they could stay in business a couple of years, probably could survive, but unfortunately their business practices were such that they didn't have the cushion. In the near future Barnes & Noble and Borders will be bigger, international, and heavily committed to selling books electronically. Maybe that will have rationalized itself in ten years. At the moment it's strictly a discount war, and only the heaviest hitters are going to survive in that. Amazon is not a heavy enough hitter to survive that. Independents are going to find themselves more and more relegated to niche markets, smaller neighborhoods, smaller towns, specialty stores. What you really have to do is let the big guys make the real estate decisions, then look around, see where the opportunities are afterward, and fill in the pockets. —MICHAEL POWELL

Sometimes, in dark days, I think to myself maybe we're in the buggy-whip business, on the wrong side of history. But Books & Books is holding its own, we're not hemorrhaging. We've been doing readings for fifteen years, and I'm very much involved with the Miami Book Fair, one of the founders of it, so our roots go pretty deep in the community, and the community's been really pretty loyal. But there's a sea change going on, in the book business, in the industry, and even in the way consumers look at things, we're seeing a real transformation. There's a huge amount of uncertainty and fear now, from major publishers all the way down to small presses. I think they're very confused in terms of what their distribution channels are, how they get their books out, who's actually buying them. What's happening is, I think, a lot of really good book people are leaving the industry. It used to be that the book business seemed to be a business wholly run by book people; now you're getting a lot of people from *TV Guide* or the entertainment world, and there's that entertainment aspect to it, which has become a little more trouble. The expectations are overblown, publishers are looking for home runs, even on smaller books. The scale is off. There is an increase in books purchased, but it's happening more in terms of depth than breadth. You've got fewer and fewer writers who might be selling more and more books; the whole vast midlist is uncertain. On top of it, the consumer's expectation is different as well. It's no longer good enough to be kind of an idiosyncratic place. But I'm hopeful that what will happen is there will be a kind of countervailing feeling, which will drive people to more original, idiosyncratic places. Ray Oldenburg wrote a book, *The Great Good Place*, about great, good places that help weave a community together. People are going to be searching and yearning for this sense of an essential experience, not a manufactured experience. I think reading gives that to you, when you're sitting alone with a book, and I think going into a weird, unusual bookstore does that to you as well. —MITCHELL KAPLAN

The Whitney's Edward Hopper show in 1981 was a blockbuster in the literal sense of the word—people were lined up around the block. Their next Hopper was a great draw, too. The biennials also brought in big crowds—as well as Andy Warhol, Nan Goldin, Cindy Sherman. People often stopped in at Books & Co., then went to the Whitney, demonstrating the positive impact we could have on each other.

Al D'Amato came in once and asked for his book. I didn't even know he had a book. That was really embarrassing. I was, like, "What book?" He was very charming. He said, "What's your name?" I said, "Penelope." He said, "I had a wife named Penelope." I was, like, "Hmmm." It was embarrassing. One time Michael Jackson came in. First a man came in with a small group of young, varying ages, black guys who were all wearing gear, trendy, but they all ran upstairs. We were like, "Gosh, that's weird. Why did all these people just run upstairs?" Then they came back, then they left and came back a little bit later. The head guy had seemed suspicious, it was just weird. He asked, "What time do you close?" "Seven." He came back at six. I'm, like, "There're those people again." But Michael Jackson was with them.   —PENELOPE BLOODWORTH

There was going to be a reading that night and, that season, Penelope and I did most of the readings, and other people would clear out, so it was just Penelope and me waiting in that dead zone between six and eight when the thing would start. So the store was open, but empty, and we were standing around the register and then Michael Jackson walked in with a little girl—she had a Texas Rangers hat on. He was all dressed in black with a black hat—he didn't look quite as freakish as I imagined, then some other people came in, some bodyguards. He spent a long time, and one of the guards asked if this was a busy time. We said, It's quiet now because of a reading starting at eight o'clock. He looked at his watch, figured they had time, so they started to look around. Michael Jackson was looking through the photography section. I remember he bought a British book, an import of skinhead photography, pretty interesting. Penelope helped the kid back in the children's section, and Michael Jackson went back there. Somebody called, "Can we get some help back here," so I went back—and this is the moment Arthur Paul loved to have me recall for him. Michael Jackson asked, his voice is really high, "Do you have *Aesop's Fables*?" I got it for him; eventually they bought more than $1,000 worth of books, tons of children's books, photography books, and the guards bought mysteries, pretty much all the new hard-cover mysteries, then they cleared out. They used one of the guard's Amex cards. They piled into this ugly-looking brown, completely undistinguished van, which was parked across the street. —FRANCIS CASH

From my perch at the bookstore, I watched the human comedy. Once quite a lively man came in, who bought a $1,000 gift certificate for his wife. A bookseller's dream. He explained that he had done it every year, given his wife this wonderful gift, and now, even though his marriage was on the rocks, he would continue to do it.

Unless someone was interested only in Danielle Steel, Tom Clancy, or Judith Krantz, Books & Co. was a general bookstore. But sometimes I worried that people would be put off when Arthur made the counter look overly intellectual. One customer suggested that if we used the little shelf in front to place a couple of best-sellers on, we might soften the way for someone entering for the first time.

In spite of the fact that Oxford's the home of William Faulkner and the University of Mississippi, there's still only ten thousand people who live here. I grew up in Oxford, and basically, there was no bookstore, so I opened Square Books in 1979. We started it with $10,000 of our own money and borrowed $10,000, opened in a little pithy upstairs location on the town square. I was talking to Jim Harris the other day, who owns Prairie Lights and opened it around the same time. We were talking about that era. I said, "I think that we have lived through the golden era of bookselling." It started about the time we opened and ended about two years ago, essentially. In many places, there was an absence of a bookstore, which had a lot to do with it. Then I think there was a carryover from the sixties culture, which created a need for bookstores in a way that there had not been a need for them previously. I think that the cultural growth of the nation and cultural trends pretty much called for bookstores. Also I think there were a lot of people like me, who were looking for something to do with their lives that was satisfying, worthwhile, a benefit to society, who, like me, were English majors in college, and it just seemed like a natural thing to do. I think that's how The Tattered Cover was started in Denver by a guy who opened it and sold it to Joyce Meskis. It failed, but Joyce decided she was simply in a poor location, and reopened the store in a different location, and now it's four stories high. An incredible store, which has had an incredible impact on that community. There's so many of my friends in this business, Chuck Robinson at Village Books, Bellingham, Washington, Neal Coonerty at Bookshop Santa Cruz in Santa Cruz, California, a lot of independent bookstores which opened in the late seventies. A lot of people who opened independent stores in this era were people who were readers. They grew up in families where people read to them, which, I think, at that time, in the forties and fifties, when those of us who were in this were born, was when there was no national awareness that reading was important.

—RICHARD HOWORTH

We were always trying to make ourselves more appealing, featuring books about Hannah Arendt, but also displaying Dick Francis and an Edith Wharton reprint. We played around with theories about why books should be placed in a certain area, what book should be next to which, which area sold best—the inside of the horseshoe or the outside. Or up on the front counter, near the cash register, where people can see it as they're buying and just grab a copy.

Peter Philbrook used to put the books upstairs in any order on the tables. Arthur, being compulsive, thought it would be better to organize them logically, so there tended to be groupings. The first table, continental, German, and French, with some Anglo-American in the middle. The second table tended to be more Marxist-oriented, the third table, history of philosophy, and cognitive science was on that third table, too, which Arthur hated—but it sold. Downstairs, start with the fiction/poetry side—in poetry you start with the more interesting titles, ideally. The more interesting things first. The Pessoa, for example, because I think we're the only bookstore in America carrying that book, so Pessoa's first—no one else is going to have it. Paul Celan from Sun & Moon would be up front, then you get into Knopf, more mainstream. Then you start with fiction, with the same kind of order. Ideally, the more interesting stuff, like university presses. Then you move to the more mainstream, and by the time you get to the end of the table, you might have Simon & Schuster. On the other side of the counter the same principle holds for philosophy: philosophy at the front, then history, psychology, and then into more purely nonfiction or biography by the end. This is ideal. Back table, the same principle, although it's where you hide books you don't really want to display. Certain books are deemphasized, because they're 20 percent off at Barnes & Noble, or some are books that a rep you like wants you to have, so you've got to listen, but the book shows up, and it's not really for the store. So you compromise, it's out but not emphasized, so you're safe. You put *The Paris Review* right near the register, because it's popular. You see it and say, I'll get the new issue. Something reassuring or recognizable, a Penguin Classic that's been long out of print but intriguing and you can be impulsive and buy it. I would not put Thomas Bernhard near the register. I took my philosophy from Arthur, and Arthur took his from Peter Philbrook.　　　　　　　　　　　　　—STEVEN VARNI

Keeping everyone happy—especially writers—was in itself a full-time job. There are thousands of writers in New York City alone. One day Larry Kramer came in and complained, "Where are my books?" "I have all your books," I said. I showed him, and he smiled broadly. I said, "I want to take a picture of you like that." Then I hung that photograph on the wall—Larry smiling, holding up his books, happy, happy, happy. It was not the way Larry Kramer was usually represented. A coup for us.

The same week that Michael Jackson came in, which was the quintessential Books & Co. celebrity thing, one morning our first customer was General William Westmoreland. He likes to talk, like the guy on the front porch, and he talked to me about everything. He and his wife were looking in the window before we opened, so I went out, let them in, and she started looking around the store, saying, This is a lovely shop—and then he faded to the back. I went back to see what he was doing, and he started asking me questions about the book business, saying things like, "Now how do ya'll choose, you know, whatever books you buy here?" I explained the sales rep system, and he said, "Now do all the stores buy the same thing?" The ins and outs of everything and how many books do you think are printed and how do they decide that—his book had been out a while then, and he was concerned about this other book that was about him [Renata Adler's *Reckless Disregard*]—he finally got around to it, which he said that he and a friend had gone through. They found a lot of inaccuracies, and he said what would happen if they changed these. I said the publisher probably wouldn't do much for the hardcover, but if they change them, it would be in the paperback. He didn't want to leave, he kept talking. But at one point, he tried to explain something that had been written about him and he said, "You know I'm . . ." He didn't want to say who he was. I said, "General William Westmoreland." He said, "That's right." I said, "Is this about CBS?" He was going to sue them for libel, because they'd said he'd underestimated enemy strength in 1967, but he withdrew his suit. Then he told me all about his family. I remember going upstairs and talking to somebody about him. Here's this guy who has a lot of history, a lot of blood on his hands. It was weird. Then later that same day Jacques Derrida came in. He had a house account. When I first got there, I looked through the house account, with names like Robert Motherwell and his Provincetown address. You'd be on the phone, and it'd be William Gaddis. He'd say, Put it on my house account.

—FRANCIS CASH

I was thrilled watching the progress of writers associated with us for many years, and I was always excited about introducing new voices at Books & Co. In 1995, poet Henri Cole read from *The Look of Things*, introduced by critic Helen Vendler:

Poets, like all imaginative writers, have an early warning system that announces change. It may be cultural change or political change, but just as it was in the pages of Richardson that we saw the new female, or whether in the pages of Stevens that some of us first met deconstruction, so, always poets show us something long before these things hit the public eye.

Nicholas Christopher gave his first reading here, from *5 Degrees and Other Poems*, and was introduced by Books & Co. favorite Richard Howard. Nicholas began to write novels, too, and the next year read from his first, *Veronica*, about a magician and alchemy. The night of his reading, he presented me with a particularly well-chosen gift, a book called *The Power-Places of Central Tibet*. One day I intend to travel to all the places of power.

I would love to come to New York and do a bookstore. Man, I think you could just knock them out. That's not saying I think you could put Barnes & Noble out of business, but I think you could do a really great, bigger sort of Books & Co. in a place that would really work and a reading room in it, do the coffee bar, and make it really nice, make it really highbrow. —RICHARD HOWORTH

For the obvious reasons, one might expect New York to have more enlightened bookstores than any other city in America. But no, I can think of four or five cities that are better for book buying than here. And what New York has isn't much—certainly there's nothing now like what Books & Co. was—and that's a major handicap for lives in which reading plays a large part. I don't want to buy only the books I already know I want to acquire. I want to discover books and writers I don't know about. That happens in a great bookstore. On-line ordering can never match the informativeness of being able to browse. —SUSAN SONTAG

My interest in alchemy intersected with another love, the library, where as a child I once journeyed alphabetically. When I joined the board of the New York Society Library, my alchemical fascination contributed to my mounting a permanent exhibition there. I had decided to go through all their archival material and discovered a collection from the first governor of Connecticut, John Winthrop Jr. He'd been a physician and a lawyer and was very interested in alchemy. The Society Library had his entire collection, which included all his alchemical books, and John Dee, Paracelsus, and others were represented. In fact, the Society Library had a John Dee book with Dee's own notes in its margins.

It was the first Library of Congress, and the library kept records of who checked which books out—George Washington, John Jay—and all are recorded. The charter was granted under King George III, so it was the oldest library in the city. Many famous writers used it. When Herman Melville was writing *Moby Dick*, he researched there. We know the books he read while he was writing it.

> I belong to the New York Society Library. It's a great old place. You pay $120 a year, you get to use it, and you can walk through the stacks and a big reading room. It's just great to be able to go through the stacks. It has an old-fashioned card catalog with actual little cards. If you do research yourself in the stacks, you find things you don't know you're looking for. I like the fact you can go through the stacks and browse in a different way. Nobody knows what's in there—you can find ancient books.
>
> —ROY BLOUNT JR.

Heading the exhibition committee, I was able to organize the exhibition myself, with some help. Mark Piel, the Society's librarian, Maggie Byard, and I decided to use time lines to denote the history of New York, books and publishers, the growth of the publishing industries—when Random House started, what the early publishing houses' names were, some of their symbols.

Doing research into the history of publishing in New York gave me an added perspective on my own situation and the current scene. Books & Co. had become an up-and-down, raucous, quiet, day-by-

222

day story, with wonderful experiences always. But it dawned on me that I might not be able to keep the store going. Another lease would be negotiated sooner than later, and no doubt the rent would go up. I didn't really want to face this unhappy fate, but it wasn't unique. Two hundred independents had closed in just two years, and many were struggling. The publishers want their Books & Co., their Prairie Lights, Books & Books, Square Books, Three Lives, St. Mark's, Barbara's, The Tattered Cover, Elliott Bay, Powell's, Midnight Special, Book Soup, Hungry Mind, Lenox Hill Bookstore, Madison Avenue Books—all the independents. Even when we can't pay their bills, many still want their books in our stores. It's their showcase. David Godine wrote me after our last Christmas and said, I haven't bugged you that much about money recently, and please order my books. I want my books at Books & Co.

We have an Internet series, science series, a Spanish language workshop now for people who speak Spanish, a writing workshop for Spanish speakers. We have poetry workshops, poetry slams, then we have a homeless series, which one of the local homeless people has been running for two years. Reading books is essential, but it's essential, from our perspective, to create a dialogue. You learn from reading but only partially, the rest of it is from exchanging ideas. You've got to struggle with ideas, and you don't struggle with them all by yourself. Mostly we are a political bookstore. It's important for us to be a little bit in changing the world, to do whatever we can in terms of enlightening people. That's the bottom thrust of this bookstore, that comes before everything. And we have a very supportive landlord.   —MARGIE GHIZ

I pondered the future and worried about what would happen with fewer independent stores, what would happen to the poets or writers whose books were not publicized, the many who required nurturing. What would happen without salespeople to know and talk about their books? Our employees were expected to read or have some knowledge of the books they were selling. Even if you don't read it all, I'd urge, during lunch, look at the front flap, read a chapter—anything so you can talk about it. Penelope and Maeve McQuillan were both reading *Remembrance of Things Past* for about six months. I love Proust, but there should be a law forbidding booksellers to read Proust while they're working.

> One of the good things about working in the store is that the people who come in are really old. Like Joe Mitchell. But they're really great people. Mr. Tucci comes in, Niccolo Tucci, and Albert Murray. He's so adorable. He started telling us all about Auden. He quoted Auden and said how wonderful he was. It was 1996, right before April, National Poetry Month, and I was, like, we should have Albert Murray talking about Auden. He seems so interested in telling people about what he loves. Hemingway, Ralph Ellison.   —PENELOPE BLOODWORTH

About 1994, I hired a publicist for the bookstore, who didn't produce any results. Then our bookkeeper, Marty Goldstein, suggested I hire a marketing person, which I did. He encouraged us to hold cross-marketing events. We did one in collaboration with the 92nd Street Y, a Carlos Fuentes reading, at which we sold his books. In fact, during that whole season we sold books at the Y. We also sold film books at the Film Forum, an independent cinema in downtown New York, hoping to entice customers to the store, which had a very good film section. I kept trying to figure out ways to sell more books and get more people into the store.

> There's a magic involved with the publishing of books, and sometimes things just take off and capture people's imaginations in ways you can hardly predict. But a lot of very, very good books, very well written books, don't sell that many copies and don't seem to get published as well

as they should have been, or don't seem to be picked up by people. A lot has to do with the fact that people have a limited amount of time to read. Then I've even heard statistics that something like 40 percent of Americans didn't buy a single book last year. You are dealing with almost half the country that doesn't read books, then there's a lot of people who like to read, but don't have that much free time, so maybe they can read six, seven, or eight books in a given year. It makes it hard. —PAUL SLOVAK

When the *New York Observer* asked what I would like for Christmas one year, I wrote, "Dear Santa: Could you bring me 10,000 poetry loving customers?" I was listed right under Ivana Trump. Poetry was on our shelves, though it was never very profitable. Our best-sellers: Mallarmé, Celan, Baudelaire, Dickinson, Stevens, Pound.

Increasingly, over the last fifteen or twenty years, major bookstores don't carry poetry. It doesn't matter who you are. Unless you're absolutely mainstream, whatever that might mean, your books are not there. If they do order a book, they order two. Then they sell the two and never re-order it. That's been my experience: If I'm lucky, when the book first comes out, there are two copies, then there are none ever again. This is terribly dispiriting, because if you imagine that there are twenty-five people who want your book, they cannot find it. The one place I was always able to tell everybody who asked me where they could find my book was Books & Co. They always ordered an enormous number of copies, at least for a book of poems, and there they were. For the most part the books have always been, one of the books or all of the books, on the shelf. That seems to me to be completely reassuring in a store that has a deserved reputation, that your work is included as part of their archive or library. —ANN LAUTERBACH

I was a reader as a kid. I don't think I brought any great focus to it, any overwhelming passion. I enjoyed the pleasure books give, and one of the reasons I stay with it is I keep looking for books that will give me as much pleasure as when I was a child. The problem is books don't give you those kinds of pleasures anymore. They give you other kinds, but not the sheer joy of a story well told. We're all too psychologically fragile for that. When I grew up, it was an easy time to read. You read biographies of Thomas Jefferson, and they didn't worry about how he stood on slavery or whether he fathered a child by a slave. It was all laudatory stuff, all good news. You weren't confronted with the underside of life, as now you are. I was a reader. But I think one of the reasons I'm in this business is I like the business. I like buying and selling books. I like finding books in odd places, new or used. I like finding books in people's garages, attics, and basements and getting them back in the mainstream, and I like making money on that. I like being able to pay my employees, or working on paying my employees a living wage. I love it that it's books we're dealing with and not something else. My company was the first company to ship a product legally into Vietnam, mostly college texts. They had to be nonpolitical books, books on technology, but it was books, and I like that. —MICHAEL POWELL

I think the literary fiction writer is going to continue to be published. But the conversation I hear reported at other houses is, how many small midlist books do we have on our list? Do we have room for another? No. We all want to publish good books, but do we have enough time, attention, and resources to dedicate to a book that's going to sell 10,000 copies, net? That means somebody's not going to get published who may have gotten published before. Is that a bad thing? I don't think so. In our desperate need not to be the one who said no to somebody who turns out to be truly great, sometimes we publish writers who are not ready to be published, or should never have been published. There's a hell of a lot of mediocre fiction out there.

—ELIZABETH BOGNER

Poetry was truly a lover's labor, not a love's labor lost. It was well represented along with literature in translation. Our customers expected us to stock foreign writers they couldn't find elsewhere. If they were traveling to other countries, they'd come to find writing from that country. For several years, we presented the Pegasus Prize, which was established by Mobil Corporation to introduce readers in the United States to distinguished works of fiction from countries whose literature was rarely translated.

I don't think the book is threatened as an entity. There's some question in my mind about how books will be delivered. The technology exists to print books on demand, which means the possibility of setting up a machine in a town with a hundred people, people coming in and saying, I want the following eight books. You say that'll be eighty dollars and print them out of a database. And there is no bookstore, hardly a bookstore. That technology causes me to think about where this is all going. It used to be reading was a recreational activity. Now, with the constant reeducation of people in their jobs, people changing careers four or five times in their life, and shifting jobs a lot, shifting locations and taking up hobbies, and all the things that people do in their leisure time, reading has almost become imperative. That's certainly driving people to books, as well as the traditional enjoyment of reading. Lots of people predicted the demise of the book. It was going to be movies, then it was going to be radio, then it was going to be God knows what, and ultimately, certainly TV, now computers. The joke, at least short term, is computers gave me my most successful store. My technical bookstore, for a long time, was my fastest growing store.

—MICHAEL POWELL

"This is it, this is it," I exclaimed to Alex. I was reading *A Stone Boat*, by Andrew Solomon. The novel was based on a mother–son relationship and the mother's death from cancer. Having three sons, I was completely absorbed. In it Solomon also examined a man who has a relationship with a man, which his mother was upset about, and with a woman. Bisexuality was one of the varieties of human sexuality that intrigued me. Andrew's reading was introduced by A. M. Holmes, another young writer whose work I supported. Andrew signed his book to me: "Without whose shop it would hardly be worth writing books. With love." To inspire that feeling was a strong reason to run a store like Books & Co. It was fuel when you're running on empty, running on credit hold.

Today it's almost impossible to have a general bookstore. Hungry Mind is even an anomaly in our town, and in most of America, since we have a 5,000- or 6,000-square-foot bookstore, and that doesn't fit anymore. The rise of these big stores, with the price pounding, turns books into just another commodity. It's only worth what you pay for it rather than what's in it. I think that's detrimental to the cause of intellectual discussion and rational discussion of ideas. We still see people who are book lovers, who care and who buy a lot of books, read them, so I don't think that it's going to end. I even see signs the other way. When Oprah Winfrey talks about books, she gets people who haven't bought books ever in their life or have never been to a bookstore, to go to a bookstore. When I'm watching the basketball game and Juwan Howard comes on in ads sponsored by the NBA, and he's reading while he's shooting baskets and says he's got this big problem, he just can't stop reading, that kind of stuff has incredible cultural impact and gets people to think about reading.

—DAVID UNOWSKY

I needed fresh outlets for my love—books, writing, reading. Meeting Jonathan Rabinowitz was a new beginning. He had a small publishing company called Turtle Point Press.

About 1992, I was getting off a Fifth Avenue bus. There was a guy named Rob Dodager, an East Village character, who sells interesting books on the street. He has a wonderful sense of humor, wonderful books. He got screwed by a clampdown on street sellers because, although so many of the booksellers are actually stealing books, Rob was not. They were all from his own collection. So I was getting off of the bus, and Rob said, Jon, this book is for you. It was *The Toys of Princes* by Ghislain de Diesbach, translated by Richard Howard. Like all these wonderful, out-of-print books, I wanted to give it to a friend. But if I gave it away, I wouldn't have it. That's when I decided to republish some of my favorites. It happened that the person I wanted to give *The Toys of Princes* to was Jeannette Haien. And she said, "Jon, if you want to republish it, why don't you get Richard Howard to write another introduction? I know Richard, and he'll do that." So I called Richard Howard, who couldn't have been nicer. He told me it was, in fact, the first book he had ever translated. I had no idea how to sell books, though. I hadn't sold one copy of the first book I published, so I thought I'd ask Rob to be my New York sales rep. He took the finished book all around, to Spring Street Books, to Burlington Books, but his first order was from Books & Co., right from Jeannette. An extraordinary number for us, ten or twelve, just tremendous. But Rob disappeared for winters, so I took over the distribution; by then we had a number of books. I'd found a book by Ford Madox Ford's sister, Juliet Soskice, called *Chapters from Childhood.* Soskice was also a great translator from the Russian. Jeannette fell in love with it, and one Christmas season, sold something like fifty books in a week. Since Jeannette was my first customer, I always felt so warmly toward her and toward Books & Co., which I'd loved anyway. I would always go to Books & Co. first, with whatever I'd published. She and I became over-the-cash-register friends. Since I did all my own selling, very often I would have some books in the backseat of my car. I could run across the street and bring her the books as soon as she ordered them—with the invoice. The funny thing about Jeannette's order of *The Toys of Princes*—I was so sure I would never sell a single book, I never had any invoices made up. When Jeannette ordered it, I had to run next door to the stationery shop—Trinins—to buy an invoice pad. —JONATHAN RABINOWITZ

In a way, I was preparing for the possibility that my life at Books & Co. was drawing to an end. I had often considered publishing, and historically bookstores did and do publish. One night I met Jon at a dinner with Jeannette Haien. He made me an offer I couldn't refuse.

Jeannette Haien's husband, Bud Ballard, is a lawyer, and my wife worked for him. We all lived in Tuxedo Park and we have dinner together periodically. One day Jeannette Haien said she thought we should have dinner with Alex Sanger and Jeannette Watson, and they had a dinner for us at the University Club. Alex was also a trust and estates attorney like my wife, Denise, so I sat next to Jeannette and Denise next to Alex, and we had all sorts of shop talk. During the shop talk, Jeannette said, "I've always wanted to have my own publishing house." I said, "Why don't you have an imprint with me? Come aboard." She thought it was a great idea. The idea was it would be the Books & Co. imprint of Turtle Point Press, but it would, in fact, be a separate corporation, set up as a limited liability corporation, so that if somebody loses interest or goes broke, the other person isn't stuck holding the bag.

—JONATHAN RABINOWITZ

I admired his books so much. Then Jon asked what my first book would be. I said Hannah Green's *The Dead of the House*. I missed having it to sell to people, I loved it. He was amazed. He said, "That's my favorite, too."

There are amazing coincidences in this little organization. Thomas McGonigle had been pushing me to publish Hannah Green's book. I finally thought, Yes, I'm going to do it. I just don't give a damn if no books are sold. I really want to do this book. But when I heard it was first on Jeannette's list, I had hopes that books would actually sell. She's terribly savvy, she really knows which books will sell, and the book did sell. We're now in our third printing. I increased the third to two thousand copies, and we've already sold that out. —JONATHAN RABINOWITZ

We signed our agreement and then we spoke to Hannah about reprinting it. She agreed, and we all had lunch together. It's funny, Hannah took about thirty years to write her book, and the lunch with her took a long time, too. She was very, very happy.

The weird thing about this is that Jeannette and I took Hannah out to lunch, and she was really ill, with lung cancer, and we asked her what her favorite book was. Hannah reached into her pocketbook and pulled out *Joan of Arc: In Her Own Words*, translated by Willard Trask. We were enchanted. Joan of Arc happens to be Jeannette's favorite saint, and we'd been talking about the fact that we both adore certain forgotten literary fiction, particularly forgotten women. The difference between us is that Jeannette has a much more spiritual, religious side, and I'm more interested in art, art history, art writing. We were thinking of some connection that would allow us to do all three areas as well as new fiction. This was perfect. This could be Jeannette's first religious book.

—JONATHAN RABINOWITZ

I loved reading about Joan of Arc; the book was in her voice, and it was out of print. But Hannah wouldn't lend me her copy, it was too precious. I was allowed to copy it, though, and did so right away. I read it immediately, sent it to Jon, and we both wanted to do it. So my first and second publishing ventures would be simultaneous, to bring out Hannah's book along with *Joan of Arc*.

Besides all the other things we do, now we're publishing. I know Jeannette is publishing. Lots of bookstores are publishing again, which is great. Hungry Mind Press, we're doing somewhere between two and four books a season.

—DAVID UNOWSKY

I felt that it was all worth it when we had a reading, signing, an author walking in, a happy customer, a good show on our walls. A special exhibition, in 1996, was of Louise Bourgeois's Burin engravings from two of her books: *Ode à Ma Mère 1991* and *The View from the Bottom of the Well* (1996).

Three Lives began almost exactly at the same time as Books & Co., in 1978. It never occurred to the three of us that we couldn't have the books that we wanted to have, have it be the way we wanted to be. It was like the dream bookstore scenario, and we were too stupid to know any better. If we had done what we did, opened up, and the neighborhood and climate were such that people wanted Gothic romances, we would have been cooked. But as it happened, we were in, luckily, pretty good harmony with the people around us, and it took off. It was a totally different world than it is now. It seemed like the more bookstores there were then, the more interesting it made it. Everybody kind of had their place. I remember Wilentz's on Eighth Street had an annex next door with remainders. A lot of places had some of the same things, but the idea of homogenization, as it is now, wasn't as powerful then.

—JENNY FEDER

In a nutshell, the Internet is a boondoggle that's going to soon fade as a bookseller to urban and suburban customers. The superstore is a basically flawed retailing concept. About 80 percent of their stock is nothing but wallpaper, designed just to overwhelm independents. At some point they'll have to use that space actually to make money. So they will change, and sometime in the relatively near future, we're going to look at the superstores and get the same feeling we had when we were in Sears in the 1980s or in Kmart today. —DON BARLIANT

The handsome reissue of Robert Musil's *The Man without Qualities*, a two-volume boxed set, made our window. Another was *Hopeful Monsters*, by Nicholas Mosley. Everyone who appreciated Thomas Bernhard, a best-seller at Books & Co., appreciated Mosley. Our reading series in 1994 celebrated Carlos Fuentes, Calvin Trillin, Abigail Thomas, and William Kotzwinkle.

I continued my support of first-time novelists, with Edwidge Danticat, who read from *Breath, Eyes, Memory*. Gloria Vanderbilt read from *The Memory Book of Starr Faithfull*. Fran Lebowitz read from her children's book, *Mr. Chas and Lisa Sue Meet the Pandas*. I especially loved selling children's books, and it was great to have one by Fran.

Writers and readers get attached to their bookstore, then they take it away, but that's what constitutes a city, the places you go to. The idea behind the chains is, Let's make a bookstore for people who don't feel comfortable in a bookstore, who are intimidated by a bookstore. Let's make a city for people who are intimidated by bookstores that keep them out. I'm not running for anything, I don't have to say I trust the people—I don't. Stay home. Do we go there? I don't know what the paradigm is of a store that America is comfortable in—a supermarket. We don't have supermarkets in New York—we still don't. I would like to be the mayor of New York for one term. I would make this place so uncomfortable for tourists you have no idea. I would give New York back to New York-ers. But I know one thing—I'm not popular enough to be the mayor. It does occasionally bring a chill to my heart that more people like Giuliani than me. It's also pretty scary to think that more people like Jesse Helms than they like me.   —FRAN LEBOWITZ

I was eternally optimistic about the fall. Business *had* to pick up. And I found in each day some pleasure or happiness. Seeing author David Plante quietly looking at the philosophy section, for instance. But of course I pestered him to sign his book. He assured me it had a happy ending. There was the anticipation about the upcoming Paul Auster and Howard Norman reading. I wanted to rent a puffin for the window, but after criticism about our coyote window for Jim Harrison and Arthur's fish window, when the fish died, I didn't dare. Instead I borrowed some bird art.

It was a glamorous night when John Giorno performed and recited from *You Got to Burn to Shine*, published by High Risk. He was introduced by Deborah Harry of Blondie fame. It was, though, really Ira Silverberg's night. Books & Co. honored his Serpent's Tail imprint and all the magnificent work he'd done as a small press publisher.

I was given the ability to publish books under Serpent's Tail's High Risk imprint and developed a line of essay books for them, a line of books called Midnight Classics, which were kind of B-movie-type books—noir classics and odd Hollywood books that were out of print, brought back under the Midnight Classics label. Essentially what I did was establish Serpent's Tail in the United States as another player on the independent publishing scene, but it didn't exactly work out, and they closed their New York office. Some books did very well; that's what's interesting about independent publishing. Sometimes you can have as large an impact in the marketplace as a large house, by working harder, by not taking certain things for granted. Every book sold counts at the bottom line, whereas, at a large house, all of the energy is getting tied up in Oprah, Katherine Graham, Walter Cronkite, Dick Morris—whatever $2 million book is, that's where all the energy is going. When you're small, working with lower overheads and investing less in each book, the return on each and every book counts a lot toward the bottom line—no book is written off.   —IRA SILVERBERG

The *New Yorker* legend Joseph Mitchell came in one day. He told me how much he enjoyed sitting on the couch upstairs. On another day I was selling a Pat Conroy book when I noticed a man who looked like him. I sent Penelope over, on a spy mission. It was Pat Conroy. He was so unassuming. Authors were sometimes quite bold, even forward, but not Conroy. He was shy. He told me he had been to readings here, but he was too modest to introduce himself. This outcome was better than the day a very distinguished looking, trim, older man entered the store with a younger man. They pointed at our Lucian Freud book, and then I realized it was Lucian Freud. I called Steven over, hoping he would make a connection, but when he failed to, I ran out onto the sidewalk, after the pair, and said, "Are you Lucian Freud?" "Yes," the older man answered. "Would you sign your book, please?" "I feel somewhat false when I sign," Freud said. "Louise Bourgeois did," I said, feebly. But he didn't sign.

An especially wonderful evening was the night we presented Roy Blount Jr. reading from his *Book of Southern Humor*.

I've been going around talking about this book here and there, and the first, most common question I find on the book tour is, as you sit down heavily next to someone and sort of cringe and wait for the first question, the first question is, "Do you get tired of hearing the same questions over and over?" Of course you can't say "Yes," the terrible thing is because then the program's just dead if you say yes. The second one lately has been, "What do you think of Newt?" I have a lot more to say about that. I've been looking for Republicans all day today. . . . They ought to come up with a new name for Newt, because you name a boy Newt, then you get a mean boy. So I thought, the Republicans should call him Jubilation T. Gingrich, or something. Or if they changed his name to Isaac Newton Gingrich they could call him Ike, but I hope they don't think of that. It might work. But one of the things about Southern humor is, as I've gotten tired of saying, that it derives from a rich, oral tradition. There's also a rich nasal tradition, obviously, in Southern humor. . . . It's a rich oral tradition but it seemed to me that the only person in the last election who seemed to be coming from that rich oral tradition was Ann Richards, who got beat. And the ones who didn't get beat came from a poor, anal tradition. So that's what I've been saying about politics. And I've also been saying that there are three essential elements of Southern humor: one is that it's very oral, it derives from the aforesaid rich oral tradition, and it also involves animals quite often. And it also involves food, eating. So if you consider an oyster an animal, the following poem, by myself, brings all those elements together. It goes like this: "I like to eat an uncooked oyster/Nothing's slicker, nothing's moister/Nothing's easier on your gorge/or when the time comes to discharge/But not to let it too long rest/within your mouth is always best/For if your mind dwells on an oyster/nothing's slicker, nothing's moister/I prefer my oyster fried/then I'm sure my oyster's died." That pretty much sums Southern humor up.

—ROY BLOUNT JR.

Books & Co. did its best to represent different voices and different kinds of writing. Among others, we presented novelist Jamaica Kincaid and psychoanalyst and theorist Slavoj Zizek. There were Benjamin Taylor, Anne Porter, Robert Jones, John Yau, Charles Simic, and Roxana Robinson, and a Robert Burns evening. The Burns night was wild, a great Scottish party, with five men, all Scots, in kilts, reading from rare books that photographer Scott Houston, who'd organized it, had borrowed from the Society Library.

We sponsored a panel on Siegfried Kracauer's *The Mass Ornament: Weimar Essays*, edited by Thomas Levin, with the writers and scholars Miriam Hansen, Annette Michelson, and Susan Sontag commenting. We also held a launch for *WORD* magazine, its one issue published and edited by M. Mark, former editor of *The Village Voice Literary Supplement*.

In honor of National Poetry Month, we toasted poetry with a tribute to Frank O'Hara.

One day Steven Varni asked me what we could do at the bookstore for National Poetry Month. Someone had reminded me that Frank O'Hara had died in the sand at Fire Island thirty years ago. I'm often annoyed by commentary on him that doesn't really seem very similar to the man and genius and delight I knew. So I suggested we have a

Frank O'Hara evening. It was hilarious, and hot and crowded. I decided to select only those who really knew O'Hara. Ron Padgett was very funny and spoke about how Frank once sang out, "I like your poetry," to which Ron could only respond, "I like yours, too." Larry Rivers read such a long play about Kenneth—a collaboration with Frank—that I kept wondering whether I should interrupt him. Thank God, I did not. I was worried that Kenneth Koch would take offense at certain parodistic lines, but he was in a rather tolerant mood that night. Kenneth read and spoke beautifully about his friend. And so did the painter Jane Freilicher. And there was a very moving report by Joe Leseur who was Frank's roommate for years and had lots to say and all of it personal and convincing. The audience was streaming and clogging up all the exits. We probably broke many fire laws. I particularly was moved by the fact that Frank's sister Maureen came. She decided not to speak, but said she loved it, and her son was there, too. —DAVID SHAPIRO

Nineteen ninety-six was the year of two venerable *New Yorker* writers. The godfather Brendan Gill read from *Late Bloomers*, and we had the rare—in fact unique—appearance and reading by Joseph Mitchell.

Late Bloomers was published by Workman Press. What's interesting about Peter Workman is he's making his money in a way nobody knew about before and that the kinds of book that he ordinarily publishes are books sold not individually, but to people who run catalogs. Some catalog company who will buy eight thousand copies of my little book, somebody else five thousand, but it doesn't mean you even see it in a bookshop, so this little book is a commodity, and we have a consumer society which has to consume everything in its sight including books. Kmart buys books, they buy five thousand books simply through the publishers catalog. It's in its third or fourth printing, and that's because, I'm afraid, for the first time in my life, I appear to have written an inspirational book, which I read from at Books & Co. I've done a couple of readings there, and I like doing readings in general. I'm sort of a clown, and I have a corrupt nature. I love applause and so I speak easily and without nervousness on any occasion. There again, it never has crossed my mind that I could fail, because I had Mommy. Freud said no man who had been his mother's favorite knows what it is to fear failure. Of course, what was he talking about? He was his mother's favorite. —BRENDAN GILL

Calvin and Alice Trillin were sitting on the stairs for Joe Mitchell's reading. They couldn't get upstairs.

Joe Mitchell hadn't published anything in the *New Yorker* for about thirty years. Then *Up in the Old Hotel* came out in 1992, then in about 1994, they put out *The Bottom of the Harbor*. He was sort of the hero to a lot of people my age, at the *New Yorker* and not at the *New Yorker*, a nonfiction writer. It was almost a cult. Most people had never heard of him, but he was the best nonfiction writer, at least in my view, the *New Yorker* ever had. He wrote not about grandiose subjects, but the Fulton Street fish market and the Bowery and various things like that. I had never heard of him until just before I came to the *New Yorker*. Somebody gave me one of his books, and it was just astonishing. I don't write the way he wrote. I don't mean that it was stylistically influential, but I think a lot of writers— roughly my contemporaries—saw him as an extraordinary figure. Then of course the mystery of his not writing added to it. When *The Bottom of the Harbor* was put out by the Modern Library, Jeannette had a reading for him. It was two or three years after *Up in the Old Hotel* came out, but still I thought of him as someone who wasn't well known, even though I think *Up in the Old Hotel* might have been on the best-seller list briefly. Alice and I had promised to be at somebody's house for dinner that night, but we thought we would stop and pay our respects. We couldn't get in the building. There were people out the door, on the street. It was fantastic, and a lot of them were young people. I was just astonished. I told Jeannette the next day that it was like a rock star or something like that. We finally edged up the stairs, just to say hello because we had to leave. It was a wonderful event, because you knew that people who went into that store appreciated Joe Mitchell. It didn't have to be somebody whose name was in the paper or in the gossip columns every day. He must have been, I guess, a retiring type.   —CALVIN TRILLIN

The reading was unbelievable. I arrived at 5:45 P.M. There were already close to two hundred people crammed in, and I had to push my way upstairs, to the reading area. It was so packed, we decided to start the reading early. Albert Murray held court downstairs, while I ran interference for Brendan Gill, to get him up the crowded stairs to see his old friend Joe.

That was one of the high moments of Joe Mitchell's life. He had never done a reading before. I was supposed to introduce him, and I got there at six or something. It was absolutely so jam-packed, there was no way for me to get upstairs. I heard Jeannette introducing him. You couldn't get through the crowd, even on the ground floor, and looking out through the shop window, I saw the street was full of people—for Joe Mitchell. He was eighty-seven years of age. What could have been more thrilling for him, and he thought he couldn't read. He was pretty much of a stammerer and very uneasy speaking, and he thought, Oh

240

god. Every word coming out was very difficult when he spoke to even old, old friends like me, but in point of fact when he got up to speak, he did an absolutely great job. It was great, and he was so happy after that. Then just a few weeks later, he was dead. He had all kinds of cancer that he didn't know about. —BRENDAN GILL

Books & Co. was hoping to build a better working relationship with the Whitney Museum, to have events with them, which would be good for both of us. Our only cross-marketing event with the Whitney, though, was in 1996. We held a reading by John Updike on the publication of *In the Beauty of the Lilies*. Steven Varni initiated the joint venture. We were hoping this was just the beginning.

The John Updike reading was our one successful collaboration with the Whitney. When I first called the Whitney, I talked to a twenty-two-year-old who had just gotten her first job there, and I was told, "Thank you very much for calling us. We're very interested, but it's just too late. We can't do anything, so thanks for thinking of us, 'bye." "Wait a minute," I said. "This is John Updike. It's his only New York reading. He hasn't read in New York for years. What are you doing?" Then I called David Ross, and David said, "I love John Updike." So then we could do it.
—STEVEN VARNI

I recognized in the store the connection between the literary world and art world, that this was sort of like neutral territory, that she was trying to be that bridge in a way. We did a wonderful Updike event together. It worked also because I have a relationship to Updike from knowing him in Boston. He, clearly, has always been a fan of Books & Co., but he's also an art writer, an art critic. He felt a certain kind of affinity. We were thinking this could be a very nice thing. We could have breakfast readings, and it could be a really nice synergy, if it could have worked.

—DAVID ROSS

A few years before we closed, David Ross, the director of the Whitney Museum, took me out to lunch. David knew business wasn't good, and he liked the store. David said that they were very interested and wanted us to be part of the Whitney, to be our own separate division. He felt that the bookstore was culturally very important. I hoped that we might become an extension of the Whitney and was encouraged. David wanted to save the bookstore—that was his instinct.

Here's the story. When I first came to the Whitney, Jeannette used to complain to me in a fun way, in a friendly way, "I'm losing money again this year." She comes from a wealthy family, and I hear a lot of wealthy people complaining, and I take it with a grain of salt. But I admired that she was putting her own money into keeping this thing going. It was a work of art. It was like investing in your own art, as an artist. I admired her for it. I would say, "Why?" She would say, "The rent. The amount of money I pay in rent. If you could just forget that." I would say, "Jeannette, we can't do that." I accepted that, in her mind, if she could be rent free she'd essentially be breaking even, and she'd be able to continue. . . . I had sympathy for what she wanted to do with her money, what she did do with her money, what she did with her time, her level of taste and intelligence, her ideological approach to the world, her philosophical approach to literature. Her approach to a bookstore that was unique, different, all those things were great. So at one point when she was complaining a little bit to me, always in a very genteel and sweet way, never on my case because she knew it wasn't really my fault, I said, Let's see if we can do something. Maybe

242

there's a way that we can merge institutions. You can become a nonprofit. If you're already losing money, become a nonprofit, and maybe you can become part of the Whitney's administrative handle. So she thought it was a good idea, I thought it was a good idea, and we had our lawyers start to meet and exchange papers and books and, looking at all those things, to try to understand what it would mean to this institution to get involved in it, but it didn't look good. Her business practices weren't sophisticated. They were what they were; they were wonderful, they were generous, they were friendly, but they were not going to allow her to survive regardless of whether or not she had rent support. Then I learned that the amount she was already paying constituted an enormous ongoing subsidy. I asked around about how that had happened, why that deal had been made, and they said that when the deal was made originally, Tom Armstrong imagined that the bookstore would be gone by the end of the eighties, because of the Michael Graves addition. —DAVID ROSS

The Whitney proposed that it acquire our inventory for book value, that our employees would become its employees, and offered me a five-year employment contract. I hired lawyers to make a counterproposal, with my demands, and I expected a round or two of negotiations. But everything stalled. From my point of view, that was the single greatest problem. Our calls and letters weren't answered; my lawyer's calls weren't returned. Obviously there was dissension at the Whitney, opposing opinions about what should be done and whether the merger was a good idea. But they didn't keep us informed.

Her lawyers were conducting the negotiations at first. Jeannette, in the spring of 1996, had submitted a proposal or letter of preliminary concerns and questions—what she would like to get out of this. Then the Whitney was supposed to respond with their own questions and concerns.

So there'd be a discussion, a back and forth. It never got that far. I remember all that summer the Whitney was completely incommunicado. Jeannette's lawyers were saying, "We've never had to do this before, but we'll just call them daily, until we get Willard Holmes to call back." Finally, in early October, they get in touch, and it's to say, "No, we can't do this thing." Jeannette came into my office crestfallen and said, "They rejected our proposal, the preliminaries to our proposal. They don't want to do a partnership deal, they want a cash cow." Now, where else but the Whitney could she have gotten that idea, I don't know—but the Whitney denies it. But Jeannette's lawyers told me they never discussed anything about Jeannette's renewing the lease, because that's not what they were hired to do. They were hired to talk about a partnership.

—STEVEN VARNI

There is the "He said, she said" thing, but the reality of it, the macropicture of it, has nothing to do with either Jeannette or the Whitney, or Books & Co., but it's that the environment for small bookstores has changed dramatically in the last ten years. I don't think it's fair to blame Barnes & Noble for that, either, but the publishing industry in general has gone through a complete sea change. The whole media industry has, through all the mergers and conglomerations of corporations that publish and distribute. Whether it's television, publishing, or the film industry, it's all changed; in some ways not for the better. There are always losers in change, and one of the losers in all those industries has been the independent voice, the independent attitudes that have been, in many cases, subsumed. At the other end it has created opportunities for new independent voices, like Harvey and Bob Weinstein of Miramax. . . . I don't think you can really cover the cost of real estate on Madison Avenue today with the kind of margins that you make selling books. I think, in a way, bookstores have to be in neighborhoods where the cost of real estate allows them to be. It's always been that way, unless there's some other form of subsidy.   —DAVID ROSS

David Ross wanted to be a white knight. I have no doubt of that. But too many different problems emerged. It became too controversial, too difficult to make happen.

David spoke to Jeannette about his interest, and it was an enthusiasm on David's part. Unfortunately, it didn't have the legs in the institution to gear it forward. I knew from talking to people that economically it doesn't make sense for the museum. What does it mean for the museum to support or be affiliated with a bookstore, which is not really what a museum does? We know that a great bookstore should work in a great museum. Casper Koenig has a bookstore in a museum in Düsseldorf, so there is a precedent. I think what happened was that when a negotiation began, the museum realized what its fiscal situation was, in terms of income, which apparently is becoming more difficult for the Whitney, as it is for any cultural institution. The hard realities made it less possible. Books & Co. was never making a great deal of money, anyway, and it became more problematic to the forces that have that responsibility to the institution. The unfortunate thing is that Jeannette didn't realize the reality of the situation soon enough. We may attribute that to David's enthusiastic belief that his will could carry it forward, but the reality of the situation couldn't make it happen. Maybe Jeannette should have known that sooner; the conversation could have been earlier: This would have been a great idea if we could do it, but we can't. That's the reality.   —JOHN G. HANHARDT

Once the museum didn't want to take the partnership through, David and I didn't communicate, either. I think that would have helped enormously. Perhaps we could have figured a way out of our relationship that wouldn't have been so painful, public, or rancorous.

Like all industries, especially any entertainment industry, the publishing industry changes, constantly, but in cycles. Fashions change cyclically. One year paperback originals are very popular, the next year we're told, people won't take it seriously if it's a paperback original. There are periods when the short story is in vogue, a lot of people are signing up collections, then five years later, you can't find a collection of short stories in a store. There are moments in our cultural history when suddenly new voices are discovered, as if somehow blacks or Asians were new to our culture. All of a sudden the front of Barnes & Noble is filled with novels about the African-American or Asian-American experience. As an industry we respond to what's going on around us probably later than many other industries. As an industry we're constantly trying to reinvent ourselves, because it is a field that technologically can never really change very much. Reading used to be the most important entertainment to the thinking person, but in the past two hundred years, with the advent of all the other technologies, it's not unimportant, but it is the most forgotten in the realm of entertainment, the least important in the realm of entertainment. It does not produce great revenue, but there's another side of the business, which is that many of us work in it because we care about literature and care about art. But now publishing firms are owned generally by media conglomerates. And aside from fashions constantly changing, what has changed *the most* in American book publishing in the past fifteen years is the retail scape. Fifteen years ago there were six hundred phenomenal independent bookstores in the U.S.A.; today there are two hundred phenomenal independent stores, two hundred quality literary stores. If you think about the size of the American public, and start doing the math, it's going to be hard for a lot of people to get to a good independent bookstore. —IRA SILVERBERG

I'd hit my stride, been in the business twenty years, knew something about it, knew the writers, and knew the ropes. I could do an even better job if I could continue. If I couldn't be a world traveler, rock star, ethnobotanist, or live with some tribe in the Amazon, I could sell books and publish them. I wanted to continue, but the climate was undermining. There was turmoil and fear in the industry. My fiery determination was burning low. Structural and other changes were affecting all of us, booksellers, publishers, writers, editors—everyone.

Jeannette's bookstore was the only bookstore in this city that for years I felt I didn't ever want to go in, because it made me sick to my stomach with jealousy. Not only could she afford to buy whatever she wanted, but she didn't have to worry that it wouldn't sell. I remember in the beginning when Burt was there, the stories about how he used to buy everything in sight, and that the main complaint was that you couldn't walk in the store because there were so many cartons that hadn't been unpacked. He was hoarding stuff, and in those days, you did hoard. There was the feeling books were special, they weren't products, and that things would disappear, and you wanted to have them, because there would always be somebody who would want them. We were huge hoarders. We had hoards and hoards. Also, in the more competitive seasons, it was much truer that if you didn't jump on something you thought was going to be "the big book," you missed it. When the stock market crashed, the economic downswing, we had to become very, very much more careful. I also think that there are very few things, if you think about it, that people hold as precious objects anymore. Things are products, items, now they have numbers on the back of them. Homogenization. While there are millions of titles that come out every year, a lot of them never see the light of day. But what you do see the most of, you see everywhere. A great percentage of what we have is available in other places, but because of how we display it, what we choose to feature, you *can* see it. Things were going downhill even before Barnes & Noble. —JENNY FEDER

There's lots of reasons people close bookstores. They get poor, they get tired, they're not making any money, and want to do something else, they're going back to school. There's a thousand reasons, only some of which are driven by competitive pressure. The thing that has changed is no one's opening new stores, because the cost of entry is so high. —MICHAEL POWELL

I had become a bolder bookseller and person in all sorts of ways. Twenty years of selling books, and of meeting and greeting the public, was enormously helpful in ridding me of my shyness. But I remained a little shy. I remember one afternoon when philosopher and art critic Arthur Danto came in. I was nervous that he'd want to hold a profound philosophical conversation, so I called Arthur Paul over, to lend some tone, if necessary. But Danto started talking about the male sperm count. I'd been reading about male infertility and knew that the count was going down, so I jumped right in. I could easily contribute to this conversation, I thought. I was very relieved Danto was thinking about the male sperm count, too.

I got arrested in Amsterdam for stealing my own book. When the Dutch translation of *The Embarrassment of*

Riches came out, there was this huge banner with the title of the book on it, and my name. It was an incredible ego trip, and I sort of walked into this bookstore carrying a book, which I was using for readings. I then sort of admired myself, the reflection of these towers of my books, and walked out again. A little bit later, because the Dutch are very discreet, I got about a hundred, two hundred feet away from the bookstore, and this enormous sort of gorilla seized my arm and said, "Come with me." Fortunately, there was a photograph. But I thought of Abbie Hoffman—steal *your* book. It was a best-seller for the longest time, and I had a huge and devoted and wonderful public in Holland, but there are some academics who hate my work and fiercely attack it. They think it's presumptuous and mistaken, in that order, and mistaken because it's presumptuous. I can understand it. I tried very hard to be very modest, and I don't want to give the impression of explaining their own culture to them, but you're doing what you're doing. I love working on cultures which, for the most part, aren't my own, so inevitably you're going to get into this situation. —SIMON SCHAMA

Artists and writers always surprised me, by making gestures of gratitude to me and the store. One of the most beautiful children's books ever was a book on Galileo by Peter Sís. We had an exhibition of Sís's drawings, in the fall of 1996, and I kept asking if I could buy some of his artwork. Instead Sís gave me a drawing and wrote, "Thank you for letting me be part of the history of Books & Co."

I had the good fortune to be born into a world of means and taught early that it has all its obligations and psychological dramas and everything else. I learned mostly by example, by contempt for wrong or unworthy or dissolute displays of means and money, the obligation that there you are fortunately situated, so you have to do better, you are obliged to do better. And that kind of obligation is fast disappearing, too. It reminds me—I read the most extraordinary piece in the *London Times*. It struck me as extraordinary because the title was "Innocent Giving," about a little boy, a seven-year-old in Sussex, with a six-year-old sister dying of an esoteric disease and needing immediately a blood transfusion of the same type, and her brother's was the absolute type. The modern sophisticated parents, thinking of the child's rights, said to the seven-year-old child, Your sister will die unless she can be given some of your blood, which will give her life. Would you be willing to give her blood? What a question to a seven-year-old child, and they asked him this in the evening, so the article tells, and he said he would like to think about it, and in the morning he said yes, he would, and so they took him to the hospital, and he was put in a bed next to his sister's bed, and they were both IV'd up, the article said. And he watched his blood being taken from his body and going over, and at the first drip of it into her body, he turned to the nurses and the two doctors gathered around him at his bed, and said, How soon do I begin to die? He thought about it, he really thought about it. So like honor, or like innocent giving, the transmission of generosity is different from giving a bunch of Godiva chocolates or the easy convenient thing. In Jeannette's generosity to writers is that pure generosity that she has earned the right to give. It isn't because she could do it. I remember being told once about a fee for a concert: You do it for less, because you don't need the money. I said, I'm sorry, that has nothing to do with it. There are all these stupid assumptions that if you have the money, you can hire people; it'll all be easy, and you can queen over it—that is not so. It's certainly not so in the running of such a place as Books & Co.; it's certainly not so in the fact that it takes me just as many hours to travel from New York to New Delhi, India, to play with the orchestra there, whether I am rich or poor. —JEANNETTE HAIEN

Glorious Jeanne Moreau, the goddess, became a loyal customer. We'd do anything to find her her books, and since she was interested in and read everything, she wanted everything. A French TV company filmed a documentary about her, some of it in the bookstore, and right in the store she declared her love for Books & Co. It was the perfect bookseller's commercial—Jeanne Moreau saying, This is the first place I come when I come to New York. This is my favorite bookstore, and then she held up our card with Flaubert's words on it: "The one way of tolerating existence is to lose oneself in literature as in a perpetual orgy." Moreau translated it back into French and then talked about her love of reading and books.

I've always had a passion for books, I believe it's a passion for life. I read newspapers in order to get news, anecdotes, and I read books in order to know life—not to forget it, but to share it with others. When I open a book, I get the impression that I'm not only with the person who wrote it, but with everyone who has found out about the writer, with everyone who has found out what the writer means, reconstructed the thoughts, discovered the analysis, a particular approach to the world. Frankly, I don't expect an author who has written a magnificent book to be magnificent; what matters is the work. I've lived long enough to know that I'm capable of amazing things, but that doesn't mean I'm always amazing. Why should I expect an exceptional author to be an exceptional person?

—JEANNE MOREAU

When Moreau was next in town to promote a movie, we created a window in her honor, an homage to the goddess. On video I showed the scene from the documentary that was filmed in the store. And Moreau chose books she wanted to have in the window with it. Her loves: Emily Dickinson, Patricia Highsmith, Jim Harrison. She also wanted Andrew Wyeth. We were out, so I called my friend Bill Wyer at Ursus Books and asked to borrow a copy of the Helga paintings. When she came in the next day, she signed the books I'd been wanting her to sign for six months.

> Writing and directing are such opposite disciplines. Writing—you can imagine anything. There's something wonderful about writing. I really love it. If I had to give up one, I suppose I would give up directing, but there is a great thing about directing—it's a communal thing. You do it. You're with people all the time—you're almost all the time with people you like a great deal. Every day, you get to the set at six in the morning, you leave at eight or nine at night, and the rush has passed. You get tired, but it's exhilarating at the same time. I can close down the computer and go for a walk, but I can't say, "Hey, you guys sit around while I go and take a nice walk." That doesn't happen. They each have their own rewards.
>
> —ROBERT BENTON

The Books & Co. imprint was launched in 1996. I did begin a new career, took up a new challenge, which was the lesson Cartier-Bresson taught me years before. He told me he was going to take up painting and had, late in life. Publishing Hannah Green's book was another dream realized, a challenge confronted. Imagine, too, what it meant to Hannah for her work to come back into print—retrieved from the dead—and to have a great clamor made for her work. Though very ill, she was able to be at her reading and party. Hannah was especially happy that William Maxwell of the *New Yorker* came.

Not long after we had reprinted her book, Hannah Green died, on October 17, 1996. Her obituary in the *New York Times* was entitled: "Hannah Green, 69, An Author Who Pursued Perfection, Dies." She was a radiant writer and woman.

Paperbacks have been great in that you find books back in print again. A lot of things have come back to life, and we always comfort ourselves with such thoughts as the fact that Emily Dickinson never published in her lifetime, that Walt Whitman sold a few hundred copies of his own books and so forth, yet they survive. Still, very good writers and their books could disappear. There's no question.

—THEODORE WILENTZ

As a publisher, I saw how difficult returns were. As a bookseller one wanted to have that ability—to return unsold books—but as a publisher, you're selling books, but you haven't gotten any money in yet, and it's 150 days after having published the book. The book is in the stores, and you have to go through a shakedown—returns—and only then do you get your pay from the distributor. The timing and delays are difficult.

There was a squib in the *New York Observer* about the fact that Jeannette was starting a publishing house with Turtle Point Press. There was an off-handed comment about Jeannette's following in the footsteps of Sylvia Beach, and, in the sentences following, connecting that to the fact that she had sort of a gilded childhood in Greenwich similar to Leila Hadley's. It wasn't until Ira Silverberg told her that it was really wonderful publicity, and it wasn't until we also started hearing from people all over the country who read the column that she realized that even an offhanded, snitty remark could be enormously helpful. For instance, the most incredible older woman came into our offices, a Danish baroness, whose grandfather was privately tutored by Hans Christian Andersen. She had written the most beautiful introduction to a new translation, which she was proposing, of Hans Christian Andersen's travel writings. We were completely enchanted by that and by this elderly baroness, who found us because of that little squib. So good things come as a result of bad things.   —JONATHAN RABINOWITZ

Before Books & Co.'s last Thanksgiving, we had a reading for *Committed to Memory: 100 Best Poems to Memorize*. I was now vice president of the Academy of American Poets, as well as a longtime board member. That connection enabled me to publish *Committed* under the Books & Co. imprint, in conjunction with the Academy. Our stellar readers were Lyn Chase, John Hollander, Brendan Gill, George Plimpton, Alice Quinn, and Susan Sontag, all poetry and bookstore lovers. Everyone memorized a poem to read aloud. Memorizing was, of course, a tradition in my family, so when Susan Sontag faltered in her recital of Gerard Manley Hopkins's "Pied Beauty," a poem that I had just spent weeks memorizing, I leaped in and fed her a few lines.

Though I had received a rejection of our joint partnership from the Whitney in October, I decided to keep the rejection secret until after Christmas. It was hard, carrying that secret inside me, not telling even my closest friends and bookstore friends. I tried to maintain the appearance—or illusion—that everything was normal. Given our sorry financial picture, we needed a good Christmas season. Ultimately, I spent $16,000 in legal fees negotiating with the Whitney.

What's valuable about independent stores is our diversity. We're as different as you can be from the chains and still be selling the same commodity. What always strikes me when I go to other independents is that I'm looking for something different, and I'm in the business. I would think that most people would appreciate that.   —BOB CONTANT

Running a bookstore twenty years is a long time. It's a long time to do anything, actually. It's like a little magazine in a way. They have a run of ten, twenty years; so

Books & Co. had a good run. But I don't know where this kind of showcasing of writers will happen now.

—JONATHAN GALASSI

After not having been kept informed, I hadn't expected a positive response from the Whitney. I had steeled myself for rejection. When it came, I tried to make the best of it. I told myself perhaps it was just the time of life when I should be doing other things. I hadn't had a relaxed Christmas in a long time—not that I had wanted one, because I've loved it at the store—but it's been frantic for twenty years. Maybe, I told myself, it will be nice to have quiet. Still, I knew, I would miss it desperately.

It was to be my last Books & Co. Christmas. I started to plan my wardrobe. I wear red in December, or bright pink, purple, sort of Advent colors. I looked at all my suits and sweaters, some of which I put on only at this time of year. Bright colors cheered people up. People would get so exhausted at Christmas, and depressed. It was one of my rules for twenty years—wear bright colors. That Christmas, knowing what I had to announce afterward, bright colors were necessary to cheer me up, too.

(Sad and shocking, at the end of 1997, and shortly after my first Christmas without Books & Co., was the unexpected news of Brendan Gill's death. No Books & Co., and now the godfather of the bookstore was gone, too. His loss to the city he loved and the people and institutions he supported was enormous. His belief in me and the bookstore had been unstinting, undying.)

What it boils down to is we have this culture full of stuff. It's not that you can't buy a book whenever you want one. You can buy more books than you will ever need or read. I am one of the victims. God forbid I should have to take all these books to heaven—I'll never get them there. But that totally misses the point about making a community of people who care about the same thing.

—ALEXANDRA ANDERSON-SPIVY

I wanted the bookstore to go out in a blaze of glory. Should I galvanize the literary community, contest the Whitney? Vindictiveness and controversy were not my way. Ira Silverberg, my imprint's publicist as well as the bookstore's, said, Either galvanize the community or embrace the Whitney, and the latter was closer to my philosophy. Ted Wilentz didn't think it was a good idea to fight the Whitney, and Alex didn't either. The response could be: Why should we bankroll Jeannette Watson and her bookstore? I understood their position. David and others had wanted to try something with us, but some of the trustees wouldn't let them. The Whitney, too, was in financial trouble. My lawyer told me that Willard Holmes had said the Whitney had had a bad summer. Their attendance was down, which was interesting, because so were our sales.

> We're underendowed, and that's dangerous from a business perspective. It also means you have less of a comfort zone to do cutting-edge programs, to maintain a progressive programming perspective. You have to do more of a balance of programming. There are many aspects to that that are good, but overall I wouldn't mind having the Walker Center's endowment. The real situation is we have to be very careful. We have to operate in a businesslike way in order to support what we're about, which is to be a museum of twentieth-century American art. It was very clear, when I had conversations with our board and with committees of our board, that even though we all admired it, and most of our board had accounts there and bought books there, none of us wanted to be business partners.
>
> —DAVID ROSS

Once our press release was issued, after the Christmas season, things went out of control. There was an unexpected, unbelievable public reaction. People were very, very upset. Everyone wanted to know the whole story. The *New Yorker* tried for an exclusive, but the *New York Times* had gotten the story first.

Books & Co. . . . will close on May 31, the owner, Jeannette Watson, announced this week. "We just cannot afford to pay the rent," Ms. Watson said. It is the latest in a series of independent bookstore closings in Manhattan. . . . "I'm heartbroken," said the writer Cynthia Ozick over the phone last week. "What does it tell us? That New York City can't support an independent bookstore?". . . . Ms. Watson's lease is up. "They were not willing to lease it on terms that were economically reasonable for Books & Co.," she said. The new lease provided for a rent increase that Willard Holmes, the deputy director of the Whitney, called "a small percentage."

—DINITIA SMITH,
The New York Times, January 18, 1997

The argument between our landlord, a great cultural institution, and us went on in the press for months and months. The thorniest bone of contention was the Whitney's claim that it offered Books & Co. a 2.5 percent interest hike for a new lease. My lawyer had reported that the Whitney had rejected our proposal for merging; he said nothing about new terms with a specific number.

The phone didn't stop ringing. John Gregory Dunne was devastated by the news of our closing, and poet Charles Wright told me he didn't want to read in a bookstore that was about to close. Friends kept calling—Ned O'Gorman, Dan Gerber of the Montana Mafia. Everyone's sadness merged with my own.

A *New York Observer* editorial in late January came out of a Saturday conversation I had with Alex Kuczynski in the store. "The Whitney is forcing Books & Co. out of business." It infuriated David Ross and the Whitney. He rushed into the store one day, practically ran up the steps, and on into Jeannette's office, unannounced, to yell at her. . . . He also wrote a letter to the *Observer* claiming, "But it was only a two and a half, three percent increase we're asking for." That appeared in early February, and that weekend I talked to a backer, who said he was willing to put money in. Then I talked to Jeannette, and said, "Would you be willing to let a store exist here?" She said yes, and in early February I called Willard on behalf of a group of people interested in supporting a new Books & Co. Soon after the main backer and I met with Willard. He told us that there had been a number of people who had inquired about the space, after it was announced that we were closing. That's very important. A number of people *inquired* about the space—not that they were in negotiations with anybody, not that they were drawing up a contract with anybody. Some people had inquired. And he told us we needed to submit a proposal, and that they would consider it along with the other proposals they were going to get. He said we'd get an answer by early March.

—STEVEN VARNI

The dam of public opinion and emotion burst. Writers, publishers, and customers were extremely disturbed. I was an angel, in need of support, or a devil, for not putting all my own money into the store to keep it going. An avalanche of argument fell upon us daily. It was an extremely confusing, tumultuous period, lasting almost six months.

Ron Rosenbaum, of the *New York Observer*, became one of the store's greatest advocates. He wrote many articles criticizing the Whitney for its shortsightedness and explaining what our disappearance would mean to the city.

Ever since I heard of the impending death of Books & Co., I have been unable to bring myself to visit the store, figuring somehow that if I got in the habit of avoiding the site now, then, when it *does* shut down, I'll never see it gone. I'll be able to imagine Books & Co. is still there, that it never died. . . . It's an indication of how much I care about the place, how much I'll miss it, what a great loss to us all it will be if this unique, idiosyncratic home for books and readers, writers and readings disappears.

—RON ROSENBAUM, "The Edgy Enthusiast,"
The New York Observer, March 17, 1997

There came an incredible, singular moment: For twenty years, we had sold Woody Allen books, but we had never had any personal exchange, any conversation, with him. Then after the announcement, Woody Allen came in and said, "Isn't there anything we can do about the bookstore? It's a real loss to the neighborhood." I was dumbstruck and very touched. And he did try to help us. Many, many people were very kind.

The Whitney was often pilloried in the press, while many customers, citizens, and writers sent letters of outrage to their offices.

From what Jeannette told my partner, Jill, there were people who were really angry with her when it was announced. She should have somehow continued to stake the bookstore, to keep it alive as this cultural icon. Our feeling is, you can't take things for granted. You have to support things you want to have. Why, in hell, just because she has the money, should she throw it down a hole to keep this icon in New York? Where are all of these people who are so angry? It is a huge, huge struggle in this city now to maintain any kind of independence or uniqueness. I think New Yorkers are more complacent than people in other places, because they're so used to having the best and the newest served up to them on a silver platter. The fact is that the economic climate can't allow you to do that anymore. It just can't. And if anybody would have stayed with it as long as they possibly could, it's her. I'm sure she struggled a lot more than anybody will ever know. I know we have. People who don't come in for months or years at a time walk in, and they expect you to have the newest and exactly what they want, and ask, "Why don't you?" The supply and demand thing is real. The fact of the matter is, if we don't start supporting these things, we're not going to have neighborhoods left or any of these icons. In my short lifetime living in this city, I can't believe what's disappeared that I still miss every day. —JENNY FEDER

No situation is black and white, but sides were starkly taken, the lines drawn. Communication between the Whitney and us became almost impossible.

People had heard only one side, or just had an emotional response to a situation, which, in fact, lends itself to emotional response. The disappearance of small bookstores with an intellectual perspective, almost a bookstore as a work of art, is something worthy of mourning and worthy of our concern. I think if I had been on the other side or outside of the situation, like so many of my friends who wrote me or called me in distress and wonderment, and sometimes anger about this institution's reported role in the demise of Books & Co., I would have understood it. In fact, I probably would have been out there with everybody else. So my desire to work with her was sincere, and it could have been a very interesting marriage. Finally, it made us look so cold and inhuman. "You're holding this entire wonderful enterprise up because it wasn't able to make business standards?" We had to say, sure. We've got a payroll of 230 people. The Whitney Museum is also a community of people, who have careers. I'm charged as director with running a business that serves the public by providing exhibitions and educational service for thousands of school students, and that buys important work from American artists when they still need that kind of support, when they're young and still untested by the market. I have all of these responsibilities, I don't also need to take on the responsibility of supporting the operation of a bookstore, no matter how good it is.   —DAVID ROSS

Letters, faxes, and phone calls deluged the store. It was overwhelming, exhausting. The bookstore actually needed that level of support all along, needed our customers to put their money where their mouths were, to realize how desperately we were fighting to survive in a changed market.

In the heady, contentious mix of feeling, half-facts, and untruths, we soldiered on, preparing for the worst, which was, I thought, inevitable. I hoped I was wrong. Occasionally it appeared as if the bookstore might be saved.

It's not too late to save Books & Co. You can make a difference. Write Leonard Lauder, chairman of the board of trustees, the Whitney Museum. . . . Tell him in a brief letter how important it is for the Whitney to find a way to save Books & Co. How grateful you'll be to the museum if it does. How angry you'll be if it fails to. . . . So that if the Whitney does turn out to be smart enough to see this as a second chance to save its own reputation, I can write a column celebrating our common victory.
       —RON ROSENBAUM, "The Edgy Enthusiast,"
          The New York Observer, March 17, 1997

In our wounded condition, various angels came forward, offering ideas and money to maintain the store. True to his word, Woody Allen offered to premiere his next film at the Whitney, as a benefit for Books & Co. He was one of the bookstore's most ardent would-be saviors.

> "What are they gonna replace it with," Woody Allen asks glumly, "another expensive foreign clothing store?" "Maybe a nail salon," I suggest bitterly. We'd been speculating about the Whitney's plans for the Books & Co. space if the museum succeeds—as it now seems intent on doing—in killing the beloved bookstore a second time.
>
> —RON ROSENBAUM,
> *The New York Observer,* March 31, 1997

The enormity of the spirited and fraught response made Steven Varni and me realize how urgently the bookstore was needed—and how symbolic Books & Co. was, too. Symbols become depleted when not supported, when market forces blow furiously in other directions. Steven kept working with several people to change the structure and finances of the store in new proposals to the Whitney. If the store had a different owner or owners, it might continue. I could participate, too, but I wouldn't have to worry about the finances or the management. I was ready to be the gray-haired lady who enters every once in a while and offers words of wisdom.

> This is less the story of the little bookstore that couldn't as much as the story of power and greed on the part of the Whitney Museum of American Art. . . . How much goodwill will the Whitney lose if it becomes Books & Co.'s executioner?   —*The New York Observer,* April 7, 1997

The ways in which they said they could provide market rent, even though they now still assure us these were legitimate proposals that they made, in fact, didn't wash. We couldn't let sentiment stand. In other words, there had to be real backers who are going to really commit themselves to real support of an institution that we all recognized was going to be very hard to be profitable. Someone had to be willing to say, "We're going to pay for this out of our own money because we believe in it. We don't think the Whitney should have to pay for it. It's a nonprofit raising money for its own goals, and yet we care about this nonprofit, even though it's not called one, and we're going to put our money in place. Here's our pledge, here it is, in writing." Nothing that concrete.

—DAVID ROSS

The trustees behaved very strangely. Some trustees called to offer their support at a certain point, but later these same people who had called and asked, "How can we help?" were totally closed to me, to us. I would call them back and ask, "So when is the trustees' meeting?" and get "I don't know," "I can't find out," or "It's out of our hands," though originally they'd said that the trustees have to approve any proposal. Then I started hearing that it would be just the people at the Whitney who'd decide—Willard and David—and the trustees would say they had nothing to do with it. We finally found out about March 26 that *somebody* had rejected our proposal. But then Woody Allen spoke to Leonard Lauder, and said that Lauder had been very receptive to his concerns about the store.

—STEVEN VARNI

Woody Allen wrote Leonard Lauder about the bookstore's importance and phoned him, too. After speaking with Lauder, Woody came into the store to tell us that Lauder was very sympathetic to us. Our hopes were raised, though I was never really optimistic.

Woody Allen says, "You should talk to Leonard Lauder." So on the 29th, I called him. Lauder was very sympathetic, even though they had just turned us down. He started saying, "We can set you up in the Store Next Door, maybe you can sell our books." That started the final round of negotiations, in which we tried to strengthen our proposal. We added on things, like paying them more money, supplementing the rent with fund-raising events. We'd pay $140,000, which is actually more than a 3 percent increase. We went into a meeting with them around April 11, Jonathan Malkin and I. Both Willard and David Ross were very upset about the press. Willard said, "If you can come up with more money, you need to quantify it. If you can do fund-raising, you need to suggest how much these fund-raising events might add up to." So Jonathan and I tried to quantify and spent that weekend quantifying and trying to think of legitimate fund-raisers that would produce money and how much. Which is what Willard requested at the meeting, after they'd finished shooting down everything Leonard Lauder had said to me—"Forget it. None of that goes." So Jonathan and I left, spent the whole weekend drawing up a new proposal, with fund-raising to add in, quantifying, giving totals, a proposal that would have added up to something like $240,000 a year. That's what they rejected again.   —STEVEN VARNI

If Books & Co. were to re-form and continue, we needed a new location. Steven and I looked at real estate. We wanted to stay in the neighborhood, where our customers were and where we were known. But it was just too expensive on Madison Avenue, and there was nothing available on Lexington Avenue in the Seventies. We didn't want to move too far away from our home base.

The block would change without us. We brought people to the area. But was our type of bookstore dead? What would bookstores be like in the future? In our last year, all the people we hired decided after a day they didn't want the job. One woman applied for the job of manager and spent a day in the bookstore trying it out, which we'd never done before. After she unpacked a few cartons, she lost interest and quit. Then the bookkeeper quit. No bookkeeper and no staff. It was crazy.

The death of the bookstore was slow and protracted, like a terminal illness. There were many swoons, breathtaking possibilities, and cries until the end. The war between the two institutions was hell.

> "The struggle between the Whitney and Books & Co. is very much a tale of a cultural institution behaving like a business and of a business behaving like a cultural institution. . . . The Whitney was giving the store what amounted to a de facto subsidy, and one that in effect became bigger every year as the potential rent of a Madison Avenue storefront continued to grow. At the same time, other forces began to play havoc with both the book business and the structure of museums. Independent bookselling became more and more difficult as large chains grew more powerful. Museums were facing a whole set of economic and social pressures of their own and they tried to respond to the curtailment of government support by marketing themselves more and more aggressively."
>
> —PAUL GOLDBERGER,
> *The New York Times*, May 5, 1997

While the roller coaster of emotion continued, taking us up and down, and even with the possibility of a new Books & Co. II emerging, Steven and I had to begin to close the shop. We discontinued house accounts and tried to call in all the cash owed us, so that we could pay our accounts. For the first time in our history, we put some books on sale at 20 percent. All the art, children's, and music books. The basement, once overstocked, once a fire hazard, looked emptier than it had in twenty years. We could not keep up with new books, we couldn't order them. Many of our regulars, our house accounts, too, stopped coming in. Perhaps it was too upsetting for them; or they could no longer find the books they wanted, or both.

On the other hand, many people began coming in every day, drawn by the drama of our interaction with the Whitney and all the news reports.

Until the end—and even after—articles appeared, stoking the fires under the store, raising hope, fueling the controversy between the Whitney and us, hardening positions, making, finally, discussion and compromise impossible. The Whitney had had a lot of bad press, and from our point of view, they'd handled the situation poorly.

> It became a polluted situation, in which nobody was any longer right. There are some in the literary world who have no respect for what you might call the art world and think of us all as a bunch of jerks and want to caricature us as eighties wanna-bes who made a lot of money quick and bought houses in the Hamptons. They don't understand the seriousness of the overall enterprise and ambition of people who straddle both worlds or who are fighting the false categorizations of the ways artists work. The fact that we were so trivialized, our mission was so trivialized and dismissed, needless to say, did not make friends among those people on our board or our staff who could have conceivably turned things around. The situation got enormously polarized. I was deeply, personally hurt by many of the things that were said. I'm sure it would seem ironic to people who are now my sworn enemies for life, but I do really miss Books & Co. and wish that it could have worked out differently. On the other hand, I have to say that we can't take the full responsibility for its demise.
>
> —DAVID ROSS

I tried to keep the staff's morale up by giving them a lunch party every week and supplying lots of chocolate. But my own morale was flagging. Even when I went with my friend Ned O'Gorman to a Mark Morris ballet, whose work I love, I would have to confront the reality of Books & Co. closing. A favorite customer,

Andrew Leigh, told me at intermission that entering Books & Co. now was like going to see a dying cancer patient.

After we presented the Whitney with our final proposal, we were supposed to get an answer on April 21. We held a vigil at the store, waiting for word. Woody Allen, Soon Yi, Erica Jong, Frederic Tuten, Oscar Hijuelos, Margot Wilkie, Helen Whitney, Quentin Crisp, Gary Indiana, so many friends, and many reporters, came to be with us. It was like a wake for the not-yet dead, but there was no answer that night.

> Being a president of a nonprofit, I have a certain sympathy for the Whitney Museum. Here they have this real estate that they're not exactly stuck with but they've bought, for their own mission and purposes, and they're obligated to maximize the return on it or use it for their own exhibits, and they had a rival cultural institution there as a tenant. But they handled it so badly, when they could have done so many creative things with this literary gem. They blew it and gave themselves a huge black eye. This will be studied in textbooks about how not to deal with a community.
>
> —ALEXANDER SANGER

The countdown for Books & Co. began. We went into our final days. A heartbreaking sale sign was placed in the window. We were discounting all books 30 percent, except for new books. The thought of not being a bookseller was unbearable. I thought after this was over, I could become a volunteer, just to be able to continue selling books.

After all the strategizing, proposals, and intense discussions, the absolute and final rejection arrived on Friday, April 25. And then it was all over.

> I was starting to close the store, ten minutes 'til seven, looking forward to having a weekend. It would have been my first weekend with no Whitney stuff to do. Closing up

and we get a letter, hand delivered. I come back upstairs from closing the basement, and before I even open the letter, the *New York Times* calls, "So, you didn't get a lease. Do you have any comments?" I said, "I haven't even read the letter yet." So they obviously sent the messenger over and called the *Times* immediately or called the *Times* first. The reporter was panicked, because his deadline was right upon him, and he wanted a comment. I had none. I hadn't read it. But because we had had the party on the 21st, every reporter there had, including the *Times* reporter, a notebook of comments. So the *Times* article on the next day, Saturday, included those comments—Sontag's comment about our being the best bookstore in New York. The Whitney had sent us a four-page letter to turn us down, which included a semblance of a counter-proposal, but it wasn't a counterproposal, because we were finished. They were empty gestures.   —STEVEN VARNI

The Whitney Museum of American Art, acting as landlord, rejected a last-minute effort to save Books & Co.... The decision followed an 11th-hour proposal by two anonymous admirers of the 20-year-old bookstore to help its owners pay the increased rent.... An announcement had been expected on Monday, which was why the bookstore convened a gathering of luminaries that included Susan Sontag, Richard Avedon, Woody Allen and Louis Auchincloss in a show of solidarity.

—DAVID W. CHEN,
The New York Times, April 26, 1997

There was an unreality to our closing. The customers couldn't believe it, even as our shelves emptied. My beloved children's section was almost gone. Many of the most popular Loebs were gone, too.

When I was talking to Ted Wilentz about the twenty years coming to an end, Ted said I should look on this as a celebration, that

I've had these years, that I've been successful, and what an important bookstore it was. I began to feel more satisfaction. I had accomplished what I set out to do. Change is good, I kept telling myself. I would need more energy than I had at that moment to think of starting another bookstore. I wouldn't want to do something that was lesser and have people moan, It's not what Books & Co. was.

> I absolutely agree with Jeannette. They can't be charities; a business has to run as a business. It's like if the language isn't used, it dies out, and you can't artificially keep it up. You can think of ways to patronize a store, but it's not a charity. It's a difficult time even for antiquarian bookstores.
>
> —CALVIN TRILLIN

> I can understand the fact that she made a decision to close the store. I don't think the idea of re-creating the store, the idea of trying to do it somewhere else, would work, especially if she can't buy a place somewhere. I know it will be sad, but it has to be.   —JOHN G. HANHARDT

> Jeannette struggled remarkably to create an atmosphere of literary life in a culture where what she's doing is a rearguard action. The kind of salon she envisions and wants to have basically doesn't exist. It's an anachronism, and in a way, it's a fantasy. And she has been very successful at making it come true. In fact making people more interesting than they actually are, because of her generosity to them. There really isn't the kind of literary community she wants there to be. The population swelled and instead of one group, there were many many many groups. It began to splinter in a way that you couldn't have any coherence.
>
> —ALEXANDRA ANDERSON-SPIVY

I suddenly, rather spontaneously, made up an image that Jeannette seemed to like very much. I was thinking back on things and said, "Yes, I remember . . ." And I talked about how awful that upstairs room was for readings, that it was such a horrible venue for readings, airless, crowded, and narrow and whatnot. I said that I, having been in both the audience and behind the podium, knew exactly what it feels like to be a hostage in a political kidnapping. In an airless, tight room. I felt like a literary hostage in that room. She seemed delighted by that, as I was. I've never given a reading in a smaller room than that, and because the audiences are usually rather full and heavy breathers, they just sort of suck all the spiritual air out of you as well. Literary heavy breathers. They're audiences that pay very close, rapt, even erotic attention to what's being read. It adds to the pressure of the situation. But I was happily kept captive there. It's as if Books & Co. were like a nice bottle of champagne on the whole of one's career. Ideal captivity.

—J. D. McCLATCHY

What was most satisfying to me was the response of people I didn't know and who didn't know me. I'd overhear their conversations about the bookstore: What a wonderful store. I knew you would have this book. That's what was truly rewarding and gave me a sense of pride. I loved the bookstore as a public arena, where I could talk to different people all day long. I knew I would miss them most. The customers always, always, were the main event, what gave me the most pleasure. I was dedicated to them, and many were dedicated to us. This was painfully clear when we had to close.

Though I loved meeting writers and being surprised when they came by, I was sustained, as was Books & Co., by the weekly and daily customers, the regulars, and the beauty of daily life in the store. It was through the bookstore that I learned to enjoy people and to be easy talking with them. It was the bookstore's gift to me.

An older man stopped in almost every day. Mr. Lutz had a ruddy face, was about 5 foot 10, and had gray hair. I always greeted him, and we had brief, pleasant conversations. When Bill Wyer, from Ursus Books, came in one day, he saw him and said, "Hello, Bob, how are you." Later I asked Bill, "How do you know Mr. Lutz?" I learned that Bob Lutz was a retired postal worker who lived with his mother, just a block away. He put everything he had into books.

There was a younger man, who came in often, who was adorable, and looked ten years younger than thirty-one. He wore a ponytail down to his waist. He loved poetry. He would remind me of what we didn't have or needed. "You don't have any Carcanet," he'd say. I thought, I have to speak to Steven, why don't we have that press? He also showed me poems he was reading or books, like one by a Russian prodigy, a fourteen-year-old girl. My customers enriched my life by telling me what they were reading. He didn't have much money, and he'd say, "Would you hold these for me for five days?" We would. I became very fond of him.

> What I have loved there: Finding a Jouve that would be very difficult to find elsewhere! bizarre marginalizing of the commercial books or even outlawing many of the poor books of the year; increasingly good philosophy and theory sections; one of the few stores where a Louise Bourgeois could have a show. *Ave et vale.* Never again will I be told that Meryl Streep just bought my book! —DAVID SHAPIRO

> She said to me, "If ever I was to close the store, you know what I would miss?" I said, "What?" She said, "I'd miss the customers, I'd miss the people I meet there every day."
> —THEODORE WILENTZ

The hardest job was telling the regulars that the store was closing. It was like telling a friend a loved one had died. I knew it would be worse if no one cared, but I cried four or five times a day. Jeanne Moreau was philosophical and kind. She called, because she couldn't come in. She told me not to worry about losing the bookstore. Sometimes, she said, these things are a blessing.

What can we learn from Books & Co.? What does it say about culture? What does it mean that this place, with the largesse that made it possible—the irony in its being lost—is in the neighborhood of a major cultural institution, neither of which could sustain the other. Books & Co. couldn't sustain itself, it couldn't bring in customers for the museum; the museum couldn't bring in customers to them. It also says something about that stretch of Madison Avenue and New York, because this had a lot of things going for it to make it work. —JOHN G. HANHARDT

I didn't know exactly what I should feel, what the bookstore represented. It was greater than any one individual's feelings. I felt sad that the city would lose this bookstore—if I were one of my customers, that's what I would say. I do feel that the bookstore, in the way it's been run by me for twenty years, is anachronistic. If the bookstore were going to continue, it would have to be totally changed, computerized, Internetted. Books & Co. was like the last nineteenth-century bookstore in the twentieth century, almost the twenty-first. I wish I could have passed on the mantle, and I wish there were someone who would be willing to take the bookstore, invent it in a new way, a modern way, and continue to have great books, the good books, and all the readings.

It's sort of like a death. I hope that Jeannette will have a sense of tremendous accomplishment that will help her transcend the disappointment of its ending. It's incredible, really, that this fragile, beautiful creature, coming from a background that is known to be very conservative and part of the power structure of America, did do something extraordinary, imaginative, and audacious and make a success of it—whether or not it's been a monetary success— so needed and loved and worthwhile. Part of our sadness must spring from the fact that we think it can't be done anymore, you don't think there'll *be* another bookstore like this, nobody will come along and do it, it evidently can't be done anymore. Jeannette's put everything into this, including a great deal of her own money. You just feel that the times don't permit it. The word anachronism comes to mind, alas.   —LYN CHASE

It's just that feeling when you look back and all of a sudden there's so many changes that have gone by, and then some people remain, and then when some people have passed on, then there are these people, together. Jeannette and I have known each other so long now.   —ALBERT MURRAY

May was our last month. Leila Hadley read on May 7 from *A Journey with Elsa Cloud*, published under my new imprint. Leila wrote in detail about everything she witnessed in India—the makeup the women put on for the dance, the different herbs, what it smelled like to walk into a bazaar. It was also a book about her past, her privileged upbringing, a spiritual journey, and a mother–daughter relationship.

I realized that the theme of the books I was committed to was family relationships. Hannah Green's book was about an American family, primarily told through the voice of a wonderful adolescent girl. Leila's was about the parent–child relationship, and the book that would follow Leila's, Rachel MacKenzie's *The Wine of Astonishment*, was the story of two sisters, and what happens to them when their mother dies. There was yet another connection. Rachel MacKenzie was Hannah Green's editor at the *New Yorker*. I realized that my imprint had a very definite and clear focus. It was also surfeited with associations, just as the bookstore was.

We placed an ad in the *New York Times*, and a huge crowd came to the store, picking over the discounted stock, like vultures. Friends came in, too, to give support and buy books. One of my loyal customers, as a protest, refused to buy the books at a discount. Fran Lebowitz went across the Wall, holding onto the ladder, setting the many books she wanted onto it. Lynn Davis photographed me, standing in a doorway upstairs. Then, finally, one day the basement was empty, absolutely empty.

There was a poignant and brilliant final party on May 29. Everyone who cared about us—our life, our death—was there. Books & Co.'s history flowed through our door, a parade of readers and writers, employees and customers, a glorious parade that moved into and out of the bookstore all night long. I saw our twenty years in everyone there.

The evening was gratifying, emotionally exciting, and devastating, too. Tremulous all night, I went home with Alex afterward and even Jane Austen couldn't comfort me. The next day we closed the store to the public and began to box up books.

> She will publish extraordinary literature, that I know. The fact that she wants to concentrate on books by and about women is music to my ears. But she's used to this incredible social milieu, and being at the intersection of the cultural life of the city, and literary life. Her friends, and thousands of people she's gotten to know over twenty years, are suddenly not going to have a place to see her, nor she to see them. She says, "How am I going to keep in touch with people? How am I going to see them?" Then she says, "Maybe I'll be part of another bookstore and be there a couple of days a week, so people know where to find me." She's an optimist and a survivor.
>
> —ALEXANDER SANGER

The bookstore was a great adventure, I told myself. It had a twenty-year run. If one viewed it as a play on Broadway, it was a long-running, successful story. My life, too, could be an encouraging story for women. Though I've been so privileged, I haven't always had a successful or easy life. It was, it is, a good life, and I hope it will always be a worthwhile life.

But I want to end this book, close its door, where Books & Co.'s heart was—with a writer reading her work to readers, to an enthusiastic audience. Our last reading was on May 15, 1997, and our last reader was the exceptional Edna O'Brien. Edna and Jeanne Moreau were longtime friends, and, another connection—only connect!—it was Jeanne Moreau who first told Edna O'Brien that she should patronize Books & Co. So it happened that our very last reader was a friend in her own Irish right.

> Good evening. I'd like to welcome all of you to Books & Co., and tonight it is a great pleasure to welcome Edna O'Brien, who will be our last reader at Books & Co. And it's sort of as though the bookstore knows, because everything has given out here. Our sound system gave out last week, and now our air-conditioning isn't working, so we're sort of down to the last gasp. But I'm so happy that our reader tonight is so distinguished, and that her publisher is Farrar, Straus, such an important publisher for us over these last twenty years. One of our early readers here was Bernard Malamud, who read from *Dubin's Lives*. Over the years we've had many Farrar, Straus & Giroux readers, including Walker Percy, Oscar Hijuelos, Carlos Fuentes four times, John Ashbery, and most recently, Howard Norman. Edna O'Brien's heartbreaking and powerful novel, *Down by the River*, about Mary's attempts to escape her father's attentions, and later to abort his child, is based on an actual case. As my husband, Alex Sanger, is the president of Planned Parenthood New York and the grandson of its founder, Margaret Sanger, this book, and the issue of a woman's right to control her own body, was especially relevant to me. I told my husband, "You have to read this immediately. It's so important for you, and it makes the militant factors on both sides of the issue come alive, more than any newspaper article you could ever read."

Jonathan Galassi, Edna's editor, an editor long associated with Books & Co., took the podium:

This is a very momentous time here. It's hard to believe this is the last night of interchange between writer and reader. We've had so many great evenings here at Books & Co. over the years. But I think this should not be a sad moment. We should give thanks for all the wonderful things that have happened here, all the marvelous experiences that Jeannette has provided for us. It's something to celebrate. We should be happy tonight for everything that Books & Co. has meant to New York and to publishing, and to writing in America. Jeannette is going on to be a publisher now. She's changing stripes. She's coming over to our side, and Jeannette, if you thought you could lose money as a bookseller, I've got news for you. She's going on to great new things, and we're just very grateful to her. And now, it's really such an honor to introduce the best reader I know, Edna O'Brien.

Edna walked to the podium, a tall, elegant, beautiful woman with an extraordinary voice.

This is an honor, and Jonathan said we should make it a happy evening. Except, this book isn't that happy, and I can't rewrite it as I sit here. I'll read some, and maybe we'll talk to each other, or have questions, or we'll see. "Ahead of them the road lay in a long, entwined, undulation of mud . . ."

Edna finished her remarkable reading—her voice is like the richest chocolate—and then addressed the audience again.

That's enough of me, thank you very much. I would just like to say one thing. That I know, for Jeannette and for all her friends, what an emotional and poignant and painful evening it must be. But the thing about whatever ends in our lives, whether it be a place or a person, they do not end in the memory and imagination and spirit of the people, and I'm sure this bookshop will be a legend forever. And I'm so honored to be a part of what's happening now, and bless you all.

I returned to the podium and gave my last speech at the store. It was a singular moment. It was the store's swan song. But I was a bookseller to the end. I thanked the audience for coming, thanked Edna for her reading and gracious remarks, and then encouraged everyone to buy a copy of her book and get it signed. Edna had ended the evening just the way I liked it—on a hopeful note. I did hope that Books & Co., and what it stood for, would live on in people's hearts and minds.

AFTERWORD

IN JANUARY of 1998, I visited the place where I had stored everything I saved from Books & Co. after our tumultuous May 1997
closing. Yorkville Storage had dragged everything out and placed it
all together, higgledy-piggledy, on the floor. Like Scrooge reawaken-
ing after being visited by the three spirits, I rushed around lovingly
touching my stuff: the green couch, the desk from my office, photos
and paintings, old Christmas ornaments, the Buddhas and elephants
I used in the window to publicize Leila Hadley's book. I tried to figure out what to do with everything. This sorting out became a meta
phor for figuring out what my new life was and would be.

When I turned the key on the lock at Books & Co. for the final
time, it was with a feeling of relief. The last year had been so stressful, after announcing my decision to close the store; then the ensu-
ing uproar from my customers; the emergence of two backers and
negotiations with the Whitney Museum about whether we could
renew the lease. I told myself I would do all the things I hadn't had
time for—take courses, pursue my different spiritual interests, continue my publishing.

During the summer I was fine working on my newsletter, publishing *The Wine of Astonishment*, and going through the renovation we had planned on our apartment. Then the fall came and the rug was yanked out from under my feet. I had no place to go and nothing to do during the day.

All the new books were coming out, but I couldn't sell them. I missed my customers desperately and also felt as though I had lost my whole identity. No one invited me to the glamorous book parties I was used to attending, and I wasn't receiving any galleys. A few kind souls treated me as though I were still "somebody." Ruth Liebmann from Knopf came over and went through all the catalogs with me as if I still had a shop on Madison Avenue. Ira Silverberg, then at Grove, invited me out to lunch, showed me catalogs, and gave me books and galleys. André Bernard from Harcourt Brace took me to lunch to discuss my publishing projects.

Lenny Golay, owner with her husband, Ray Sherman, of the Corner Bookstore and Lenox Hill Bookstore, invited me for breakfast. We discussed bookselling, and she suggested the possibility of my working in her bookstore. I declined politely, thinking to myself, Why on earth would I want to work in a bookstore after being Queen Bee?

By Thanksgiving I was so depressed I spent the holiday in my nightgown—no makeup (oh, the horror)—lying in bed, watching TV, and eating Ben & Jerry's Chocolate Fudge Brownie ice cream out of the carton. After nearly hitting bottom, I gradually began to put things back together.

I decided to accept Lenny Golay's gracious offer. So I have been working at Lenox Hill Bookstore two days a week since January 1998 and really enjoying my colleagues Saul Katz, Josh Mrvos, Jade Zapotocky, Jeannine Bartel, and Christina Pelech, who have been so kind to me. Many of my former customers now buy books from me there, and I cherish the continuity. I have continued the Books & Co. newsletter, publishing it twice a year, and work on it with Steven Varni, the last manager of Books & Co., whose book will be published by Morrow. Wonderful Ted Wilentz, formerly the owner and founder of Eighth Street Bookstore, continues to give me great advice about all my various book-related projects. Peter Philbrook, manager and buyer of Books & Co. for fifteen years and now the manager of the Urban Center Bookstore, has given me the opportunity to work with him in continuing the Books & Co. reading series at the Municipal Art Society, where the Urban Center Bookstore is located. Fran Lebowitz had suggested we do a reading series together, and we all combined forces. Fran's generosity in showcasing other writers is phenomenal. It has been a great joy doing the series.

Jon Rabinowitz and Helen Marx, my publishing partners, are delightful to work with. Brilliant Steven Aronson, who encouraged and helped me start the bookstore, worked with me editing Jacqueline Weld's *Rara Avis*. And I feel very privileged to be part of Margot Wilkie's meditation group, which meets every Thursday to meditate, read, pray, and talk.

I want to thank Lynne Tillman for taking on the herculean task of writing this book. I think she has done a brilliant job of writing my story and weaving together all the different stories in *Bookstore*. Through the process—even after sharing all the secrets of my soul—Lynne has become a close and treasured friend. I keep joking that in twenty years she'll do a sequel entitled *"Publisher"* at which she slightly cringes! I am so excited that a book has been written about Books & Co. and is being published by a great publisher, whose books I love selling. I am thankful to André Bernard, its editor, for wanting to publish it.

I am also blessed with three wonderful sons, Ralph, Andrew, and Matthew, and a fabulous husband. Alex's love, belief in me, and understanding during this period have been constant and so very important. My beautiful mother, Olive Watson, and my four terrific sisters, Olive, Lucinda, Susan, and Helen, and my brother, Tom, have been a great source of comfort and support, as well as my honorary sisters the "Glad Girls"—Helen Houghton, Barbara Lazear Ascher, Barbara Liberman, Joan Jakobson, and Virginia Mailman, and the "Breakfast Club"—Clara Dale, Bicky Kellner, and Pam Loxton. And of course Jackie Weld whose book *Rara Avis* I am so excited about having published, and my friends Prudy Fryberger, the Connor family, Janie Hitchcock Hoagland, Jocelyn Kress, Wendy Gimbel, Joyce Ravid, Susan Cheever, Leila Hadley, Ann Lauterbach, Marcie Braga, Esty Brodsky, Alexandra Anderson-Spivy, Abadia Cristo, and Janet Stromberg. I'd like to thank Alex's family for their support—particularly my mother-in-law, Edwina Sanger, for her wise advice and counsel, and Ralph's grandmother, Betsy McElvenny, for her support and love. And everybody who contributed to this book.

My photos from Books & Co. are in my office in my New York apartment. The Books & Co. sign, the little rocking chair from the children's section, and a lot of Books & Co. artwork have gone to my barn in Maine. The green couch, used by Joseph Mitchell, Brendan Gill, and so many others, now resides in the North Haven Library in Maine, where it is around books and where I can visit it.

Life is sweet!

—JEANNETTE WATSON

JEANNETTE WATSON'S
SECRET LIST OF FIFTY BOOKS,
HER BEST-SELLERS IN ALPHABETICAL
ORDER BY AUTHOR

Lives of the Monster Dogs / KIRSTEN BAKIS ✦ Daisy Bates in the Desert / JULIA BLACKBURN ✦ The Wilder Shores of Love / LESLEY BLANCH ✦ Invisible Cities / ITALO CALVINO ✦ The Book of Mercy / KATHLEEN CAMBOR ✦ A Month in the Country / J. L. CARR ✦ On the Black Hill / BRUCE CHATWIN ✦ The Deptford Trilogy / ROBERTSON DAVIES ✦ The Book of Ebenezer Le Page / G. B. EDWARDS ✦ Deep River / SHUSAKU ENDO ✦ The Dead of the House / HANNAH GREEN ✦ A Journey with Elsa Cloud / LEILA HADLEY ✦ The All of It / JEANNETTE HAIEN ✦ Mariette in Ecstasy / RON HANSEN ✦ Dalva / JIM HARRISON ✦ Hidden Journey / ANDREW HARVEY ✦ Winter's Tale / MARK HELPRIN ✦ The Mambo Kings Play Songs of Love / OSCAR HIJUELOS ✦ Ancient Futures: Learning from Ladakh / HELENA NORBERG-HODGE ✦ The Book of Bees: And How to Keep Them *and* A Country Year: Living the Questions / SUE HUBBELL ✦ Mrs. Caliban / RACHEL INGALLS ✦ The Remains of the Day / KAZUO ISHIGURO ✦ Niels Lyhne / JENS PETER JACOBSEN ✦ Shoeless Joe / W. P. KINSELLA ✦ The Monk / MATTHEW G. LEWIS ✦ The Storyteller / MARIO VARGAS LLOSA ✦ Changing Places: A Tale of Two Campuses / DAVID LODGE ✦ The Wine of Astonishment / RACHEL MACKENZIE ✦

Palace Walk / Naguib Mahfouz ◆ The Assistant / Bernard Mala-mud ◆ Love in the Time of Cholera / Gabriel García Márquez ◆ So Long, See You Tomorrow / William Maxwell ◆ The Rector's Daughter / F. M. Mayor ◆ Monkeys / Susan Minot ◆ The Enlightened Mind: An Anthology of Sacred Prose *and* The Enlightened Heart: An Anthology of Sacred Poetry / Stephen Mitchell ◆ My Old Sweetheart / Susanna Moore ◆ The Tree of Life / Hugh Nissenson ◆ Under the Eye of the Clock: The Life Story of Christopher Nolan / Christopher Nolan ◆ The Pagan Rabbi and Other Stories / Cynthia Ozick ◆ The Moviegoer / Walker Percy ◆ A Glastonbury Romance / John Cowper Powys ◆ The Tongues of Angels / Reynolds Price ◆ Wide Sargasso Sea / Jean Rhys ◆ Dusk and Other Stories / James Salter ◆ Rameau's Niece / Cathleen Schine ◆ Keep the River on Your Right / Tobias Schneebaum ◆ The Emigrants / W. G. Sebald ◆ A Stone Boat / Andrew Solomon ◆ The Volcano Lover / Susan Sontag ◆ Waterland / Graham Swift ◆ The Makioka Sisters / Junichiro Tanizaki ◆ A Confederacy of Dunces / John Kennedy Toole ◆ Joan of Arc: In Her Own Words / Willard Trask ◆ Frost in May / Antonia White

Twenty Years

OF BOOKS & CO. READINGS

1979

(Jan. 9)

The First Books & Co. "Official" Reading: JOHN HOLLANDER, RICHARD HOWARD, JAMES MERRILL & HOWARD MOSS. Introduced by HAROLD BRODKEY

(Jan. 16)

BERNARD MALAMUD—*Dubin's Lives* (Farrar, Straus & Giroux)

(Jan. 23)

ANN BEATTIE—*Secrets and Surprises* (Random House)

(Jan. 30)

HANNAH GREEN—*The Dead of the House* (Doubleday)

(Feb. 6)

WILLIAM GOYEN—*The Collected Stories of William Goyen* (Doubleday)

(Feb. 13)

ROBERT STONE—*A Flag for Sunrise* (Knopf)

(Feb. 20)

JOEL OPPENHEIMER—*Names & Local Habitations: Selected Poems* (St. Andrews Press)

(Feb. 27)
MICHELE WALLACE—*Black Macho and the Myth of the Superwoman* (Dial Press)
(March 1)
JACK GILBERT—*Views of Jeopardy* (Yale University Press)
(March 6)
DONALD WINDHAM—*Tanaquil: A Novel* (Holt, Rinehart and Winston)
(March 9)
ALFRED KAZIN—*New York Jew* (Knopf)
(March 13)
HORTENSE CALISHER—*The Collected Stories of Hortense Calisher* (Arbor House) and CURTIS HARNACK—*Limits of the Land* (Doubleday)
(March 20)
JONATHAN WILLIAMS—*Elite/Elate Poems: Selected Poems 1971–1975* (Jargon Society) and THOMAS MEYER—*Staves Calends Legends* (Jargon Society)
(March 26)
FRAN LEBOWITZ—*Metropolitan Life* (Dutton)
(March 27)
BRENDAN GILL—*Summer Places* (Methuen)
(March 30)
The Liverpool Poets: BRIAN PATTEN—*Grave Gossip* (Allen & Unwin) & ROGER McGOUGH—*Holiday on Death Row* (Cape)
(April 3)
EDMUND WHITE—*Nocturnes for the King of Naples* (St. Martin's Press)
(April 10)
MANUEL PUIG—*Kiss of the Spider Woman* (Knopf)
(April 17)
LIONEL TIGER—*Optimism: The Biology of Hope* (Simon & Schuster)
(April 24)
JOHN IVAN SIMON—*Paradigms Lost: Reflections on Literacy and Its Decline* (Crown Publishers)

(May 1)
LESLIE ULLMAN—*Natural Histories* (Yale University Press)
(May 8)
MAUREEN OWEN—"A Brass Choir Approaches the Burial Ground"
(in *Big Deal* magazine, part 2, Barbara Barracks, ed.); ARMAND
SCHWERNER—*Triumph of the Will* (Perishable Press); QUINCY
TROUPE—*Snake Back Solos: Selected Poems, 1969–1977* (I. Reed Books)
(May 15)
RAY DIPALMA—*Planh* (Casement Books); TED GREENWALD—
Common Sense (L Publications); MICHAEL LALLY—*Catch My Breath*
(Salt Lick Press)
(May 22)
GILBERT SORRENTINO—*Mulligan Stew* (Grove)
(May 25)
A Bilingual Reading: CLAYTON ESHLEMAN (English) and LUISA
VALENZUELA (Spanish) reading from: *Cesar Vallejo's Complete
Posthumous Poetry* (University of California Press)
(May 29)
WALTER ABISH—*In the Future Perfect* (New Directions) and JOSEPH
McELROY—*Plus* (Knopf)
(May 31)
CHARLES SIMIC—*Selected Poems* (Edge Press) and JAMES TATE—*Riven
Doggeries* (Ecco Press)
(June 5)
STEPHEN KOCH—*Night Watch* (Marion Boyars)
(June 12)
RICHARD PRICE—*Ladies' Man* (Houghton Mifflin)
(June 17)
BARBARA HOLLAND—*The Pony Problem* (Dutton); SPENCER HOLST—
Spencer Holst Stories (Horizon Press); VERA LACHMANN—selected
poems; JACKSON MAC LOW—*Prophets* (Permanent Press)
(June 19)
NIKKI GIOVANNI—*Cotton Candy on a Rainy Day* (William Morrow)
(June 26)
RITA MAE BROWN—*Plain Brown Rapper* (Doubleday)

287

(Jan. 29)
JONATHAN BAUMBACH AND CO.—*Statements 2: New Fiction from the Fiction Collective* (Braziller)
(Feb. 8)
RON PADGETT—*Tulsa Kid* (Z Press)
(Feb. 15)
RUDY BURCKHARDT—*Mobile Homes* (Z Press)
(Feb. 19)
SUSAN FROMBERG SCHAEFFER—*Bible of the Beasts of the Little Field* (Dutton)
(Feb. 22)
JOANNE KYGER—*The Wonderful Focus of You* (Z Press) and BERNARD WELT—selected poems
(Feb. 29)
KENWARD ELMSLIE—*Moving Right Along* (Z Press)
(March 11)
IRVING FELDMAN—*New and Selected Poems* (Viking)
(March 18)
FRAN LEBOWITZ—from *Metropolitan Life*
(April 30)
DAVID IGNATOW—*Tread the Dark: New Poems* (Little, Brown & Co.)
(Sept. 11)
NAOMI LAZARD—*Ordinances* (Ardis) and ROBERT PETERS—*Selected Poems* (Crossing Press)
(Sept. 18)
HARVEY SHAPIRO—*Lauds and Nightsounds* (Sun & Moon Press) and TOBY OLSON—*Bird Songs: Eleven New Poems* (Perishable Press)
(Sept. 25)
The Writer on Her Work (W. W. Norton): JANET STERNBERG, HONOR MOORE, INGRID BENGIS, et al. reading essays
(Oct. 2)
WILLIAM VIRGIL DAVIS—*One Way to Reconstruct the Scene* (Yale University Press) and ISHMAEL REED—*Conjure: Selected Poems, 1963–1970* (University of Massachusetts Press)

(Oct. 9)
MARILYN HACKER—*Taking Notice: Poems* (Knopf) and MARY
OLIVER—*Twelve Moons* (Little, Brown & Co.)
(Oct. 16)
ISRAEL HOROWITZ and Friends: A staged reading of his play, *The
Good Parts*
(Oct. 23)
Editors Introduce: JOHN ROBERT REED—*A Gallery of Spiders* and TOM
WAYMAN—*Tom Wayman: Selected Poems, 1973–1980.* Introduction by
JOYCE CAROL OATES and RAYMOND J. SMITH, in celebration of their
new publishing endeavor, the *Ontario Review Press*
(Oct. 27)
E. L. DOCTOROW—*Loon Lake* (Random House)
(Oct. 30)
HILMA WOLITZER—*Hearts* (Farrar, Straus & Giroux)
(Nov. 6)
MARVIN COHEN and Friends: A staged reading of selected prose-
poems, mini-plays, and dialogues written by Cohen
(Nov. 13)
A Memorial Reading in Honor of Millen Brand: with friends of the
late poet
(Dec. 4)
JACK ANDERSON—*Toward the Liberation of the Left Hand* (University
of Pittsburgh Press) and MARC KAMINSKY—*Daily Bread* (University
of Illinois Press)

1981

(Jan. 20)
DANIEL HALPERN—*Life among Others* (Viking) and MARK STRAND—
Selected Poems (Atheneum)
(Jan. 27)
PAOLI VIOLI—*Splurge: Poems* (Sun & Moon Press) and MARJORIE
WELISH—*Handwritten* (Sun & Moon Press)
(Feb. 3)
CALVIN TRILLIN—*Floater* (Ticknor & Fields)

(Feb. 12)

Carol Muske—*Skylight* (Doubleday) and Susan Wood—*Bazaar* (Henry Holt & Co.)

(Feb. 17)

Screenwriters Close up: Panel discussion of the process of adapting novels to stage, screen, and TV. Moderated by Manya Starr, with Tad Mosel, Perry Miller Adato, et al.

(Feb. 24)

Paul Fussell—*Abroad: British Literary Traveling between the Wars* (Oxford University Press)

(March 3)

Latin American Poets: Enrique Lihn—*The Dark Room and Other Poems* (New Directions) and Herberto Padilla—*Legacies: Selected Poems* (Farrar, Straus & Giroux); David Unger and Jonathan Cohen, translators

(March 5)

Donald Finkel—*What Manner of Beast* (Atheneum) and Constance Urdang—*The Lone Woman and Others* (University of Pittsburgh Press)

(March 8)

Toby Talbot—*A Book about My Mother* (Farrar, Straus & Giroux) and Dr. Otto Kernberg—lecture

(March 10)

Alexis De Veaux—*Don't Explain: A Song of Billie Holiday* (Harper & Row) and Sara Miles—selected poems

(March 19)

Pushcart Prize V: 1980–1981 (Avon Books): A Gala Celebration: Bill Henderson, et al.

(April 5)

The New York City Poetry Marathon: Based on Howard Moss's anthology, *New York: Poems* (Avon Books). A benefit for the P.E.N. Writers Fund. Readings by John Lithgow, Marion Seldes, Tammy Grimes, Barbara Feldon, Christopher Walken, John Guare, May Swenson, Reed Whitmore, James Merrill, Nikki

GIOVANNI, HARVEY SHAPIRO, PHILIP LEVINE, PAUL ZWEIG, PATRICIA
SPEARS JONES, et al.
(April 9)
TONI MORRISON—*Tar Baby* (Knopf)
(April 14)
LOUISE GLÜCK—*Descending Figure* (Ecco Press) and GREGORY
ORR—*The Red House* (Harper & Row)
(April 21)
FRAN LEBOWITZ—*Social Studies* (Random House)
(April 26)
STUART SCHNEIDERMAN—*Returning to Freud: Clinical Psychoanalysis
in the School of Lacan* (Harvard University Press)
(April 28)
ANNETTE JAFFEE—*Adult Education* (Ontario Review Press) and
JOYCE CAROL OATES—*A Sentimental Education: Stories* (Dutton)
(May 6)
Fiction Collective Two: A second reading with members of the
Fiction Collective, reading *Statements 2: New Fiction from the Fiction
Collective* (Braziller); with JONATHAN BAUMBACH, et al.
(May 7)
CARLOS FUENTES—*Burnt Water* (Farrar, Straus & Giroux)
(May 12)
LYNNE SHARON SCHWARTZ—*Rough Strife* (Harper & Row) and ANN
ARENSBERG—*Sister Wolf* (Knopf)
(May 19)
WALTER ABISH—*How German Is It* (New Directions) and DAVID
SHAPIRO—*Lateness: A Book of Poems* (Overlook Press)
(May 26)
FRANCINE DU PLESSIX GRAY—*World Without End* (Simon &
Schuster) and SUSAN CHEEVER—*Looking for Work* (Simon &
Schuster)
(June 3)
ANN LAUTERBACH—*Many Times, but Then* (University of Texas Press)
(Sept. 23)

JOHN IRVING—*Hotel New Hampshire* (Dutton)
(Sept. 25)
DENISE LEVERTOV—*Pig Dreams: Scenes from the Life of Sylvia*
(Countryman Press)
(Sept. 29)
FRONTIER WOMEN: JENNIFER MOYER—selected poems and JUDITH
JOHNSON SHERWIN—*Dead's Good Company (Waste, Part Three)*
(Countryman Press)
(Oct. 14)
JOHN HOLLANDER—*Looking Ahead* (Nadja) and J. D. MCCLATCHY—
Scenes from Another Life (Braziller)
(Oct. 19)
MARIAN SELDES—*Time Together* (Houghton Mifflin) and WILLIAM
HAMILTON—*The Love of Rich Women* (Houghton Mifflin)
(Oct. 27)
CIRCLE REPERTORY COMPANY—A staged reading of a new play, with
audience feedback to the playwright after the performance
(Nov. 3)
The Best American Short Stories 1981 (Houghton Mifflin): HORTENSE
CALISHER, ed., leads authors, including Elizabeth Hardwick and
Walter Abish, from the anthology in a panel discussion
(Nov. 10)
PAUL GOLDBERGER—*The Skyscraper* (Knopf)
(Nov. 17)
GILBERT SORRENTINO—*Crystal Vision* (North Point) and WILLIAM
BRONK—*Life Supports* (North Point)
(Nov. 24)
FREDERICK FEIRSTEIN—*Fathering: A Sequence of Poems* (Applewood
Books) and FREDERICK TURNER—*The Return* (Countryman Press)

1982

(Jan. 12)
HILMA WOLITZER, MARY GORDON, et al., writers from *Fine Lines:
The Best of* Ms. *Fiction* (Scribners): panel/reading: RUTH SULLIVAN
and SUZANNE LEVINE, eds.

(Jan. 19)
GAIL GODWIN—*A Mother and Two Daughters* (Viking) and GERALD
JAY GOLDBERG—*Heart Payments* (Viking)
(Jan. 27)
DAVID IGNATOW—*Whisper to the Earth: New Poems* (Little, Brown &
Co.) and ROBERT PHILLIPS—*Running on Empty: New Poems*
(Doubleday)
(Feb. 1)
James Joyce Centennial Celebration: Group reading of Joyce's
Dubliners: BARBARA FELDON, MICHAEL TOLIN, et al.
(Feb. 9)
Jazz/Poetry: TED JOANS with an homage to Langston Hughes and
André Breton
(Feb. 16)
DIANA TRILLING—*Mrs. Harris: The Death of the Scarsdale Diet Doctor*
(Harcourt Brace)
(March 2)
PAUL THEROUX—*The Mosquito Coast* (Houghton Mifflin)
(March 9)
Editors Introduce: RICHARD MOORE—*Empires: Poems,* introduction
by JOYCE CAROL OATES and RAYMOND J. SMITH of the *Ontario
Review* Press
(March 16)
ALICE ADAMS—*Listening to Billie* (Knopf) and SARA McAULAY—
Chance (Knopf)
(March 23)
The Second Annual Screenwriters Forum: A panel discussion
moderated by MANYA STARR
(March 30)
CAROLYN FORCHE—*The Country between Us* (Harper & Row) and
JANA HARRIS—*Manhattan as a Second Language* (Harper & Row)
(April 6)
HOPE COOKE—*Time Change* (Simon & Schuster)
(April 13)
Editors Introduce: *The Cross-Cultural Review* Chapbooks: (bilingual)

293

American Indian, Romanian, Swedish writers, et al. reading their work. Introduction by STANLEY BARKIN, editor of *The Cross-Cultural Review*
(April 20)
Editors Introduce: Poets KATHA POLLITT—*Antarctic Traveller* and NICHOLAS CHRISTOPHER—*On Tour with Rita* and Brad Leithauser—*Hundreds of Fireflies: Poems*. Introduction by ALICE QUINN of Knopf
(April 27)
JACK GILBERT—*Monolithos: Poems 1962 and 1982* (Knopf)
(May 4)
A First Reading from *The Random Review 1982* (Random House)
RAYMOND CARVER, PETER TAYLOR, et al. Introduction by Gary Fisketjon and Jonathan Galassi, eds.
(May 11)
FREDERICK MORGAN—*Northbook* (University of Illinois Press) and JAY PARINI—*Anthracite Country* (Random House)
(May 18)
TED MOONEY—*Easy Travel to Other Planets* (Farrar, Straus & Giroux) and RICHARD SENNETT—*The Frog who Dared to Croak* (Farrar, Straus & Giroux)
(Sept. 14)
CHARLES HENRI FORD—*Om Krishna, Vol. II: Secret Haiku* (Red Ozier Press)
(Sept. 21)
WILLIAM M. SPACKMAN—*A Presence with Secrets* (Dutton/Obelisk) and JANE HOWARD—*A Different Woman* (Dutton/Obelisk)
(Sept. 28)
A Memorial in Honor of James Wright: with reminiscences of James Wright, and a reading of *This Journey* (Random House); ROBERT PHILLIPS, ANNIE WRIGHT, et al.
(Oct. 5)
JONATHAN AARON—*Second Sight: Poems* (Harper & Row) and BOBBIE ANN MASON—*Shiloh and Other Stories* (Harper & Row)
(Oct. 11)

IGGY POP—*I Need More* (2.13.61 Publishers)
(Oct. 12)
SUSAN CHEEVER—*A Handsome Man* (Simon & Schuster) and
SUSANNA MOORE—*My Old Sweetheart* (Houghton Mifflin)
(Oct. 19)
RICHARD HOWARD—*Lining Up: Poems* (Atheneum) and CHARLES
SIMIC—*Classic Ballroom Dances* (Braziller)
(Nov. 2)
EDMUND WHITE—*A Boy's Own Story* (Dutton) and STANLEY
ELKIN—*George Mills* (Dutton)
(Nov. 9)
ISRAEL HOROWITZ and Friends: a staged reading of his play, *Park
Your Car in Harvard Yard*
(Nov. 16)
ROY BLOUNT JR.—*One Fell Soup: Or, I'm Just a Bug on the Windshield
of Life* (Little, Brown & Co.)
(Nov. 30)
JOHN GUARE—*Three Exposures* (Harcourt Brace)
(Dec. 3)
STEPHEN PHILBRICK—*No Goodbye* (Horizon Press) and CELIA
WATSON STROME—*The Drum and the Melody* (Horizon Press)
(Dec. 7)
A Panel Discussion on Art: A Forum: Panel discussion with INGRID
SISCHY, et al.; JOHN BERNARD MYERS, moderator

1983

(Feb. 1)
MAUREEN HOWARD—*Grace Abounding* (Little, Brown & Co.) and
JOYCE JOHNSON—*Minor Characters: A Young Woman's Coming of Age
in the Beat Orbit of Jack Kerouac* (Houghton Mifflin)
(Feb. 8)
A Commemorative Reading on the Birthday of Elizabeth Bishop:
RICHARD HOWARD, AMY CLAMPITT, and HOWARD MOSS reading from
Bishop's works

(March 1)
Editors Introduce: CYNTHIA OZICK—*Trust* and ALICE MUNRO—*The Moons of Jupiter: Stories.* Introduction by ANN CLOSE of Knopf
(March 15)
Poetry in Translation: A reading and panel with RICHARD HOWARD, RIKA LESSER, GRACE SCHULMAN, and PAUL SCHMIDT
(March 22)
WENDY LAW-YONE—*The Coffin Tree* (Knopf) and EDWARD SWIFT—*Principia Martindale: A Comedy in Three Acts* (Harper & Row)
(April 5)
The Third Annual Screenwriters Panel Discussion, moderated by MANYA STARR
(April 12)
ISABEL EBERSTADT—*Natural Victims* (Knopf)
(April 17)
STUART SCHNEIDERMAN—*Jacques Lacan: The Death of an Intellectual Hero* (Harvard University Press)
(April 19)
JAMES MERRILL—*From the First Nine: Poems 1946–76* (Atheneum)
(April 24)
A "Bloomsbury" Special Benefit Program: Actors reading from the work of Virginia Woolf with comments and reminiscences by NIGEL NICOLSON. Proceeds to Royal Oak Foundation's Restoration Project
(May 3)
STEVEN ARONSON—*Hype!* (William Morrow)
(May 10)
HILMA WOLITZER—*In the Palomar Arms* (Farrar, Straus & Giroux)
(May 17)
JOHN CALVIN BATCHELOR—*The Birth of the People's Republic of Antarctica* (Dial Press) and RAYMOND ANDREWS—*Baby Sweet's* (Dial Press)
(May 24)
CARLOS FUENTES—*Distant Relations* (Farrar, Straus & Giroux)
(Oct. 25)

HORTENSE CALISHER—*Mysteries of Motion* (Doubleday)
(Nov. 1)
LYNNE SHARON SCHWARTZ—*Disturbances in the Field* (Harper &
Row) and ROBERT TOWERS—*The Summoning* (Harper & Row)
(Nov. 3)
BERNARD MALAMUD—*The Stories of Bernard Malamud* (Farrar, Straus
& Giroux)
(Nov. 8)
DANIEL MARK EPSTEIN—*The Book of Fortune: Poems* (Overlook Press);
ROLAND FLINT—*Resuming Green: Selected Poems, 1965–1982* (Dial
Press); and BARON WORMSER—*The White Words* (Houghton Mifflin)
(Nov. 15)
JAY CANTOR—*The Death of Che Guevara* (Knopf) and DENIS
JOHNSON—*Angels* (Knopf)
(Nov. 22)
RENATA ADLER—*Pitch Dark* (Knopf)
(Nov. 29)
A Dramatic Poetry Reading: BARBARA FELDON, MICHAEL TOLAN, et al.
(Dec. 6)
JAMAICA KINCAID—*At the Bottom of the River* (Farrar, Straus &
Giroux)

1984

(Feb. 14)
ELIZABETH SPENCER—*The Salt Line* (Doubleday)
(Feb. 28)
JAMES PURDY—*On Glory's Course* (Viking) and BARBARA PROBST
SOLOMON—*Short Flights* (Viking)
(March 6)
H. D. [Hilda Doolittle] Remembered: With BARBARA GUEST [*Herself
Defined* (Doubleday)], plus poets reading from H. D.'s work
(March 25)
First-Person Singular: Writers on Their Craft (*Ontario Review* Press),
compiled by JOYCE CAROL OATES; with GAIL GODWIN, GRACE
SCHULMAN, et al., reading from and discussing their craft

(April 3)

ANTHONY GIARDINA—*Men with Debts* (Knopf) and RON LOEWINSOHN—*Magnetic Field(s)* (Knopf)

(April 10)

STRATIS HAVIARAS—*The Heroic Age* (Simon & Schuster)

(April 17)

ROBERT PINSKY—*History of My Heart* (Ecco Press) and STANLEY PLUMLY—*Summer Celestial* (Ecco Press)

(April 24)

ROSELLEN BROWN—*Civil Wars* (Knopf)

(April 29)

Prize Stories: The O. Henry Award (Doubleday): Prize-winning authors read and discuss their work; hosted by WILLIAM ABRAHAMS and SALLY ARTESEROS, editors

(May 1)

JOHN ASHBERY—*A Wave* (Viking) and ALFRED CORN—*Notes from a Child of Paradise* (Viking)

(May 8)

HOWARD MOSS—*Rules of Sleep* (Atheneum)

(May 15)

PATRICIA BOSWORTH—*Diane Arbus: A Biography* (Knopf)

(May 22)

JAMES MCCOURT—*Kaye Wayfaring in "Avenged"* (Knopf)

(May 24)

The Best of Modern Humor: A fund-raiser for the 939 Foundation; ROY BLOUNT JR., GEORGE PLIMPTON, et al.

(Sept. 18)

JOSEF SKVORECKY—*The Engineer of Human Souls* (Knopf); plus a discussion with Skvorecky concerning the topic of the writer in exile

(Oct. 14)

A Reading from the new Vintage Contemporaries Series: JANET HOBHOUSE—*Dancing in the Dark;* PAULE MARSHALL—*The Chosen Place, the Timeless People;* PETER MATTHIESSEN, *Far Tortuga;* and JAY MCINERNEY, *Bright Lights, Big City*

(Nov. 11)

A Celebration of the 40th Anniversary Issue of *The Quarterly Review of Literature:* THEODORE WEISS, RENEE WEISS, HARVEY SHAPIRO, DAVID IGNATOW, et al.

(Nov. 13)

A Tribute to Tennessee Williams: Actors, directors and friends in readings and reminiscences; with FRANK CORSARO, RUTH FORD, RICHARD GILMON, JAMES LAUGHLIN, LYLE LEVERICK, NED ROREM, et al.

(Dec. 2)

A Celebration of the Life and Work of Delmore Schwartz: A group reading celebrating *The Letters of Delmore Schwartz* (*Ontario Review* Press); with JAMES ATLAS, WILLIAM BARRETT, JAMES LAUGHLIN, ROBERT PHILLIPS, ELISABETH POLLET, KARL SHAPIRO, EILEEN SIMPSON, et al.

(Dec. 9)

The Second Annual General Electric Awards for Younger Writers: Recipients of the awards in a special group reading

1985

(Jan. 22)

PHILLIP GRAHAM—*The Art of the Knock* (William Morrow)

(Jan. 29)

GRACE SCHULMAN—*Hemispheres* (Sheep Meadow Press) and PHILIP SCHULTZ—*Deep within the Ravine* (Viking)

(Feb. 5)

BREYTEN BREYTENBACH—*Mouroir: Mirrornotes of a Novel* (Farrar, Straus & Giroux)

(Feb. 12)

SUSAN CHEEVER—*Home before Dark* (Houghton Mifflin)

(Feb. 19)

CAROLYN KIZER—*The Mermaid in the Basement: Poems for Women* (Copper Canyon) and DONALD FINKEL—*The Detachable Man* (Atheneum)

(Feb. 26)
MARY JO SALTER—*Henry Purcell in Japan* (Knopf) and BRAD
LEITHAUSER—*Equal Distance* (Knopf)
(March 5)
RUSSELL BANKS—*Continental Drift* (Harper & Row) and DOUGLAS
UNGER—*Leaving the Land* (Harper & Row)
(March 10)
QUENTIN CRISP—*Manners from Heaven: A Divine Guide to Good
Behaviour* (Harper & Row)
(March 19)
An Evening in Celebration of Young Poets
(March 24)
VIRGIL THOMSON—*Virgil Thomson* (Dutton/Obelisk) and CYNTHIA
OZICK—*The Cannibal Galaxy* (Dutton/Obelisk)
(March 26)
An Edith Wharton Evening: With WENDY GIMBEL, JANE
HITCHCOCK, et al.
(April 2)
A Staged Poetry Reading: The poetry of Neruda; with BARBARA
FELDON and MICHAEL TOLAN, et al.
(April 9)
ROBERT FERRO—*The Blue Star* (Dutton)
(April 16)
MARY GORDON—*Men and Angels* (Random House)
(April 22)
GUY DE ROTHSCHILD—*Whims of Fortune* (Random House)
(April 30)
FERNANDA EBERSTADT—*Low Tide* (Knopf) and AMY HEMPEL—
Reasons to Live (Knopf)
(May 14)
Editors Introduce: T. CORAGHESSAN BOYLE—*Greasy Lake and
Other Stories* and MICHAEL THOMAS—*Hard Money*. Introduction
by ELISABETH SIFTON, editor of new Sifton imprint from
Viking

(May 21)
AMY CLAMPITT—*What the Light Was Like* (Knopf) and MARILYN
HACKER—*Assumptions* (Knopf)
(May 23)
Gala Fifth Birthday Reading and Party: LOUIS AUCHINCLOSS, ANDRE
GREGORY, ERICA JONG, GRACE PALEY, and CALVIN TRILLIN, master of
ceremonies, and introduction by ROBERT PHILLIPS
(Sept. 17)
EDMUND WHITE—*Caracole* (Dutton)
(Oct. 8)
GREGOR VON REZZORI—*The Death of My Brother Abel* (Elisabeth
Sifton/Viking)
(Oct. 15)
MARY MORRIS—*The Bus of Dreams and Other Stories* (Houghton
Mifflin) and JULIA MARKUS—*Friends Along the Way* (Houghton
Mifflin)
(Oct. 22)
MICHAEL ONDAATJE—*Secular Love* (W. W. Norton) and ROSANNA
WARREN—*Each Leaf Shines Separate* (W. W. Norton)
(Oct. 29)
JONATHAN RABAN—*Foreign Land* (Viking) and ALEXANDER
KALETSKI—*Metro: A Novel of the Moscow Underground* (Viking)
(Nov. 5)
E. L. DOCTOROW—*World's Fair* (Random House)
(Nov. 12)
FRANCINE DU PLESSIX GRAY—*October Blood* (Simon & Schuster)
(Nov. 17)
A STANLEY KUNITZ 80th Birthday Celebration Reading
(Nov. 19)
F. FORRESTER CHURCH—*Father and Son: A Personal Biography of
Senator Frank Church of Idaho* (Harper & Row)
(Nov. 26)
JENNIFER BARTLETT—*The History of the Universe* (Moyer Bell) and
AUGUST KLEINZAHLER—*Storm over Hackensack* (Moyer Bell)

1986

(March 20)
EDUARDO GALEANO—*Genesis (Memory of Fire,* Part I) (Pantheon)
(April 8)
JACQUELINE BOGRAD WELD—*Peggy: The Wayward Guggenheim*
(Dutton)
(April 17)
*Orchards: Seven Stories by Anton Chekhov and Seven Plays They Have
Inspired* (Knopf): MARIA FORNES, SPALDING GRAY, JOHN GUARE,
DAVID MAMET, WENDY WASSERSTEIN, MICHAEL WELLER, and SAMM-
ART WILLIAMS
(April 29)
PAUL AUSTER—*The New York Trilogy: City of Glass, Ghosts, and The
Locked Room* (Sun & Moon Press)
(May 9)
DEBORAH EISENBERG—*Transactions in a Foreign Currency* (Knopf)
and STEVEN MILLHAUSER—*In the Penny Arcade* (Knopf)
(May 18)
SCOTT SPENCER—*Waking the Dead* (Knopf) and ROBERT STONE—
Children of Light (Knopf)
(May 27)
SUSAN MINOT—*Monkeys* (Seymour Lawrence/Dutton)
(Sept. 16)
DAPHNE MERKIN—*Enchantment* (Harcourt Brace)
(Oct. 7)
CHRISTOPHER LEHMAN-HAUPT—*Me and DiMaggio: A Baseball Fan
Goes in Search of His Gods* (Simon & Schuster)
(Oct. 29)
JEANNETTE HAIEN—*The All of It* (Godine)

1987

(Jan. 20)
MONA SIMPSON—*Anywhere But Here* (Knopf)
(Jan. 27)
TERRY MCMILLAN—*Mama* (Houghton Mifflin)

(Jan. 28)
HUGH NISSENSON—*The Tree of Life* (Harper & Row)
(Feb. 24)
ANN LAUTERBACH—*Before Recollection* (Princeton University Press)
(March 10)
PHILLIP LOPATE—*The Rug Merchant* (Viking)
(April 15)
WALKER PERCY—*The Thanatos Syndrome* (Farrar, Straus & Giroux)
(April 21)
HOWARD NORMAN—*The Northern Lights* (Summit Books)
(April 28)
WADE DAVIS—*The Serpent and the Rainbow* (Warner Books)
(May 12)
SUSAN CHEEVER—*Doctors and Women* (Crown Publishers)
(Sept. 22)
CHRISTOPHER COE—*I Look Divine* (Ticknor & Fields)
(Sept. 30)
The Quarterly 3: ANN PYNE, MARK RICHARD, and SUNNY ROGERS
reading selected stories from Gordon Lish's magazine the *Quarterly
Review of Literature*
(Oct. 20)
HARRY MATHEWS—*Cigarettes* (Weidenfeld & Nicolson)
(Nov. 17)
BRENDAN GILL—*Many Masks: A Life of Frank Lloyd Wright*
(Putnam)

1988

(Jan. 26)
TOBIAS SCHNEEBAUM—*Where the Spirits Dwell* (Grove Press)
(March 21)
"Spring Training": A Baseball Evening: ROGER ANGELL—*Season
Ticket: A Baseball Companion* (Houghton Mifflin) and IRA BERKOW—
Pitchers Do Get Lonely (Atheneum)
(April 12)
JAMES SALTER—*Dusk and Other Stories* (North Point Press)

(April 25)
JIM HARRISON—*Dalva* (Dutton)
(April 28)
JOHN BRADLEY—*Tupelo Nights* (Atlantic Monthly Press)
(May 3)
JAMES LASDUN—*A Jump Start* (W. W. Norton & Co.)
(May 10)
BRADFORD MORROW—*Come Sunday* (Weidenfeld & Nicolson)
(Oct. 20)
Books & Co. Tenth Anniversary Reading: HAROLD BRODKEY, JOHN HOLLANDER, JAMES MERRILL, HOWARD MOSS

1989

(Jan. 17)
SUSAN SONTAG—*AIDS and Its Metaphors* (Farrar, Straus & Giroux)
(Feb. 7)
ROBERTSON DAVIES—*The Lyre of Orpheus* (Viking)
(April 16)
American Fiction: Where Have We Been, Where Are We Going? A panel discussion with BRUCE BAWER, TOM DISCH, FRAN LEBOWITZ, and PHILLIP LOPATE; moderated by WENDY GIMBEL
(April 18)
JOYCE JOHNSON—*In the Night Cafe* (Dutton)
(April 25)
GREIL MARCUS—*Lipstick Traces: A Secret History of the Twentieth Century* (Harvard University Press)
(May 2)
PHILLIP LOPATE—*Against Joie de Vivre* (Poseidon Press) and PATRICK MCGRATH—*The Grotesque* (Poseidon Press)
(May 16)
SUSAN MINOT—*Lust and Other Stories* (Houghton Mifflin) and LYNNE SHARON SCHWARTZ—*Leaving Brooklyn* (Houghton Mifflin)
(May 24)
MARK RICHARD—*The Ice at the Bottom of the World* (Knopf) and JOHN BURNHAM SCHWARTZ—*Bicycle Days* (Summit Books)

(June 7)
A Celebration of Edith Wharton: Fund-raiser for restoration of
The Mount; R. W. B. LEWIS, NANCY LEWIS, WENDY GIMBEL, JANE
STANTON HITCHCOCK, and JEAN-CLAUDE VAN ITALLIE
(Sept. 12)
An Evening in Celebration of Jean-Paul Sartre
(Sept. 20)
THOMAS MCGUANE—*Keep the Change* (Houghton Mifflin)
(Sept. 26)
HOWARD NORMAN—*Kiss in the Hotel Joseph Conrad* (Summit Books)
(Oct. 3)
PAUL WEST—*Lord Byron's Doctor* (Doubleday)
(Oct. 24)
PHYLLIS ROSE—*Jazz Cleopatra: Josephine Baker in Her Time* (Bantam
Doubleday Dell)

1990

(Jan. 12)
AMY HEMPEL—*At the Gates of the Animal Kingdom* (Knopf)
(April 26)
PETER GAY—*Reading Freud* (Yale University Press)
(May 22)
LAURIE COLWIN—*Goodbye without Leaving* (Poseidon Press)
(May 23)
THOMAS J. WATSON JR., with PETER PETRE—*Father, Son & Co.: My
Life at IBM and Beyond* (Bantam Books)
(Sept. 11)
BROOKS HANSEN and NICK DAVIS—*Boone* (Summit Books)
(Sept. 25)
In Memory of Pablo Neruda: ALASTAIR REID reads from *Pablo
Neruda: Selected Poems* (Houghton Mifflin)
(Oct. 2)
AGNES DE MILLE—*Portrait Gallery* (Houghton Mifflin)
(Oct. 16)
MARK STRAND—*The Continuous Life* (Knopf)

(Oct. 17)
CHINA GALLAND—*Longing for Darkness: Tara and the Black Madonna, a Ten Year Journey* (Viking)
(Oct. 25)
CEES NOOTEBOOM—*The Knight Has Died* (Louisiana State University Press) and PAUL AUSTER—*The Music of Chance* (Viking)
(Nov. 6)
TED MOONEY—*Traffic and Laughter* (Knopf)

1991

(Jan. 10)
CHARLES BAXTER—*A Relative Stranger* (W. W. Norton)
(Jan. 15)
JAMAICA KINCAID—*Lucy* (Farrar, Straus & Giroux)
(Jan. 29)
ISABEL ALLENDE—*The Stories of Eva Luna* (Macmillan)
(Feb. 6)
MICHAEL CUNNINGHAM—*A Home at the End of the World* (Farrar, Straus & Giroux)
(Feb. 19)
JOHN RICHARDSON—*A Life of Picasso: 1881–1906, Volume I* (Random House)
(Feb. 26)
MARY MCGARRY MORRIS—*A Dangerous Woman* (Viking Penguin)
(March 12)
An Evening in Honor of North Point Press: GARY SNYDER—*The Practice of the Wild* and *Riprap & Cold Mountain Poems*
(April 2)
SUSAN CHEEVER—*Treetops: A Family Memoir* (Bantam Books)
(April 16)
ANDREW HARVEY—*Hidden Journey: A Spiritual Awakening* (Henry Holt & Co.)
(May 16)
REYNOLDS PRICE and KATHRYN WALKER—*The Foreseeable Future* (Macmillan)

(June 4)

FERNANDA EBERSTADT—*Isaac and His Devils* (Knopf)
(June 11)

MARC REISNER—*Game Wars: The Undercover Pursuit of Wildlife Poachers* (Viking)
(June 18)

BRADFORD MORROW—*The Almanac Branch* (Simon & Schuster)
(Sept. 10)

EDWARD SAID—*Musical Elaborations* (Columbia University Press)
(Sept. 17)

ANN LAUTERBACH—*Clamor* (Viking)
(Sept. 24)

FRED FERSTEIN—*City Life* (Story Line Press)
(Oct. 1)

An Evening in Honor of Lyons & Burford Publishers: ROBERT KIMBER—*Upcountry* and RANDY WAYNE WHITE—*Batfishing in the Rainforest*
(Oct. 8)

ETHAN CANIN—*Blue River* (Houghton Mifflin)
(Oct. 15)

JEANNE SCHINTO—*Children of Men* (Persea Books) and WAYNE KOESTENBAUM—*Ode to Anna Moffo and Other Poems* (Persea Books)
(Oct. 24)

JULIAN BARNES—*Talking It Over* (Knopf)
(Oct. 29)

A Celebration of Clark City Press: RUSSELL CHATHAM, DAN GERBER, and JIM HARRISON
(Nov. 5)

NICCOLO TUCCI—*Before My Time* (Moyer Bell) (read by his daughter Maria)
(Nov. 10)

Afternoon in Celebration of the Year of Tibet: ROBERT THURMAN, ANDREW HARVEY, GALEK RINPOCHE, et al.
(Nov. 14)

HAROLD BRODKEY—*The Runaway Soul* (Farrar, Straus & Giroux)

(Jan. 14)
RICHARD BAUSCH—*Violence* (Seymour Lawrence/Houghton Mifflin)
(Jan. 21)
MARY STEWART HAMMOND—*Out of Canaan* (W. W. Norton)
(Feb. 12)
ALAN EREIRA—*The Elder Brothers* (Knopf)
(Feb. 13)
A Valentine's Day Reading: With the Academy of American Poets:
WILLIAM J. KISTLER, ANN LAUTERBACH, MARY JO SALTER, and
CYNTHIA ZARIN
(Feb. 18)
MADISON SMARTT BELL—*Save Me Joe Louis* (Harcourt Brace) and
THOMAS MCGONIGLE—*Going to Patchogue* (Dalkey Archive Press)
(Feb. 20)
An Evening of Thomas Bernhard: Presented with *Pequod* magazine:
HAROLD BRODKEY, RICHARD BURGIN, STEPHEN DIXON, JOHN
GRIESEMER, PHILLIP LOPATE, MARK RUDMAN, and KATHERINE
WASHBURN; hosted by MARK RUDMAN
(March 1)
An Afternoon in Celebration of Anthony Trollope: Presented by
the Trollope Society—N. JOHN HALL, JANE HITCHCOCK, RANDY
WILLIAMS; hosted by RANDY WILLIAMS, president
(March 10)
BILL BARRETTE and JOHN YAU—*Big City Primer* (Timken
Publishers)
(March 17)
Modern Painters Panel Discussion: Participants: DAVID CARBONE,
LOUIS FINKELSTEIN, DEBORAH ROSENTHAL, JOHN SNYDER, and
TREVOR WINKFIELD; hosted by JED PERL, panel moderator
(March 31)
CARYL PHILLIPS—*Cambridge* (Knopf) and GRAHAM SWIFT—*Ever
After* (Knopf)
(April 13)
DAVID LODGE—*Paradise News* (Viking Penguin)

(April 23)
CARLOS FUENTES—*The Buried Mirror* (Houghton Mifflin)
(May 12)
DEBORAH EISENBERG—*Under the 82nd Airborne* (Farrar, Straus &
Giroux) and SIRI HUSTVEDT—*The Blindfold* (Poseidon Press)
(May 19)
CHRISTOPHER BOHJALIAN—*Past the Bleachers* (Carroll & Graf) and
SHEILA BOSWORTH—*Slow Poison* (Knopf)
(May 26)
ROBERT ROBIN—*Above the Law* (Pocket Books)
(June 2)
DAN WAKEFIELD—*New York in the 50s* (Seymour Lawrence/
Houghton Mifflin)
(June 18)
ELLEN CHESLER—*Woman of Valor: Margaret Sanger and the Birth
Control Movement in America* (Simon & Schuster)
(Sept. 15)
JANE STANTON HITCHCOCK—*Trick of the Eye* (Dutton)
(Sept. 22)
A Reading to Benefit the Homeless: SUSAN FROMBERG-
SCHAEFFER—*First Nights* (Knopf) and SCOTT SPENCER—*Men
in Black* (Knopf)
(Sept. 29)
THOMAS McGUANE—*Nothing but Blue Skies* (Seymour Lawrence/
Houghton Mifflin)
(Oct. 1)
ARTHUR MILLER and LOUISE BOURGEOIS—*Homely Girl, A Life* (Peter
Blum Edition)
(Oct. 5)
SOGYAL RINPOCHE—*The Tibetan Book of Living and Dying*
(HarperSanFrancisco)
(Oct. 27)
NICK LYONS—*Spring Creek* (The Atlantic Monthly Press)
(Nov. 10)
SUSAN SONTAG—*The Volcano Lover* (Farrar, Straus & Giroux)

(Jan. 19)
Louis Begley—*The Man Who Was Late* (Knopf)
(Jan. 26)
Paul Watkins—*The Promise of Light* (Random House)
(Feb. 2)
Barry Hannah—*Bats Out of Hell* (Seymour Lawrence/Houghton Mifflin)
(Feb. 9)
Fae Myenne Ng—*Bone* (Hyperion Books)
(March 2)
Barbara Lazear Ascher—*Landscape without Gravity: A Memoir of Grief* (Delphinium)
(March 9)
John Gruen—*Keith Haring: The Authorized Biography* (Prentice Hall Editions)
(March 11)
Oscar Hijuelos—*The Fourteen Sisters of Emilio Montez O'Brien* (Farrar, Straus & Giroux)
(March 23)
Svend Age Madsen—*Virtue and Vice in the Middle Time* (Garland)
(April 13)
Stephen Mitchell—*A Book of Psalms* (HarperCollins)
(April 19)
Victor Erofeyev—*Russian Beauty: A Novel* (Viking)
(April 20)
Jacques Roubaud—*Hortense in Exile* (Dalkey Archive Press)
(April 27)
Peter Straub—*The Throat* (Dutton)
(May 10)
Dominick Dunne—*A Season in Purgatory* (Crown Publishers)
(May 11)
Frances Fyfield—*Shadow Play* (Pantheon)
(May 18)
Frederick Busch—*Long Way from Home* (Houghton Mifflin)

(May 25)
LEONARD MICHAELS—*The Men's Club* and *To Feel These Things*
(Mercury House)
(May 27)
ROSANNE DARYL THOMAS—*The Angel Carver* (Random House) and
CATHIE PELLETIER—*The Bubble Reputation* (Crown Publishers)
(June 15)
FREDERIC TUTEN—*Tintin in the New World* (William Morrow)
(Sept. 14)
CHRISTOPHER COE—*Such Times* (Harcourt Brace)
(Sept. 18)
A New York Is Book Country Reading: LAURIE COLWIN—*A Big
Storm Knocked It Over: A Novel* (HarperCollins)
(Sept. 21)
JAMES MERRILL—*A Different Person: A Memoir* (Knopf)
(Sept. 26)
A Celebration of Two Editions of Edith Wharton's *The Buccaneers*:
MARION MAINWARING (who completed the novel for Viking) and
VIOLA HOPKINS WINNER (editor of the original edition for the
University of Virginia Press): a discussion moderated by WENDY
GIMBEL and texts read by BARBARA FELDON
(Sept. 28)
FRANK CONROY—*Body and Soul* (Seymour Lawrence/Houghton
Mifflin)
(Oct. 5)
LINDA FAIRSTEIN—*Sexual Violence: Our War Against Rape* (William
Morrow)
(Oct. 12)
HOWELL RAINES—*Fly Fishing through the Midlife Crisis* (William
Morrow)
(Oct. 18)
MARTIN SIMECKA—*The Year of the Frog* (Louisiana State University
Press) and WILLIAM STYRON—*A Tidewater Morning* (Random House)
(Oct. 19)
SUSANNA MOORE—*Sleeping Beauties* (Knopf)

(*Oct. 26*)

BRUCE BAWER—*A Place at the Table: The Gay Individual in American Society* (Poseidon Press)

(*Nov. 2*)

CAROL HILL—*Henry James' Midnight Song* (Simon & Schuster)

(*Nov. 9*)

JACQUELINE DEVAL—*Reckless Appetites: A Culinary Romance* (Ecco Press)

(*Nov. 16*)

ANTHONY HECHT—*The Hidden Law: The Poetry of W. H. Auden* (Harvard University Press)

(*Nov. 18*)

The Best American Erotica 1993 (Macmillan): Hosted by SUSIE BRIGHT, editor

1994

(*Jan. 18*)

KARL KIRCHWEY—*Those I Guard* (Harcourt Brace) and CYNTHIA ZARIN—*Fire Lyric* (Knopf)

(*Jan. 20*)

MARK SALZMAN—*The Soloist* (Random House)

(*Jan. 25*)

WILLIAM PARK—*The Idea of Rococo* (University of Delaware Press)

(*Jan. 27*)

A Celebration of Robert Burns and Scottish Literature: REVEREND DAVID HAXTON CARSWELL READ, D.D.; DUNCAN ARCHIBALD BRUCE, and SCOTT HOUSTON

(*Feb. 1*)

CAMPBELL MCGRATH—*American Noise* (Ecco Press)

(*Feb. 8*)

JOHN GIORNO—*You Got to Burn to Shine* (Serpent's Tail/High Risk)

(*Feb. 15*)

DONALD KEENE—*On Familiar Terms* (Kodansha)

(*Feb. 22*)

IVA PEKAKROVA—*Truck Stop Rainbows* (Knopf) and WENDY LAW-
YONE—*Irrawaddy Tango* (Knopf)
(Feb. 24)
TIM BINDING—*In the Kingdom of Air* (W. W. Norton)
(Feb. 28)
ETHAN CANIN—*The Palace Thief* (Random House)
(March 1)
RICHARD HOWARD—*Like Most Revelations* (Pantheon)
(March 16)
J. P. DONLEAVY—*The History of the Ginger Man* (Seymour Lawrence/
Houghton Mifflin)
(March 22)
FRANCINE DU PLESSIX GRAY—*Rage and Fire: A Life of Louise Colet—
Pioneer Feminist, Literary Star, Flaubert's Muse* (Simon & Schuster)
(March 31)
TOM DRURY—*The End of Vandalism* (Seymour Lawrence/Houghton
Mifflin)
(April 4)
CALVIN TRILLIN—*Deadline Poet: My Life as a Doggerelist* (Farrar,
Straus & Giroux)
(April 7)
CARLOS FUENTES—*The Orange Tree* (Farrar, Straus & Giroux)
(April 12)
MICHAEL STEPHENS—*The Brooklyn Book of the Dead* (Dalkey Archive
Press)
(April 19)
GRACE PALEY—*The Collected Stories* (Farrar, Straus & Giroux)
(April 26)
GWENDOLYN M. PARKER—*These Same Long Bones* (Houghton Mifflin)
(May 3)
ABIGAIL THOMAS—*Getting over Tom* (Algonquin Books of Chapel Hill)
(May 10)
KELVIN CHRISTOPHER JAMES—*Secrets* (Vintage) and EDWIDGE
DANTICAT—*Breath, Eyes, Memory* (Vintage)

(May 12)
JIM HARRISON—*Julip* (Seymour Lawrence/Houghton Mifflin)
(May 17)
DENNIS MCFARLAND—*School for the Blind* (Houghton Mifflin)
(June 8)
WILLIAM KOTZWINKLE—*The Fan Man* (Vintage)
(June 15)
SUSAN CHEEVER—*A Woman's Life: The Story of an Ordinary American and Her Extraordinary Generation* (William Morrow)
(Sept. 8)
PAUL AUSTER—*Mr. Vertigo* (Viking) and HOWARD NORMAN—*The Bird Artist* (Farrar, Straus & Giroux)
(Sept. 13)
ANDERSON FERRELL—*Home for the Day* (Knopf)
(Sept. 19)
JAYNE ANNE PHILLIPS—*Shelter* (Seymour Lawrence/Houghton Mifflin)
(Sept. 20)
GIANNINA BRASCHI—*Empire of Dreams* (Yale University Press), with TESS O'DWYER, translator
(Oct. 3)
A Memorial Reading for Christopher Coe: With CORK SMITH, ANDERSON FERRELL, et al.
(Oct. 13)
IRVING FELDMAN—*The Life and Letters* (University of Chicago Press)
(Oct. 17)
GLORIA VANDERBILT—*The Memory Book of Starr Faithfull* (Knopf)
(Oct. 18)
JANE STANTON HITCHCOCK—*The Witches' Hammer* (Dutton)
(Oct. 25)
ANDREW SOLOMON—*A Stone Boat* (Faber & Faber)
(Nov. 1)
ANN LAUTERBACH—*And for Example* (Penguin)

(Nov. 6)
FRAN LEBOWITZ—*Mr. Chas and Lisa Sue Meet the Pandas* (Knopf)

1995

(Jan. 10)
ROY BLOUNT JR.—*Roy Blount's Book of Southern Humor* (W. W. Norton)
(Jan. 17)
HENRI COLE—*The Look of Things* (Knopf)
(Jan. 24)
NICHOLAS CHRISTOPHER—*5° and Other Poems* (Penguin)
(Jan. 31)
PEARSON MARX—*On the Way to the Venus De Milo* (Simon & Schuster)
(Feb. 1)
LUCY GREALY—*Autobiography of a Face* (Houghton Mifflin)
(Feb. 7)
WILLIAM EISNER—*The Sévingé Letters* (Baskerville) and MARCIA GOLUB—*Wishbone* (Baskerville)
(Feb. 14)
DAVID IVES—*All in the Timing: Fourteen Plays* (Vintage)
(Feb. 21)
KATHERINE MOSBY—*Private Altars* (Random House)
(March 7)
J. M. McDONNELL—*Half Crazy* (Little, Brown & Co.)
(April 18)
HOPE COOKE—*Seeing New York: History Walks for Armchair and Footloose Travelers* (Temple University Press)
(April 25)
MARY WESLEY—*An Imaginative Experience* (Viking)
(May 2)
CHARLIE SMITH—*Before and After: Poems* (W. W. Norton) and MARK RUDMAN—*Realm of Unknowing: Meditations on Art, Suicide, and Other Transformations* (Wesleyan University Press)

(May 23)

BILL BARRETTE and JOHN YAU—*Berlin Diptychon* (Timken)

(Sept. 5)

FRANCINE PROSE—*Hunters and Gatherers* (Farrar, Straus & Giroux)

(Sept. 11)

JULIA BLACKBURN—*The Book of Color* (Knopf)

(Sept. 12)

RICHARD WHELAN—*Alfred Stieglitz: A Biography* (Little, Brown & Co.)

(Sept. 14)

A Panel Discussion of Siegfried Kracauer's *The Mass Ornament: Weimar Essays*, edited by Thomas Levin. Panelists: MIRIAM HANSEN, ANNETTE MICHELSON, and SUSAN SONTAG; moderated by THOMAS LEVIN

(Sept. 19)

Word Magazine Launch Celebration: Hosted by M. MARK, former editor of *The Village Voice Literary Supplement*

(Sept. 20)

JOHN GREGORY DUNNE—*Playland* (Plume Books)

(Sept. 26)

WILLIAM KISTLER—*Poems of the Known World* (Arcade)

(Oct. 5)

ARTHUR DANTO—*Playing with the Edge: The Photographic Achievement of Robert Mapplethorpe* (University of California Press)

(Oct. 10)

BARRY GIFFORD—*Baby Cat-Face* (Harcourt Brace)

(Oct. 17)

LUCIE BROCK-BROIDO—*The Master Letters* (Knopf)

(Oct. 23)

CARLOS FUENTES—*Diana: The Goddess Who Hunts Alone* (Farrar, Straus & Giroux) (a joint reading done in presentation with the 92nd Street Y)

(Oct. 25)

WILLIAM CORBETT—*New & Selected Poems* (Zoland Books)

(Nov. 1)

BENJAMIN TAYLOR—*Tales Out of School* (Turtle Point Press)

(Nov. 7)

PAUL WILLIAM ROBERTS—*In Search of the Birth of Jesus* (Riverhead Books)

(Nov. 14)

ANNE PORTER—*An Altogether Different Language: Poems 1934–1994* (Zoland Books)

(Nov. 21)

R. S. JONES—*Walking on Air* (Houghton Mifflin)

1996

(Jan. 12)

JAMAICA KINCAID—*The Autobiography of My Mother* (Farrar, Straus & Giroux)

(Jan. 23)

NICHOLAS CHRISTOPHER—*Veronica* (Dial Press)

(Feb. 6)

JOSEPH MITCHELL—*Joe Gould's Secret* (Viking)

(Feb. 16)

JOHN UPDIKE—*In the Beauty of the Lilies* (Knopf) (a joint presentation with the Whitney Museum)

(March 19)

ROXANA ROBINSON—*Asking for Love* (Random House)

(April 18)

SLAVOJ ZIZEK—*The Indivisible Remainder* (W. W. Norton)

(April 24)

Extraordinary Liberty: A Celebration of Frank O'Hara: JANE FREILICHER, KENNETH KOCH, RON PADGETT, LARRY RIVERS, JOE LESEUR, and DAVID SHAPIRO. In honor of National Poetry Month

(May 1)

WILLIAM T. VOLLMANN—*The Atlas* (Viking)

(May 14)

Books & Co./Turtle Point Press Celebration: HANNAH GREEN—*The Dead of the House* (Books & Co./Turtle Point Press) and DONNA TARTT [reading from the text of]—*Joan of Arc: In Her Own Words* (Books & Co./Turtle Point Press)

(June 4)
BRENDAN GILL—*Late Bloomers* (Artisan Books)
(Oct. 30)
Books & Co./Turtle Point Imprint Inaugural Address: A speech
given by JEANNETTE WATSON and JONATHAN RABINOWITZ of Turtle
Point Press
(Nov. 8)
CHARLES SIMIC—*Walking the Black Cat* (Harcourt Brace) and JOHN
YAU—*Forbidden Entries* (Black Sparrow Press)
(Nov. 12)
SHENA MACKAY—*The Orchard on Fire* (Moyer Bell)
(Nov. 20)
Committed to Memory—100 Best Poems to Memorize (Books & Co./
Turtle Point Press): Presented by the Academy of American Poets;
with LYN CHASE, JOHN HOLLANDER, BRENDAN GILL, GEORGE
PLIMPTON, ALICE QUINN, and SUSAN SONTAG

1997

(Feb. 13)
ARTHUR DANTO in Conversation with DAVID REED—*After the End of
Art* (Princeton University Press)
(Feb. 28)
STANLEY CAVELL—*Contesting Tears: The Hollywood Melodrama of the
Unknown Woman* (University of Chicago Press)
(March 13)
FREDERIC TUTEN—*Van Gogh's Bad Café* (William Morrow)
(March 24)
FERNANDA EBERSTADT—*When the Sons of Heaven Meet the Daughters
of the Earth* (Knopf)
(April 22)
PATRICIA BOSWORTH—*Anything Your Little Heart Desires* (Simon &
Schuster)
(May 7)
LEILA HADLEY—*A Journey with Elsa Cloud* (Books & Co./Turtle
Point Press)

(May 15)
Edna O'Brien—*Down by the River* (Farrar, Straus & Giroux)
(May 29)
The Books & Co. Farewell Party: Twenty Years of Bookselling and
Readings

LIST OF CONTRIBUTORS

ALEXANDRA ANDERSON-SPIVY (editor/art critic)

STEVEN M. L. ARONSON (writer/editor)

BARBARA LAZEAR ASCHER (writer/essayist)

PAUL AUSTER (novelist/filmmaker)

DON BARLIANT (owner, Barbara's Books, Chicago)

DUNCAN BENTLEY (retired writer)

ROBERT BENTON (director/screenwriter)

ANDREW BERGEN (research scientist/former Books & Co. employee)

LISA BERNHARD (bookstore manager/former Books & Co. employee)

PENELOPE BLOODWORTH (bookstore employee/former Books & Co.
employee)

ROY BLOUNT JR. (writer/humorist)

ELIZABETH BOGNER (editor/former Books & Co. employee)

FRANCIS CASH (writer/former Books & Co. employee)

MAY CASTLEBERRY (librarian and associate curator, Whitney Museum of
American Art)

LYN CHASE (chairman of the board, the Academy of American Poets)

SUSAN CHEEVER (writer)

BOB CONTANT (owner, St. Marks Bookshop, New York)

MICHAEL CUNNINGHAM (novelist)

CLARA DALE (architect)

JAMES FALKIN (political scientist/theorist)

JENNY FEDER (owner, Three Lives bookstore, New York)

CHARLES HENRI FORD (poet/filmmaker/artist)

JONATHAN GALASSI (editor/poet/translator)

MARGIE GHIZ (owner, Midnight Special bookstore, Los Angeles)

BRENDAN GILL (writer) (deceased 1997)

WENDY GIMBEL (writer/critic)

LEILA HADLEY (novelist/travel writer)

JEANNETTE HAIEN (novelist/pianist)

JOHN G. HANHARDT (senior curator, Guggenheim Museum/former curator, Whitney Museum of American Art)

JAMES HARRIS (owner, Prairie Lights bookstore, Iowa City)

JIM HARRISON (novelist/screenwriter/poet)

AMY HEMPEL (short-story writer/novelist)

JANE STANTON HITCHCOCK (novelist)

RICHARD HOWARD (poet/translator)

RICHARD HOWORTH (owner, Square Books, Oxford, Miss.)

MAX KAPLAN (poet/short-story writer)

MITCHELL KAPLAN (owner, Books & Books, Miami)

ANN LAUTERBACH (poet/essayist)

FRAN LEBOWITZ (writer)

J. D. MCCLATCHY (poet)

TERRY MCCOY (owner, St. Marks Bookshop, New York)

TED MOONEY (novelist/editor)

JEANNE MOREAU (actress)

ALBERT MURRAY (novelist/critic)

PETER PHILBROOK (manager, out-of-print and rare books, bn.com/ former Books & Co. buyer and manager)

BUD POMERANZ (foreign policy consultant/writer)

MICHAEL POWELL (owner, Powell's bookstore, Portland)

JONATHAN RABINOWITZ (publisher)

DAVID ROSS (director, San Francisco Museum of Modern Arts/former director, Whitney Museum of American Art)

ALEXANDER SANGER (president, Planned Parenthood NYC)

SIMON SCHAMA (historian)

SUSAN SCOTT (bookstore manager/former Books & Co. employee)

DAVID SHAPIRO (poet/critic)

IRA SILVERBERG (agent/former editor and publicist)

PAUL SLOVAK (editor/publicist)

ED SOLOWITZ (sales representative)

SUSAN SONTAG (novelist/critic)

CALVIN TRILLIN (writer/humorist)

DAVID UNOWSKY (owner, Hungry Mind bookstore, St. Paul)

STEVEN VARNI (novelist/former Books & Co. buycr and manager)

OLIVE WATSON (real estate)

JACQUELINE WELD (novelist/biographer)

THEODORE WILENTZ (retired publisher and bookstore owner, Eighth Street Bookshop)

MARTHA WILSON (performance artist/director, Franklin Furnace Archive)

PAUL YAMIZAKI (manager, City Lights bookstore, San Francisco)

JOHN YAU (poet/critic)

INDEX